SHERLOCK HOLMES DETECTED

SHERLOCK HOLMES DETECTED

The Problems of the Long Stories

IAN McQUEEN

DRAKE PUBLISHERS
New York

LCCCN 74–1324

ISBN 0–87749–615–3

Published in 1974 by
Drake Publishers Inc
381 Park Avenue South
New York, N.Y. 10016

Printed in Great Britain

CONTENTS

	page
List of Illustrations	7
Preface	9
ONE—A Study in Scarlet	11
FIRST INTERVAL—Financial Problems	36
TWO—The Sign of Four	73
SECOND INTERVAL—Some Chronological Problems of the Marriage Period	108
THREE—The Hound of the Baskervilles	127
THIRD INTERVAL—A Note on The Five Orange Pips	171
FOUR—The Valley of Fear	177
Notes	213
Select Bibliography	218
Acknowledgements	220
Index to the Sherlock Holmes Stories	221
General Index	223

ILLUSTRATIONS

	page
'I've found it! I've found it!'	22
The unfortunate creature's tongue	24
He struck a match on his boot	34
'Pretty sort o' treatment this!'	65
Pattered off upon the trail	66
We were clear of the town	83
'Look at that with your magnifying glass'	84
We all three shook hands	101
'The murderer has escaped'	102
It passed with a rattle and a roar	119
His body was discovered	120
'Welcome, Sir Henry!'	137
'I'll fill a vacant peg, then'	138
'Holmes,' I cried, 'you are too late'	155
The lady sprang from her chair	156
Our visitor sprang from his chair	173
I sprang to my feet	174
Then suddenly he hauled something in	191
The tall and portly form of Mycroft	192

PREFACE

I first discovered Sherlock Holmes at about the age of ten, and for many years managed to keep the sacred writings in proper perspective as one of the most enjoyable experiences of English literature. But one day I remarked, semi-jocularly, to my children that Holmes was a real person, who really lived, and was living still. My sons and daughter greeted this with unfilial derision, whereupon my wife saw fit to abandon parental solidarity and sided with them.

They were not particularly impressed when I told them that many Baker Street enthusiasts throughout the world also regarded Holmes and Watson as real people. I pointed out that American *aficionados*—and some English ones—had gone so far as to claim that the adventures were written by Dr Watson and that they had relegated Sir Arthur Conan Doyle to the role of literary agent who introduced Dr Watson to his publisher.

Thinking along this amiably tongue-in-cheek line, a new slant on the saga occurred to me. Holmes and Watson were only *pretending* to be characters of fiction and had employed Conan Doyle to edit their scripts and have them published as if they were only stories. To re-read the Holmesian saga with this thought in mind may not open up an entirely new dimension, but it certainly leads along many fascinating trails. In short, there is an immense amount of fun to be had, without diminishing in any way one's enormous admiration for the genius of Sir Arthur Conan Doyle.

Unlike Holmes' monograph on 'The Polyphonic Motets of Lassus', which was said by experts to be 'the last word on the subject', this book has been written for the general reader and does not attempt detailed comparison with the conclusions of earlier chronologists of the Baker Street scene. I naturally hold these pioneers in the highest regard and have listed the main books in the Bibliography, in case any reader wishes to embark upon further research independently. That there is ample scope may be judged by the fact that when William Baring-Gould became the sixth chronologist in the field in 1955 he lamented that the sextet had so far been able to agree as to year, month, date of month and days of week on fewer than ten of the sixty stories which comprise the canon.

In addition to the researches of the chronologists, a great deal of commentary on all aspects of the canon, including the dating of individual adventures, has been published, much of the material having appeared first in the *Baker Street Journal* (New York) and the *Sherlock Holmes Journal* (London). It is sad to note that so many of the authorities now have to be referred to as 'the late'. They include William Baring-Gould, H. W. Bell, Gavin Brend, Jay Finley Christ, Sir Sydney Roberts, Dorothy M. Sayers, Edgar Smith and E. B Zeisler.

CHAPTER ONE

A STUDY IN SCARLET

Sherlock Holmes said it:

'What you do in this world is a matter of no consequence. The question is, what can you make people believe you have done.'

A Study in Scarlet, one of the earliest cases and the first to be published, is essentially the basis and starting-point of our knowledge of Holmes and Watson. When the time comes to deal in detail with *The Sign of Four* we shall find ourselves immersed in problems specially affecting Watson; but, as he begins *A Study in Scarlet* with an autobiographical sketch, it is not inappropriate here to say something of his early life, which led up to his first meeting with Holmes

WATSON'S BACKGROUND AND EDUCATION

When Watson took his degree in 1878 he can hardly have been younger than twenty-five, which would fix the year of his birth as 1853 at the latest. Possibly he was born earlier than that because, even if he had pursued his studies without interruption, he could well have been nearer thirty upon gaining his qualification. In *The Naval Treaty* Watson introduces his school-fellow, Percy Phelps, 'who was of much the same age as myself, though he was two classes ahead of me'. Despite Phelps having been 'a very brilliant boy', it sounds as if Watson may have slightly lagged behind his contemporaries in academic performance. There is also, as we shall see, the possibility that Watson had suffered a break in his medical studies which would have contributed towards making him an older-than-average graduate. It seems reasonable to suggest that his birth date was probably in the region of 1850–2.[1]

Of his parents very little is known. Watson's mother is not mentioned anywhere in his writings and may have died while he was still a child. His father had, if Holmes remembered right, 'been dead many years' at the time of *The Sign of Four*.[2] Neither parent had been living in England when Watson returned home from India in 1881, invalided out of the service. However, there are some deductions which may be made with reasonable confidence. The Watson family was fairly well-to-do, for the elder son 'was left with good prospects' in addition to his father's 'fifty-guinea watch'. And the younger son,

John, was educated at one of the more notable public schools, before proceeding to the University of London to read medicine and play rugby for Blackheath. It was in a match at the Old Deer Park that Watson was thrown 'over the ropes into the crowd' by Robert Ferguson, the Richmond three-quarter, who was later to figure in *The Sussex Vampire.* Watson's school cannot be identified with certainty, but Winchester is a distinct possibility: firstly, it was a school of the standing to which the nephew of 'Lord Holdhurst, the great Conservative politician', might well have been sent, as a prelude to Cambridge and the Foreign Office; and secondly it was situated in that part of England for which Watson retained great pride and affection, noticeable in several of the stories, particularly *The Copper Beeches.*[3] The classical side of his education made a permanent impression, for at the conclusion of *A Study in Scarlet* Watson was able to trot out a quotation from Horace, to console Holmes for having seen the credit for the case go to the official police:

> Populus me sibilat at mihi plaudo
> Ipse domi simul ac nummos contemplar in arca.

The doctor's childhood home was probably in or near London. It was thither that he 'naturally gravitated' after landing from the *Orontes* on Portsmouth jetty, and there he chose to remain. Short of money as he was, and 'leading a comfortless, meaningless existence', he would surely have revisited, for a while at least, the scenes of his early life, where his health might have had a better chance to improve and where his means might have been sufficiently stretched to buy some additional comforts. Watson appears to have had no hankering then for 'the old English capital', or any yearning 'for the glades of the New Forest or the shingle of Southsea'. The idea that he might be compelled to 'leave the metropolis and rusticate somewhere in the country' was a prospect about as alarming as the state of his finances. The 'great cesspool into which all the loungers and idlers of the Empire are irresistibly drained' was home, so far as Watson was concerned.

But Watson had travelled abroad no small amount, if the claims made in *The Sign of Four* about his familiarity with the fair sex are to be taken literally. As Mary Morstan entered his life and attracted his love Watson recalled that, 'in an experience of women which extends over many nations and three separate continents, I have never looked upon a face which gave a clearer promise of a refined and sensitive nature'. *Many* nations, *three* separate continents; experience indeed. The suggestion has been made that one of the continents was Australia, that Watson probably lived there for a while as a boy before entering public school or possibly spent some time there during or prior to his medical studies. The theory cannot be disproved, and indeed there is a measure of support for it in Watson's remark to Miss Morstan in *The Sign of Four*, as they stood outside Pondicherry Lodge, looking at 'the traces of the treasure-seekers' in the grounds. 'What a strange place!' said the lady, to which Watson replied, 'It looks as though all the moles in England had been let loose in it. I have seen something of the sort on the side of a hill near Ballarat, where the prospectors had been at work.' Perhaps it is fair to speculate that Watson's 'unhappy brother', and possibly also his father, may have been living in Australia at the time of *A Study in Scarlet* and that he had visited them at some earlier time; even so, the remark to Miss Morstan may involve no more significance than that Watson had seen a picture of the Ballarat diggings which the disordered grounds of Pondicherry Lodge called to mind and that he had not in fact experienced the Australian gold-fields at first hand.

What is not generally appreciated is that, if Watson's boast about the women of three continents is literally true, Australia is not required as one of them. Indeed, if Watson really had visited or lived in Australia, we should have expected to hear of his experience of women extending to *four* continents, rather than three, the others being Europe, Asia and Africa. His experience in Asia and Africa must necessarily have been exceedingly limited, but he probably had some spare time available for amorous excursions in such places as Bombay and Peshawur, as well as in Egypt, while on the way to join his regiment. In his early years, before the ruin of his health in Afghanistan, Watson seems to have been the sort of young man who was not slow to indulge such opportunities as came his way. In his confession to Holmes on the occasion of their very first meeting in the chemical laboratory Watson admitted that, when he was well, he had 'another set of vices', and sexual encounters were probably not excluded.

Between taking his degree and going to Netley for the army surgeons' course, Watson spent a short while at St Bartholomew's Hospital, where he made the acquaintance of young Stamford, who was later to figure so significantly in *A Study in Scarlet*, making the all-important introduction to Holmes. Mention of Stamford calls to mind his description of Watson's appearance as they sat in their hansom and 'rattled through the crowded London streets' on their way from the Criterion Bar to the Holborn Restaurant. 'As thin as a lath and as brown as a nut' were the metaphors employed by the Barts dresser. Holmes continues in similar vein, noticing that Watson's 'face is dark, and that is not the natural tint of his skin, for his wrists are fair'. Whether these observations can possibly be accepted as accurate is a problem. Watson's memory may have been playing him false, so that he got it only partly right when writing his account of this momentous day, and the descriptions as he reported them may have become coloured by his own impression of what he hoped he looked like.

WATSON AND AFGHANISTAN

It can hardly have been earlier than the spring of 1880 when Watson left England for Bombay, whence he reached Candahar, found his regiment, transferred on attachment to the Berkshires and served with them 'at the fatal battle of Maiwand' in July. Having been rescued and brought back to the British lines, he 'was removed, with a great train of wounded sufferers, to the base hospital at Peshawur', where he rallied. There, 'struck down by enteric fever, that curse of our Indian possessions', he spent some months in hospital during which his 'life was despaired of'. Then, convalescent at last, he was hastily dispatched home and 'stayed for some time at a private hotel in the Strand', ultimately drifting into the Criterion Bar, where he 'recognized young Stamford' and took pleasure at 'the sight of a friendly face'. It is plain enough how Watson became 'as thin as a lath'; but how, exactly, did he contrive to present to two independent observers the dark tan of an Englishman who has spent his life in the tropics?

His trip to and through India can have taken, at the most, about three months, May to July 1880. As an Englishman taking what was in all probability his first journey to a hot climate, Watson would have taken care to avoid excessive exposure to the elements, though it is only reasonable to expect that he would have acquired some sun-tan. We know, from *The Reigate Squires*, that Watson's 'old friend Colonel Hayter' had come under his professional care in Afghanistan, and he refers, in *The Musgrave Ritual*, to 'the rough-and-tumble work' there, but there can have been little time available for the ordinary business of doctoring before the battle of Maiwand.

Watson was then confined in the base hospital having treatment for his wound for possibly two months, August and September, and became sufficiently improved in health 'to be able to walk about the wards, and even to bask a little upon the verandah'. Then there followed the months during which his life was despaired of, until, at last, he was able, as a convalescent, to be shipped back to England, arriving in London in about March or April 1881 and then staying 'for some time' in the meaningless life of a private hotel. In so far as Watson had the opportunity to acquire an obviously apparent facial brownness, it seems clear that it must have been insufficient to survive the prolonged incarceration in hospital, the sea voyage home, and the period of residence in London; assuredly it would no longer be so obvious that Stamford could say with any truth that Watson was 'as brown as a nut', nor that Holmes could have been so impressed by Watson's dark face that he should draw a deduction from it in the course of his reasoning that the doctor had just returned from Afghanistan.

If this is thought to be a bad point the reader is of course at liberty to reject it, but, though one hates to spoil the story, it does seem unlikely—to say the least—that Watson can have been wandering around London in the summer or autumn of 1881[4] with such a brown face that two people who met him are supposed to have commented immediately upon it. (We should have thought it far less improbable had Watson recollected taking an evening's leisure and visiting the Opera Comique for one of the early performances of Gilbert and Sullivan's *Patience*.) Watson, revelling in his role as the old campaigner, seems to have wildly exaggerated the dark tint of his skin, partly for understandable reasons of vanity, partly with the object of enabling Holmes to display his remarkable deductive capacity. It may be that Holmes was not so quick with his inference about Afghanistan as Watson would have the reader believe.

DATING OF 'A STUDY IN SCARLET'

Turning now to the dating of *A Study in Scarlet*, the murder of Drebber was committed in the early hours of the morning of Saturday 4 March 1882 and Jefferson Hope was arrested in Holmes' room after 'a terrific conflict' during the morning of the following day Sunday 5 March. However, since the more generally held opinion—though based on flimsy evidence—is that *A Study of Scarlet* is an 1881 adventure, it is no more than just to state the case and consider the problems.[5]

The case for 1881 necessarily presupposes that Watson returned to England from India in late 1880, meeting Holmes and taking up residence in Baker Street by the end of January 1881. That year must be favoured, so it is asserted, because otherwise too long a period would elapse between the 'fatal battle of Maiwand' and Watson's introduction to Holmes. Even Watson, it is thought, would not have remained in idleness for a year or more. More specifically, if 1882 were chosen, the second day of the adventure would be a Sunday and the papers from which Watson quotes at length, the *Daily Telegraph*, the *Standard* and the *Daily News*, would not have been published. Furthermore, a study of the shipping records made by Percy Metcalfe reveals that the *Orontes* made a trip to England from India in October–November 1880. But that is the sum total of the evidence supporting 1881, and the chief objection to 1882, the little matter of the daily papers, carries less weight when set against other evidence which makes it impossible for the second day of the mystery to have been a Saturday either. When 1882 is examined, even with the most critical eye, there is found an overwhelming case in favour of that year.

Consider first the timing of Watson's adventures. Is it even conceivable that by 4 March 1881 he can have been ready to accompany Holmes to the Brixton Road? After meeting Holmes and arranging 'to go halves with him in some nice rooms which he had found', Watson allowed the weeks to go by, while his curiosity deepened and the two men 'gradually began to settle down' in their new surroundings. The whole tenor and spirit of Watson's remarks in the chapter 'The Science of Deduction' implies a fairly long period of observation. 'Be it remembered how objectless' was Watson's life at this time and how many of the 'nondescript individuals put in an appearance' who were Holmes' clients. The date of the Lauriston Gardens mystery is definite: 4 March, as Watson had 'good reason to remember'. On the time factor alone it should be possible to dismiss any suggestion that this particular 4 March was the Friday in 1881. The minimum plausible periods of time to cover this stage of Watson's life must have been:

In hospital following wounds	2 months
In hospital with enteric fever	4 months
Travelling home	1 month
Staying at the private hotel	2 months
With Holmes at Baker Street	2 months
Total	11 months

It is stressed that these are minimum periods and were, in all probability, longer, extending in all to a period in excess of a full year. Working forward from the battle of Maiwand, we are confronted with late June, 1881, eleven months afterwards, as the earliest possible date for *A Study in Scarlet*, in other words nearly four months after the date which so many others have learnedly, if unconvincingly, propounded. Is it not far more feasible that the 'months my life was despaired of' were themselves three or four, followed by a prolonged period of gradual recovery, and that the time spent at the private hotel in the Strand was also of several months' duration? After all, Watson had been leading his 'comfortless, meaningless existence' for a sufficient time to allow him to refer to it as his 'style of living'.

But this is not all. When *The Five Orange Pips* is consulted, Watson is seen glancing over his 'notes and records of the Sherlock Holmes cases between the years '82 and '90'. Why no mention of 1881 if he had been collaborating with Holmes since the early days of March in that year? By itself, the passage can hardly be regarded as conclusive, but it is at least suggestive of the proposition that Watson's notes began only in 1882. Certainly he retained a detailed account of *A Study in Scarlet*, which was 'duly recorded in Dr. Watson's Journal'.

Some additional support may be forthcoming from *The Speckled Band*, one of the cases in which Watson had 'during the last eight years' studied the methods of his friend Sherlock Holmes. It seems likely that Watson intended those last eight years to indicate the same period as his notes and records, ie, 'between the years '82 and '90', and had forgotten that these would have amounted to nine years *inclusive*. This view is fortified by the doctor's statement that *The Speckled Band*, which is dated 'early in April, in the year '83', had 'occurred in the early days of my association with Holmes'. If Holmes and Watson had been together since about January 1881, a necessary requirement if *A Study in Scarlet* took place that year, they could scarcely be said to be still 'in the early days' of their association as late as April 1883. Upon this basis, an 1882 date for *A Study in Scarlet* is obviously far more probable.

We have already noticed that the most telling point against 1882 is the fact that, on the evidence of the newspapers, 5 March could not have been a Sunday. There are, however, two equally cogent arguments that it cannot have been a Saturday, as is bound to have been the case if 1881 was the correct year.

Jefferson Hope was never brought to trial because 'on the very night after his capture' he died in his cell through the bursting of his aortic aneurism. (Parenthetically, one wonders whether the coroner had any harsh words to say about Gregson and Lestrade for leaving him overnight without attendance or medical aid, so that 'he was found in the morning stretched upon the floor of the cell'.) And yet Watson, Holmes and the other witnesses 'had all been warned to appear before the magistrates upon the Thursday', which indicates that, following the arrest, Hope had been brought before a court to be remanded to a fixed date when 'our testimony' would be given. This is most unlikely to have been done on a Sunday and was presumably, and quite properly, attended to on the Monday morning, prior to the prisoner's death on the night of Monday/Tuesday. If the mystery had been solved on the Saturday, as would have been the position if 1881 was the year, Hope's fatal collapse on the 'night after his capture' would have prevented the fixing of Thursday for the committal proceedings, as the murderer must then have been dead before he could have appeared in any court.

The case for 1882 is made complete when, as J. F. Christ noted, it is recalled that on the afternoon of the first day of the story, 4 March, Holmes attended one of Hallé's concerts, which were regularly performed on Saturday afternoons. *A Study in Scarlet* must, therefore, belong to a year in which 4 March fell on a Saturday; 1882 suits that requirement perfectly, but not 1881, when 4 March was a Friday, an impossible day for the concert. So 1882 it must have been.

INTRODUCTION TO HOLMES

We therefore imagine a winter's day, perhaps November or December 1881, or even January of the following year, foggy, damp and rather cold, with Watson, fortified by his refreshment in the Criterion and his Holborn lunch, looking on with amazement while his new acquaintance, delighted at having made 'the most practical medico-legal discovery for years', looked as though he had unearthed a gold mine. 'Dr. Watson, Mr. Sherlock Holmes', said Stamford, introducing them; and so it all began.

Stamford and Watson have both recorded some extraordinarily detailed impressions of Holmes at this time. Stamford begins by describing Holmes simply as 'a fellow who is working at the chemical laboratory up at the hospital'. He then continues by telling Watson that 'I know nothing more of him than I have learned from meeting him occasionally in the laboratory'—but actually he did know quite a lot more. 'I believe he is well up in anatomy, and he is a first-class chemist; but, as far as I know, he has never taken out any systematic medical classes. His studies are very desultory and eccentric, but he has amassed a lot of out-of-the-way knowledge which would astonish his professors.'

Watson seems to have agreed that such activities as 'beating the subjects in the dissecting rooms with a stick' were bizarre enough to have astounded any professor. And there was yet a further word of warning to the proposed fellow-lodger: 'I could well imagine his

‘“I’ve found it! I’ve found it!” he shouted.’
By Geo Hutchinson, from page 9 of the 1891 edition of *A Study in Scarlet*.

giving a friend a little pinch of the latest vegetable alkaloid, not out of malevolence, you understand, but simply out of a spirit of inquiry in order to have an accurate idea of the effects.' And how wise that warning was. Fifteen years later, in *The Devil's Foot*, Watson kept himself just sufficiently alert to enable him to rescue himself and Holmes from the toxic fumes which had been created in that self-same spirit of inquiry. Holmes had to apologise afterwards that 'it was an unjustifiable experiment even for oneself, and doubly so for a friend'. Stamford deserves our thanks not only for the original introduction but also for his timely admonition that Holmes should be carefully watched when dabbling with poisons.

Watson apparently thought it safe enough to chance joining up with Holmes, but we wonder what the doctor's bull pup thought of the arrangement. The animal figures in the story no more, and may have been disposed of before Watson moved in to Baker Street, but we have a sneaking suspicion that it died, possibly through a slight overdose of vegetable alkaloid. Holmes was not averse to experimenting upon dogs. The landlady's 'poor little devil of a terrier' was dispatched quite mercifully with half of one of Jefferson Hope's pills. By this time Watson may have influenced Holmes sufficiently to prevent him from pursuing his chemical researches except upon very sickly animals.

Watson perhaps transferred his doggy affections to Holmes himself. As E. V. Knox and others have noted, he frequently uses canine metaphors in his descriptions of Holmes' detective activities. 'His nostrils seemed to dilate with a purely animal lust for the chase,' and there are several passages in which Holmes reminds Watson of a foxhound. When the murderer was arrested in *A Study in Scarlet* we read that 'Gregson, Lestrade and Holmes sprang upon him like so many staghounds'. It was, to Watson, an irresistible association of ideas. Even when supposed to be taking a restful holiday in Cornwall, Holmes, unexpectedly consulted by the local vicar, 'sat up in his chair like an old hound who hears the view-holloa'. It is only fair to mention, however, that Watson also noticed feline characteristics in his companion, among them a 'cat-like love of personal cleanliness'.

Whatever the reason for the bull pup's disappearance may have

'THE UNFORTUNATE CREATURE'S TONGUE SEEMED HARDLY TO HAVE BEEN MOISTENED IN IT BEFORE IT GAVE A CONVULSIVE SHIVER IN EVERY LIMB, AND LAY AS RIGID AND LIFELESS AS IF IT HAD BEEN STRUCK BY LIGHTNING.'

By Geo Hutchinson, from page 111 of the 1891 edition of *A Study in Scarlet*. Sherlock Holmes displaying his vivisectionist tendencies. An interesting picture, showing the rat-faced Lestrade and, seated, his colleague Gregson, 'the smartest of the Scotland Yarders'. The stout, bearded Gregson, modelled, perhaps, as a younger edition of the Prince of Wales, hardly lives up to Watson's description of him earlier in the book, 'a tall, white-faced, flaxen haired man'.

been, Watson is soon to discover that Holmes is, by profession, a consulting detective, 'the only one in the world'. What, to use an expression often heard in the criminal courts, were his antecedents?

He was about the same age as Watson, possibly a little younger. The only direct reference to his age comes from the very last adventure of all, *His Last Bow*, when Holmes, alias the Irish-American Altamont, is described as 'a tall, gaunt man of sixty'. (Watson, who has acted as chauffeur, figures then as 'a heavily built, elderly man, with a grey moustache'.) The age sixty may not have been precise, but is suggestive of Holmes having been born about 1853 or 1854. His ancestors, we learn from Holmes himself in *The Greek Interpreter*, 'were country squires, who appear to have led much the same life as is natural to their class'. His 'grandmother, who was the sister of Vernet, the French artist', was to some extent held responsible for the art in his blood, his love of music and the opera, of dropping in at art galleries, and writing learned papers on such subjects as tattoo marks. It was also, according to Holmes, a basis for his 'faculty of observation' and his 'peculiar facility for deduction'.

Of his education Watson tells us nothing, probably because Holmes, for his part, told Watson nothing. He referred 'hardly ever to his own early life', and it was not for a long time after taking up lodgings together that Watson even discovered the existence of Holmes' brother, Mycroft. While Mycroft seems sufficiently conformist to have been the product of the nineteenth-century English public school, Sherlock Holmes does not. His teaching may have been left in the hands of a governess and tutor, but it is not impossible that he followed Mycroft to school only to be expelled for exhibiting too individualistic a behaviour and maintaining a stout refusal to conform. One can imagine that his ability in the noble art of self-defence was acquired for the very practical purpose of getting the bigger boys to leave him alone. It may have been at school that Holmes began to 'dabble with poisons a good deal', and he probably made discoveries about the masters which they would have preferred to keep secret. The likelihood is that his parents were requested to remove him and to arrange for the continuance of his education elsewhere. He may, at this time, have travelled extensively abroad, accompanied by his tutor.[6]

Aided by a private tutor and equipped with a first-class brain, Holmes could well have gone up to the university at the age of sixteen or seventeen, far younger than the main body of freshmen, and this may explain why, at first, he found it difficult to make friends. By the time Holmes reached the varsity it must be assumed that his parents were dead and that, advised by brother Mycroft, who was probably also one of his trustees, he spent most of his share of the family money in completing his education and fitting himself for his chosen profession.

Holmes maintained rooms in London from his undergraduate days, but, by the time he met Watson, 'he was bemoaning himself.. because he could not get someone to go halves with him in some nice rooms which he had found, and which were too much for his purse'. Watson's income at this time was little more than the four pounds a week contributed by a grateful nation, and the Baker Street rooms were modest enough—'a couple of comfortable bedrooms and a single large airy sitting-room'—so it would appear that Holmes' personal fortune had dwindled to fairly small proportions; he was, after all, earning some fees from his occasional consultations. Holmes, as he tells Watson in *The Musgrave Ritual*, had by this time 'established a considerable, though not a very lucrative, connection'. It appears, therefore, that Holmes was left by his parents sufficiently well provided for to enable him to finish his education, but that there was very little over.

Much detailed research has been done and many arguments joined over the rival claims of the universities and colleges to have counted Holmes among their students. But, since this is a subject worthy of a monograph to itself and since it has already been exhaustively treated by others, we content ourselves here with stating that, as far as can be ascertained upon very sketchy evidence, Holmes was up at Oxford between 1870 and 1874.

However, some attention must be given to the varsity reminiscence cases, if only to check their chronologies against the datings postulated for Holmes and his career at the time of *A Study in Scarlet*. Because there are so many internal contradictions in *The Gloria Scott*, the more helpful memoir to study first is *The Musgrave Ritual*. 'Reginald Musgrave had been in the same college' as Holmes; he was 'an exceedingly aristocratic type' and 'a scion of one of the very oldest families in the kingdom'. The detective had seen nothing of him for four years until one morning he walked into Holmes' room in Montague Street. Since his father's death, two years previously, Musgrave had been managing the Hurlstone estates. He then goes on to explain that 'as I am member for my district as well, my life has been a busy one'.

Unfortunately, it is not clear whether Musgrave succeeded to his father's seat by contesting a by-election after his death, or whether he had entered Parliament earlier or later than that. However, Musgrave speaks as though he had become member for his constituency first and had subsequently had to undertake the extra burden of looking after the family property. If this is right, it is not unreasonable to infer that Musgrave commenced his political career at the general election of 1874, very soon after going down from Oxford. He would have been very young and inexperienced, but it is by no means impossible that a safe Sussex seat fell into the lap of this rich young heir within a short time of taking his degree. If Musgrave graduated in 1873, which may have been a year ahead of Holmes, he could have secured election in 1874 and called upon Holmes as a client in 1877. I believe I may be the only researcher who has opted for this year. The major chronologists divide their preferences among the years 1878, 1879 and 1880.

At this time, Holmes observes, 'I have taken to living by my wits', though there are still many years of patient study to ensue before his practice becomes established on a full-time basis. The early years of Holmes' 'turning to practical ends those powers with which you used to amaze us' were to produce in all a pile of packages and bundles making a large tin box one-third full. Holmes was probably no older than twenty-three at the time he deciphered the ritual, and must have taken great encouragement at being able to command the patronage of an MP at this early stage of his career.

There seems to be nothing in *The Musgrave Ritual* inconsistent with the datings and ages suggested here; so let us now examine the other case of Holmes' university days, *The Gloria Scott*. Here we are introduced to Victor Trevor, the young man described by Holmes as 'the only friend I made during the two years that I was at college', and who invited him down to his father's place at Donnithorpe, in Norfolk, for a month of the long vacation. At first, the old man underestimated Holmes' mental powers, but, unexpectedly convinced of his ability, recommended the choice of a career and made Holmes 'feel that a profession might be made out of what had up to that time been the merest hobby'. Natural aptitude and hard work did not enable Holmes easily to make progress in his chosen profession; later he is to remark to Watson, when recounting the memoir of *The Musgrave Ritual*, 'how difficult I found it at first, and how long I had to wait before I succeeded in making any headway'.

However, *The Gloria Scott* affords little or no assistance in confirming or contradicting the chronology of the early part of Holmes' life. The adventure itself is undated, although, according to Trevor senior's statement recovered from the Japanese cabinet, it purports to be thirty years after the trial in 1855. An 1885 date is quite impossible on any showing and, however one may juggle with ages and dates, there always appears some insuperable objection to any proposition which might be advanced. The reader who has an hour to spare can entertain himself handsomely by testing the various permutations in a quest for an acceptable solution. The date of this adventure, as Martin Dakin has observed, 'is one of the thorniest problems in Holmesian chronology'. A measure of the difficulties involved may be seen from the variety of dates assigned by others: 1873 Brend, Folsom, Dakin; 1874 Baring-Gould, Blakeney; 1875 Bell; 1876 Christ and Zeisler. But the chief interest of *The Gloria Scott* lies in its explanation of how it was that Sherlock Holmes came to decide upon his vocation.

BREAKFAST AT 221B

It is now time to turn to some of the problems of the Baker Street menage which first present themselves in *A Study in Scarlet.* To start with, there is breakfast. In *A Study in Scarlet* Watson seems to make the position absolutely clear. He refers to his own 'late habits' and confesses that 'I get up at all sorts of ungodly hours'. Holmes 'had invariably breakfasted and gone out' before Watson rose in the mornings, though on that memorable day, 4 March 1882, the doctor was up 'somewhat earlier than usual, and found that Sherlock Holmes had not yet finished his breakfast'. His appearance at breakfast at such an early hour must have been most exceptional, for his place at table had not been laid, nor his coffee prepared.

If the evidence stopped there, some impression could be gained of the early morning domestic habits of the two friends. But the breakfast arrangements of *A Study in Scarlet* did not always apply. Only just over a year later, in early April 1883, Watson describes himself as 'regular in my habits' and Holmes as 'a late riser as a rule'. What can have happened in the thirteen months between *A Study in Scarlet* and *The Speckled Band* to demand such drastic changes? So far as Watson is concerned, the answer may be that his regular habit was to be late; it was 'only a quarter past seven' when Holmes wakened Watson with the news that a lady client had arrived, and the doctor 'blinked up at him in some surprise, and perhaps just a little resentment'. Much later, in *The Abbey Grange*, Holmes roused Watson very early and they both departed from Baker Street without their breakfasts. But presumably, at the time of *The Speckled Band*, Holmes had never disturbed Watson's slumbers before. He may have done so upon that occasion merely because he required a chaperon or medical attendant while he interviewed the lady client, Miss Helen Stoner, who had 'arrived in a considerable state of excitement'.

Possibly all Watson meant in describing Holmes as a late riser was that 7.15 was considerably earlier than his usual time for getting up. But, if so, his habits had changed again by 1889 because Watson, in *The Engineer's Thumb*, is expecting to discover Holmes taking his breakfast soon after seven o'clock. In that adventure the wounded Hatherley has called on Watson just before 7 am and, after receiving only the most perfunctory medical attention, is bundled into a cab and whisked off to consult Holmes, the doctor remarking that they will 'just be in time to have a little breakfast with him'. In fact they find Holmes smoking 'his before-breakfast pipe'.

And to make the mystery deeper still, the habits of Holmes apparently changed yet again, for Watson asserts, in *The Hound of the Baskervilles*, that the detective was 'usually very late in the mornings, save upon those not infrequent occasions when he stayed up all night'. This is supported in *Black Peter*, in which Inspector Stanley Hopkins is invited to breakfast at nine-thirty, and in *The Valley of Fear*, in which Holmes is found sitting before 'his untasted breakfast' at about ten o'clock in the morning. He had also refused his breakfast on the second day of *The Norwood Builder*; that must have been one of those times when he stayed up for most of the night, for his eyes were surrounded by dark shadows and 'the carpet round his chair was littered with cigarette ends'. Watson was ready first in *The Naval Treaty*, but that was because he was looking after the haggard Percy Phelps and Holmes really *had* stayed up all night. But what a breakfast the three of them eventually had, curried chicken, ham and eggs, and, for the client, 'a touch of the dramatic', the missing naval treaty hidden beneath a third cover! Mrs Hudson 'has as good an idea of breakfast as a Scotchwoman', was Holmes' remark. However, this was something very special in breakfasts. More usually the fare would have been what Holmes consumed very early before going off to investigate the alleged losses of *The Retired Colourman*; Watson described the debris as 'some toast crumbs and two empty egg-shells'.

But even before Watson's marriage further changes had been brought about in the morning routine at 221B Baker Street. In *The Five Orange Pips*[7] Watson remarks that 'Sherlock Holmes was already at breakfast when I came down'. Presumably they usually breakfasted together at this time, because Holmes immediately excuses himself for not waiting until Watson arrived. At the resumption of partnership after the *Return* the two friends are breakfasting together again, for at the opening of *The Norwood Builder* they have a discussion at table in which Holmes remarks that 'sensational cases had disappeared out of our papers'. In *Black Peter* Watson has begun without Holmes, but that was only because the latter has gone out early to experiment with his harpoon, and one infers that their usual practice at this time was to have breakfast together. And it seems likely that this was still their custom in *Thor Bridge*, wherein Watson 'descended to breakfast', expecting to find Holmes in depressed spirits, but instead 'found that he had nearly finished his meal, and that his mood was particularly bright and joyous', despite his two eggs having been served hard-boiled.

There are so many contradictions about breakfast-time that one hesitates to express a certain view; save possibly one, that Watson, ready as always to submit to his very human failings, was not very good at getting up in the mornings. I am fortified in this belief by the remark made by Mgr Ronald Knox: 'Both in *A Study in Scarlet* and in *The Adventures*, we hear that Watson breakfasted after Holmes: in *The Hound* we are told that Holmes breakfasted late. But then, the true inference from this is that Watson breakfasted very late indeed.'

Early birds are not always very easy to live with, and, when the time came for the famous detective's retirement, Watson went his own way. His horror of being awakened soon after dawn may well have been one of the reasons why he paid Holmes no more than 'an occasional week-end visit'. Holmes had surrendered himself not only to that peculiar English addiction, the 'early cup of tea', but also to a liking for cliff-top walks and sea-bathing before breakfast. Watson kept out of the way!

HOLMES' ADDICTIONS

Holmes' early addiction to cocaine and Watson's efforts to wean him away from it have been dealt with in varying detail by other writers, the most recent being Martin Dakin. Whatever Watson's part may have been in trying to save Holmes from the consequences of his infirmities, it is an undeniable fact, clearly set out in *The Devil's Foot*, that it was 'in the spring of the year 1897 that Holmes' iron constitution showed some symptoms of giving way in the face of constant hard work of a most exacting kind, aggravated, perhaps, by occasional indiscretions of his own'. Indiscretions there must certainly have been, and Watson seems to have been exceedingly frightened of them. When he saw Holmes at Cambridge, in *The Missing Three-Quarter*, 'holding his tiny hypodermic syringe', he at once 'feared the worst', but the detective was able to reassure him that 'it is not upon this occasion an instrument of evil'.

If Watson *was* ever able to wean Holmes from the drug mania which so beset him throughout his career, it seems to have been most effectively accomplished during the later years, following the holiday in Cornwall. Perhaps Watson, having seen success elude him for so long, inserted this passage in *The Missing Three-Quarter*, when it was published in 1904, to let his readers know that his persistence had been worthwhile and had at last resulted in a complete cure. He would have been less than human to let the opportunity slip of advertising to his public that he had, after all, acquired some influence over the great man.

Watson never seems to have tried to stop Holmes smoking. Presumably this is because he was such a heavy smoker himself and failed to recognise any serious danger in the excessive use of tobacco. There is a passage in *The Devil's Foot* which suggests that Watson was not entirely unaware of the injury to health which smoking might cause, for Holmes, asked by Mortimer Tregennis what he is going to do about the Cornish horror, replies: 'I think, Watson, that I shall resume that course of tobacco-poisoning which you have so often and so justly condemned.' But it was said with a smile, and Holmes probably meant it as a joke. He knew as well as Watson that neither of them could possibly manage without the solace and stimulation of tobacco. Watson, an avid reader of medical periodicals, can be imagined over the years teasing Holmes about his addiction to smoking and reminding him light-heartedly of the risks they were both running in their inability to give it up.

For Watson was as hooked on the weed as his companion. The pair must rank as two of the most famous smokers of their time. An exchange of details about their smoking habits forms the very first swapped confidence between them, when they were considering taking up residence together at the rooms which Holmes had found in Baker Street. 'You don't mind the smell of strong tobacco, I hope?' asked Holmes. 'I always smoke Ship's myself,' replied the doctor. 'That's good enough,' Holmes rejoined; and then went on to talk about his chemical experiments.

To smoke a pipe was, for Holmes, his favourite manner of relaxing and the stimulus he needed for prolonged mental effort. Over and over again, as the stories unfold, we find him—and often Watson, too—puffing away contentedly.

The frequent references to smoking have been dealt with in detail by other writers, as is the case with Holmes' drug addiction. Here, however, are a few comments we should like to make. Though

Holmes was most often found smoking a pipe or a cigar, it was to cigarettes that he turned on that fateful day in May 1891 when he set out on the hike which was to lead to the hand-to-hand death-struggle with Professor Moriarty. With him was the silver cigarette-case which, Watson recalled, 'he used to carry'. Holmes was to describe it with a certain lack of precision in *The Empty House* as a 'cigarette-box', but there is no doubt that his silver cigarette-case was meant, because he had deliberately left it behind at Reichenbach, accompanying the note to his friend, as corroboration of the authenticity of his disappearance. Holmes may have been particularly attached to it. The suggestion is that he was, and that Watson knew that he was; hence its choice, with the stick, as an object to leave behind, so that Watson might be drawn to no other plausible conclusion except that he had really been killed.

What pleasure it must have given the doctor to observe how Holmes, still 'dressed in the seedy frock-coat of the book merchant', and back at Baker Street alive and well, 'lit a cigarette in his old nonchalant manner'. And what joy Watson must have felt, only a short while later, to see Holmes 'pushing his case across' to offer a cigarette to McFarlane. We feel reasonably sure that it was the same cigarette-case, the silver one, which had been carefully deposited on the top of the boulder alongside the narrow pathway by the waterfall, for his friend to find. And we think it may have been a present to Holmes from Watson himself, possibly to commemorate the occasion when Holmes acted as best man at the doctor's wedding to Mary Morstan. But that is only a guess.

Before leaving the subject of Sherlock Holmes and tobacco, be it noted that this was a topic which helped to bring him to the fore as one of the earliest exponents of forensic science. His famous 'little monograph on the ashes of 140 different varieties of pipe, cigar, and cigarette tobacco' was just one of the many handbooks and articles which he published in aid of the detection of crime. Even as early as *A Study in Scarlet* he was telling Watson about some of them and, indeed, giving a practical demonstration of one piece of research in the chemical laboratory at Barts. And one of the first clues which he was able to provide for Lestrade and Gregson was that the murderer of

'HE STRUCK A MATCH ON HIS BOOT AND HELD IT UP AGAINST THE WALL.'
By Geo Hutchinson, from page 49 of the 1891 edition of *A Study in Scarlet*. Holmes and Watson, on their first adventure together, and in company with the little, rat-faced Inspector Lestrade, examine marks on a wall. A picture which is worth contrasting with Sidney Paget's portrayal of a similar scene after the *Return* (see p 84).

Drebber had smoked a Trichinopoly cigar. During the cab journey to Audley Court, Holmes was at pains to let Watson know how sure he was:

> I gathered up some scattered ash from the floor. It was dark in colour and flakey—such an ash as is only made by a Trichinopoly. I have made a special study of cigar ashes—in fact, I have written a monograph upon the subject. I flatter myself that I can distinguish at a glance the ash of any known brand either of cigar or of tobacco. It is just in such details that the skilled detective differs from the Gregson and Lestrade type.

This particular brochure must have been one of Holmes' favourites. He mentions it again in *The Sign of Four* and *The Boscombe Valley Mystery*. Obviously it was a fine production, distinguished not only by its detailed and authoritative text but also by its 'coloured plates illustrating the difference in the ash'. Presumably the monograph was compiled during those early years when Holmes occupied rooms in Montague Street, just round the corner from the British Museum where, as he was to explain to Watson in *The Musgrave Ritual*, 'I waited, filling in my too abundant leisure time by studying all those branches of science which might make me more efficient.'

And how efficient Holmes became, and how efficient his biographer was in his self-appointed task of glorifying the exploits of the great detective, are matters which we may now proceed to examine more closely in the context of the many problems which present themselves in the other stories of the saga.

FIRST INTERVAL

FINANCIAL PROBLEMS

Sherlock Holmes said it:

'I cannot agree with those who rank modesty among the virtues.'

'Then, as to money?' asked the business-like Sherlock Holmes at his first interview with the King of Bohemia. A generous advance towards expenses must have seemed a good idea. But he was not always business-like, or even consistent, in the financial affairs of his professional life. To let Holmes continue in his own words:

> The status of my client is a matter of less moment to me than the interest of his case.[1] I listen to their story, they listen to my comments, and then I pocket my fee.[2] My professional charges are upon a fixed scale. I do not vary them, save when I remit them altogether.[3] I play the game for the game's own sake.[4] I never make exceptions. An exception disproves the rule.[5] The work itself, the pleasure of finding a field for my peculiar powers, is my highest reward.[6] My work is its own reward.[7] It's Art for Art's sake, Watson. I suppose when you doctored you found yourself studying cases without thought of a fee.[8] I have taken to living by my wits.[9] I am a poor man.[10] I should be glad if you would make me out a cheque for six thousand pounds.[11]

Was it art? Or was it money? Or a bit of both? This is no idle inquiry. The financial problems of Sherlock Holmes lie at the very root of his literary fame. It was—never let it be forgotten—owing to shortage of money that Watson was in the first place introduced to Holmes as a prospective fellow-lodger, as someone who could 'go halves with him in some nice rooms which he had found, and which were too much for his purse'. As he remarked later, when telling Watson the story of *The Musgrave Ritual*, he 'had already established a considerable, though not a very lucrative, connection'. Hard cash was at a premium in those early days. Had Holmes been rich enough to manage on his own there can be no doubt that he would have done so Watson speaks of 'his proud, self-contained nature' and asserts that Holmes 'loathed every form of society with his whole Bohemian soul'. Holmes was not the kind of man who desired company; his need to find someone to share the Baker Street rooms was purely financial. Later, when Watson left to get married, there was no question of Holmes seeking another companion. By that time he was financially secure, and well able to pay the rent without assistance.

So is it not fortunate for the reading public of several successive generations that Holmes found it difficult, at first, to establish himself in his profession? For without the concerns of money there would have been no meeting with Watson; and without Watson there could have been no published adventures.

Even the good Watson, true friend that he was, had problems in getting his stories into print. It was an off-hand 'You may do what you like, Doctor' which Watson interpreted as permission to publish his first book, that 'small brochure with the somewhat fantastic title of *A Study in Scarlet*'. Thereafter Holmes did his best to discourage the doctor from any further attempts. He refused to offer any congratulations, and he irritated Watson by his 'criticism of a work which had been specially designed to please him'. It is amazing enough that Watson troubled again to take up his pen. And, when he did, he was to face 'the charge of sensationalism which has been urged against my records'.

After the *Return*, Holmes was still reticent and disapproving. 'His cold and proud nature was always averse, however, to anything in the shape of public applause, and he bound me in the most stringent terms to say no further word of himself, his methods, or his successes,' reported Watson in *The Norwood Builder*. Even after Holmes retired, Watson's problems were not over. In *The Devil's Foot* he complained about having 'continually been faced by difficulties caused by his own aversion to publicity'. Watson bemoaned the fact that it was 'this attitude upon the part of my friend' which 'caused me of late years to lay very few of my records before the public'. There is no doubt that Holmes was a very difficult man to please.

But the good doctor, bless his heart, persevered, urged on, no doubt, by financial considerations of his own; for his eagerly awaited reminiscences of the great detective were by this time bringing in a very useful income for the retired 'Army surgeon with a weak leg and a weaker banking account'.

Sherlock Holmes was not an extravagant man. His needs were simple, and money was not regarded as a matter of great importance. Luxurious living held few attractions. He was particularly fond of music, concerts, and the opera, and especially the more intimate recital, when he could transport himself 'to violin-land, where all is sweetness, and delicacy, and harmony'. Fine art interested him, and he formed the habit of dropping in at picture galleries, but he never seems to have bought any expensive paintings. Of food and wine he was something of a connoisseur, and would, on occasions, treat himself to some special delicacy, perhaps 'oysters and a brace of grouse, with something a little choice in white wines', but his normal diet was frugal enough. A beef sandwich, even just a loaf of bread, would be ample to satisfy his 'simple wants'. We may be sure that he never paid 'eightpence an ounce' for his tobacco, nor frequently as much as 'eightpence for a glass of sherry'. He had only himself to support and could, according to his own modest standards, exist very comfortably on a fairly low income, judged by the requirements of other professional men of his day. So long as he had enough, he was more than content. His remark in *The Naval Treaty* about 'Lord Holdhurst, the great Conservative politician' has a touch of pathos about it: 'He is far from rich, and has many calls'. Even Sherlock Holmes, we surmise, had never been so poor as to be compelled to have his boots re-soled.

It has been conjectured, for reasons outlined in the previous chapter, that during his early years, while fitting himself for his chosen career, Holmes used up most of the small inheritance which had been left him by his parents. Clients were few and money was short, but prospects were improving. The rooms in Baker Street represented an increase in his fortunes, though his professional activities did not yet involve a full-time commitment, and he was unable to manage the expense of Mrs Hudson's apartment on his own. Within the next decade, however, the payments to his landlady had become 'princely'. Watson was to comment, in *The Dying Detective*, that 'I have no doubt that the house might have been purchased at the price which Holmes paid for his rooms during the years that I was with him'.

The original arrangement between Holmes and Watson over the rooms was that they were shared, and the expenses were shared too. 'Go halves' was the expression used by Stamford, and Watson himself remarked that 'so moderate did the terms seem when divided between us, that the bargain was concluded upon the spot, and we at once entered into possession'. Watson paid half, and he occupied half, except when Holmes 'used to beg for the use of the sitting-room', and then the doctor would retire to his bedroom. This confirms that, in the early days, they were equal partners in the tenancy and Watson paid his full share. But how much was the rent? It cannot have been 'princely' at that stage, for Watson was alarmed at the state of his finances and was searching London for 'comfortable rooms at a reasonable price'. His income, so he tells us, was only 'eleven shillings and sixpence a day', or about four pounds a week.

Watson's disclosures about himself provide more than a clue to what Holmes could afford. Though possibly a little better off than Watson, Holmes must have counted most of his fees in shillings, rather than pounds, and it is doubtful whether they commenced by paying Mrs Hudson more than three or four pounds a week between them. If Holmes had then had an income exceeding about six pounds a week, there would have been no compulsion upon him to share. Therefore the probability must be that his earnings at the time of *A Study in Scarlet* amounted only to something in the region of four to six pounds weekly.

In the currency of the time this was no penury. Mary Sutherland, in *A Case of Identity*, had 'a hundred a year in my own right, besides a little that I make by the machine', which Holmes described as 'so large a sum', upon which his client could 'no doubt travel a little' and indulge herself in every way. 'I believe', he continued, 'that a single lady can get on very nicely upon an income of about sixty pounds.'

And a governess, living in with all found, might reckon to earn no more than £40 a year. Violet Hunter, in *The Copper Beeches*, thought an offer of £30 a quarter sufficiently eccentric to induce her to call upon Holmes for advice as to whether or not she should take such a post.

Watson's income seems to have remained static until he went into harness as a general practitioner at about the time of his marriage. When Mrs Hudson, as was only to be expected, sought a rent increase from time to time, he was quite unable to pay anything more. He was still referring to his weak bank account at the time of *The Sign of Four*, and he seems consistently to have failed to make a profit out of his bookmaker. 'Watson, you know something of racing?' asked Holmes in *Shoscombe Old Place*. 'I ought to,' the doctor ruefully replied, 'I pay for it with about half my wound pension.' By this time, however, in the years following the *Return*, the payments to Mrs Hudson had already assumed princely proportions, and it is clear that the extra expenses were paid entirely by Holmes, as some compensation to the long-suffering landlady for harbouring 'the very worst tenant in London'. Watson's opinion expressed in *The Dying Detective* about the value of the Baker Street house may even indicate that, within a few years of moving in, Holmes had become sufficiently prosperous, through rewards and fees for his professional services, to take on the entire responsibility of the establishment, even perhaps to the extent of allowing the wounded veteran to live there rent-free.

There had obviously occurred an upsurge in Holmes' fortunes, and a substantial one at that. How did it happen?

The first point to note is that throughout his career Holmes did a great deal of work 'without thought of a fee'. His services were freely available, provided the problem was worthwhile, to clients from all walks of life; 'and the humbler are usually the more interesting', said Holmes, smiling, in *The Noble Bachelor*. 'His increasing fame had brought with it an immense practice,' wrote Watson in the introductory paragraph of *Black Peter*, but 'Holmes, however, like all great artists, lived for his art's sake', and the doctor had 'seldom known him claim any large reward for his inestimable services' Watson continued:

> So unworldly was he—or so capricious—that he frequently refused his help to the powerful and wealthy where the problem made no appeal to his sympathies, while he would devote weeks of most intense application to the affairs of some humble client whose case presented those strange and dramatic qualities which appealed to his imagination and challenged his ingenuity.

SERVICES AVAILABLE TO THE YARD

But although Holmes never consciously sought riches, his genius, his single-mindedness of purpose, above all his basic kindness, all too often concealed beneath a rather pompous and forbidding exterior, brought him the material rewards which guaranteed his independence, fearlessness and incorruptibility in the cause of his clients. Again and again his services were gratuitously placed at the disposal of the official police who, more often than not, took the credit they all too seldom deserved. Lestrade was calling for guidance as frequently as 'three or four times in a single week' at the time of *A Study in Scarlet*. But the inspector also had other uses, in keeping Holmes 'in touch with all that was going on at the police headquarters' and occasionally introducing clients who could be charged a fee in the normal way.[12]

However, there is, in contrast, one example of a case in which Lestrade did his best to dissuade a prospective client from sending for Holmes. This was *The Boscombe Valley Mystery*, in which Alice Turner sensibly concluded that the Scotland Yard official was getting out of his depth. She insisted on employing Holmes and her attitude was not altogether to Lestrade's liking. As he explained to Holmes upon his arrival in Herefordshire:

> The case is as plain as a pikestaff, and the more one goes into it the plainer it becomes. Still, of course, one can't refuse a lady, and such a very positive one, too. She had heard of you, and would have your opinion, though I repeatedly told her that there was nothing which you could do which I had not already done.

It is at least reassuring to find Lestrade speaking so frankly, for these words run counter to the original message which invited Holmes to investigate the matter. Holmes had explained the summons clearly enough to Watson during the train journey from London, that 'Lestrade, being rather puzzled, has referred the case to me, and hence it is that two middle-aged gentlemen are flying westward at fifty miles an hour, instead of quietly digesting their breakfasts at home'. At this stage Lestrade had given Holmes the plain impression that he was recommending the new client; but that was a little deception which had to be abandoned when Holmes and Watson reached Ross.

Lestrade's feelings of professional jealousy, tinged perhaps with some sense of inferiority, are understandable. Nevertheless, it may be assumed that Holmes did rely from time to time upon introductions from police officers. One is reminded particularly of Cyril Overton of Trinity College, Cambridge, in *The Missing Three-Quarter*, who was recommended to Holmes by another police colleague, Stanley Hopkins, and of Colonel Ross, in *Silver Blaze*, who seems at least to have been prompted or encouraged to send for Holmes by Inspector Gregory.

Of the fully recorded cases there are at least nine, *The Reigate Squires*, *Black Peter*, *The Six Napoleons*, *The Golden Pince-Nez*, *The Abbey Grange*, *The Cardboard Box*, *The Dying Detective*, *A Study in Scarlet* and *The Valley of Fear*, in which Holmes participated solely in order to assist the police. For Holmes there can have been little reward save the experience, and the privilege of paying his own expenses in following up the clues.

He may, nevertheless, have managed to recoup something in *The Six Napoleons*, for the 'famous black pearl of the Borgias', which Holmes succeeded in recovering, was 'enormously valuable' and had undoubtedly been insured for a very considerable sum. It is noteworthy that Holmes had 'been looking up the dates in the old files of the paper', and it surely goes without saying that he would have kept an eagle eye open for the loss adjuster's advertisement. Why otherwise should he have taken such meticulous care, at the end of the case, to procure a document of transfer signed in the presence of two witnesses? The reward for that one discovery must have compensated Holmes tenfold for his work on all the police cases put together. His modest outlay of £10 for the purchase of Mr Sandeford's Napoleon bust turned out to be a very lucrative investment.

It was not only the English police who turned to Holmes for help in their more difficult cases. His study of criminology was unlimited by national boundaries, and he was sometimes able to quote 'parallel cases' from crimes which had been committed abroad. As Watson carefully noted in his first assessment of his new friend, in *A Study in Scarlet*: 'He appears to know every detail of every horror perpetrated in the century.' Foreign detectives were thus able to look to him occasionally for assistance, like François Le Villard, the official who 'has come rather to the front lately in the French detective service', who consulted Holmes in a case 'concerned with a will' which is mentioned in *The Sign of Four*. 'My practice has extended recently to the Continent,' said Holmes somewhat proudly, starting up a new line of conversation. Watson confessed to having 'observed that a small vanity underlay my companion's quiet and didactic manner'. Holmes may have been musing to himself that it did no harm to indulge in a little vanity over a case like that; after all, nobody was going to pay him for it. It was truly an example of his profession being its own reward.

PRIVATE CASES WITHOUT FEE

In a large number of private cases, too, Holmes had to rub along without the consolation of a fat cheque at the end of the chase. The reasons were many and various. In *The Five Orange Pips* and *The Dancing Men* the clients were murdered after engaging Holmes to protect them; and, as we shall see in a later chapter, Holmes was guilty of gross negligence towards them both and must have had their deaths on his conscience for a long while afterwards. In *The Retired Colourman* the client turned out to be himself the murderer, and was probably sent to the criminal lunatic asylum before he got round to paying his personal debts. Holmes would have immensely enjoyed being able to collect a fee from Amberley. But he had the last laugh, anyway, of seeing the client who had attempted to fool him put firmly in his place.

The Missing Three-Quarter poses a problem in that the original client, Cyril Overton, may have escaped having to pay upon the basis that he was merely an agent. He has assumed that Godfrey Staunton, when found, would be prepared to meet the cost of engaging a detective, or, if he were not found, that his family would. Holmes goes to the miserly Lord Mount-James, who refuses to pay anything, changing his tune only when Holmes hints that there may have been a kidnapping. 'Spare no pains, Mr. Detective. I beg you to leave no stone unturned to bring him safely back. As to money, well, so far as a fiver, or even a tenner, goes, you can always look to me.' But later Holmes assured Dr Armstrong that he was 'not employed by Lord Mount-James' and, as he had to keep Godfrey Staunton's confession a closely guarded secret, it seems ridiculous to suppose that he was ever able to claim any reward from the parsimonious nobleman. Presumably nobody paid Holmes anything, despite the relatively heavy expenses which he must have incurred in investigating the case.

Melas, in *The Greek Interpreter*, and Hatherley, in *The Engineer's Thumb*, were introduced to Holmes by brother Mycroft and Doctor Watson respectively, and neither of these clients would have expected to be charged. It was also Mycroft, acting on behalf of the government, who consulted his younger brother over *The Bruce-Partington Plans*, and it was made clear from the outset that a fee was not even contemplated, though, 'If you have a fancy to see your name in the next honours list——'. Holmes waved aside any question of an honour, as he later refused to accept a knighthood, but a piece of jewellery was always acceptable as a souvenir of success,[13] not least the 'remarkably fine emerald tie-pin' which Holmes had presented to him at Windsor by 'a certain gracious lady in whose interests he had once been fortunate enough to carry out a small commission'.

There were no fees, either, in *The Gloria Scott* or *The Devil's Foot*, when Holmes was on holiday, or in *The Lion's Mane*, which took place in Sussex after his retirement. In both *The Red Circle* and *The Veiled Lodger* Holmes was originally consulted by a landlady; and although in the latter case the client was Mrs Ronder, the lodger, who was talked out of committing suicide, it would be entirely contrary to the spirit of the adventure for Holmes to have sought any remuneration for his efforts. The detective's reward in *The Red Circle* was specifically 'education' only. 'Mrs. Warren's whimsical problem' became somewhat enlarged, and assumed a more sinister aspect than

Holmes can originally have divined; so much so that Watson questioned whether it was worthwhile for them to continue with the investigation. Their conversation gives a clear enough insight into Holmes' attitude in such circumstances:

> 'It is very curious and complex, Watson.'
>
> 'Why should you go further in it? What have you to gain from it?'
>
> 'What, indeed? It is Art for Art's sake, Watson. I suppose when you doctored you found yourself studying cases without thought of a fee?'
>
> 'For my education, Holmes.'
>
> 'Education never ends, Watson. It is a series of lessons, with the greatest for the last. This is an instructive case. There is neither money nor credit in it, and yet one would wish to tidy it up.'

A wish to 'tidy it up' rather than a quest for financial profit led Holmes to *The Final Problem* and *The Empty House*. It was also, doubtless, his motive in investigating a host of other matters which presented a challenge to his thirsting talents. He would grow impatient when the case was trivial or the problem lacked interest, even when the client could afford to pay. 'As to my own little practice', he grumbled to Watson in *The Copper Beeches*, 'it seems to be degenerating into an agency for recovering lost lead pencils and giving advice to young ladies from boarding-schools.' This was the adventure in which Violet Hunter, who favourably impressed Holmes, was the attractive female client; she was probably quite able to afford a moderate fee for the services rendered, but there was another, even more favoured, lady client whose affairs put Holmes and Watson to no end of trouble and close to being murdered, but who never, we feel sure, was charged anything. And this was the charming Miss Morstan, of *The Sign of Four*.

To draw hard and fast conclusions about Holmes' professional fees from the published adventures is a difficult task, and one which cannot be achieved with any guarantee of accuracy, for Watson understandably selected a not necessarily representative series of memoirs for the world to enjoy. Some cases which might have deserved publication he was forced to omit for reasons of confidentiality; others, because they were devoid of interest except to the seeker of sensation. Holmes, as we have already observed, was a difficult man to please. Despite his often-repeated complaint that Watson was prone to embellish his accounts with 'romanticism, which produces much the same effect as if you worked a love-story or an elopement into the fifth proposition of Euclid', Holmes was content, when discussing 'these little records of our cases' with Watson in *The Copper Beeches*, to observe that 'you have given prominence not so much to the many *causes célèbres* and sensational trials in which I have figured, but rather to those incidents which may have been trivial in themselves, but which have given room for those faculties of deduction and of logical synthesis which I have made my special province'.

It is plain that Watson's published stories were never intended as a characteristic cross-section of the detective's exploits. 'Some facts should be suppressed,' Holmes decreed; and doubtless the dutiful Watson sometimes complied in suppressing them. So, as it remains unknown what and how much he was constrained to censor, the problem of how much reliance can be placed upon the published adventures as an accurate or typical sample of the whole continues to vex and tantalise. And in no inquiry are these deficiencies more baulking to the presentation of a faithful picture than in research into Holmes' professional emoluments.

SMALL FEES FOR EARLY CASES

If the client called for a consultation and no more, a fee was collected there and then in cash, though if the problem was interesting and the visitor poor Holmes would probably waive any payment whatever. Watson never revealed how much Holmes charged for his advice. It may well have varied according to the value or complexity of the matter and the amount of time spent. His remark to ex-Senator Gibson that his professional charges were upon a fixed scale, even if meant seriously, does not prevent the scale being sufficiently elastic to cater for reasonable remuneration, having regard to the amount of effort expended. It can be no more than a guess, but the normal or average consultation fee was probably about five shillings, though this may have been increased during the later years, after the detective had achieved world-wide fame. The small-scale nature of some of Holmes' cases was hinted at by Brother Mycroft in *The Bruce-Partington Plans* when he said: 'Never mind your usual petty puzzles of the police-court.'

When a great deal of time, trouble and travelling were involved the charges must have become very considerable. Even in his early days Holmes would have required a fairly substantial fee when the importance of the case justified it. There is every reason to believe that Reginald Musgrave, with whom Holmes had only 'some slight acquaintance' previously despite the two of them having belonged to the same college, paid handsomely. He could well afford it, and 'the large issues which proved to be at stake', which Holmes successfully fathomed, indubitably merited some proportionate recompense. He had, after all, recovered 'nothing less than the ancient crown of the Kings of England', and at the end of the subsequent investigations ('legal bother', Holmes called it) Musgrave was allowed to retain the treasure for himself upon paying 'a considerable sum'.

It would also have been during the early period of Holmes' professional life, when he had set himself up in rooms in Montague Street, that he earned a goodly fee from Mrs Farintosh, a lady whom Holmes had 'helped in the hour of her sore need'. This client was sufficiently grateful for the services rendered to recommend Miss Helen Stoner to consult Holmes about her fears and suspicions which culminated in the thrills and horrors of *The Speckled Band.* Mrs Farintosh's case, as Holmes remarked, was 'concerned with an opal tiara'. The detective recalled having devoted some care to the matter, so it had involved more than just an interview. The case was a success and concerned an object of obvious value; it is clear that Mrs Farintosh was only too delighted to pay Holmes a fitting recompense. This fact she had probably imparted to Miss Stoner, for the latter had the question of fees very much in mind when she called at Baker Street: 'At present it is out of my power to reward you for your services, but in a month or two I shall be married, with the control of my own income, and then at least you shall not find me ungrateful.' Then Holmes, having reminded himself about the Farintosh case, possibly in order to satisfy himself that the recommendation was a respectable one, politely reassured her: 'As to reward, my profession is its reward;

but you are at liberty to defray whatever expenses I may be put to, at the time which suits you best.'

Such reticence about discussing his charges is typical of Holmes and appears to reflect no more than the understandable reluctance of a professional man to regard his perquisites as of any importance when compared with the affairs of the client. Hence the euphemistic defraying of expenses being made to serve for the more literal payment of fees. Watson displays a similar perception in the introductory paragraph of *The Speckled Band*, when he describes Holmes as working 'rather for the love of his art than for the acquirement of wealth', meaning not that his friend enjoyed working for nothing but that the client's interests were very properly regarded as of far greater concern than the amount of the final reckoning.

It is difficult to propound any confident conclusions from these early cases, except that Holmes' earnings must have varied a lot, between cases which he undertook for the experience and those which paid him well. *A Study in Scarlet*, like so many other cases in which Holmes helped the police, involved him in financial loss rather than profit. Episodes like 'Vanderbilt and the Yeggman' probably depended for their cash value upon whether Holmes had his services retained by the American millionaire or the wandering gypsy. The other 'pretty little problems' of the early years, among them 'the Tarleton murders, and the case of Vamberry, the wine merchant, and the adventure of the old Russian woman, and the singular affair of the aluminium crutch, as well as a full account of Ricoletti of the club foot and his abominable wife', may or may not have been remunerative. However, Holmes could have obtained some compensation at the hands of Vamberry, who possibly ensured that the detective's cellar was well stocked 'with something a little choice in white wines', perhaps some Montrachet, or 'a group of ancient and cobwebby bottles'.

If only Watson had written full accounts of more than just a handful of Holmes' cases during their early years together at Baker Street, the task of trying to deduce an acceptable pattern of the detective's professional rewards would be less perplexing. As it is, we have to make do with Watson's general observations about Holmes' rising fame and growing riches, and to infer what we can from the facts surrounding those few adventures which have been adequately reported.

The Yellow Face and *Charles Augustus Milverton*, though both are undated, must be two of the earliest. Holmes was dismayed at having missed Mr Grant Munro. A departed client who had 'no need to practise economy', as Holmes was quick to observe, gave cause for regret; 'I was badly in need of a case,' he confessed to Watson. He may have been badly in need of a fee as well. 'You wish to employ me as a consulting detective?' Holmes eagerly asked when the hop merchant returned. Munro's case turned out to be fairly simple, though Holmes was wrong about the presumed blackmailing. Nevertheless, the client would hardly have cavilled at sending Holmes a most welcome cheque for his services. With 'an income of seven or eight hundred', he was, as Holmes had shrewdly noticed at the outset, well able to afford them.

Lady Eva Brackwell, and the illustrious client who 'placed her piteous case in my hands', could also well afford to pay. Holmes offered £2,000 to Milverton for the return of her 'sprightly' letters, and the blackmailer was probably not far wrong in suggesting that it was possible 'for her friends and relations to make some little effort upon her behalf' and raise £7,000. The time which Holmes occupied upon this investigation, including masquerading as 'a plumber with a rising business' and his lightning courtship of Agatha the housemaid, not to mention the risks of the eventual burglary, justified the payment of a very considerable fee.

But one wonders whether the client thought all these efforts worthwhile, even whether he got to know of them all, because Milverton was fortunately dead, and the compromising papers destroyed, and Holmes was probably never able to tell his illustrious patron exactly how it happened. For how could he ever assure Lady Eva that the letters would never be found? Having become an accessory to the murder by burning 'the letter which had been the messenger of death', he would scarcely have risked telling the whole truth to his client, however illustrious. He may have had to rest content in the circumstances with a fairly nominal fee. Furthermore, it is not without interest to speculate how much effort Lestrade wasted in hunting the supposed murderers and taking statements from Agatha in quest of the vanished Escott. The inspector's eyebrows must have been raised to their fullest height when he read the whole story upon its appearance in 1904. No wonder Watson delayed so long in publishing it.

There was also during this early period the 'little domestic complication' which Holmes was able to unravel for Mrs Cecil Forrester. This good lady was sufficiently impressed by his kindness and skill to want to send her governess to Holmes for assistance over the mysterious appointment 'outside the Lyceum Theatre' which led to the adventure of *The Sign of Four* and Watson's first meeting with his future bride. The facts of Mrs Forrester's case are not available, and may have involved no more than some petty dishonesty among her servants, but this matter, too, might have concerned the recovery of indiscreet letters, as Lady Eva's had. Holmes made light of the case to Miss Morstan, remarking that it was 'a very simple one'. But Mrs Forrester herself did not think so, and Holmes may have preferred not to discuss the details for reasons of confidentiality. Whatever it was, the problem was obviously an important one for the client and Holmes was presumably paid a commensurate fee.

'EUROPE WAS RINGING WITH HIS NAME'

By the mid-eighties Holmes' reputation was international. European royalty were numbered among the clients. Noblemen, politicians, bankers and businessmen, more than enough to pay Holmes richly for his esteemed services and still leave him time for gratuitous assistance to the police and leisure for pursuing those stimulating problems which he loved so much, 'all that is bizarre and outside the conventions and humdrum routine of everyday life'. He took a mocking pleasure in reminding Lord Robert St Simon that in acting for him he was descending in the class of society from which his clients came. The King of Scandinavia and Lord Backwater were among those who had placed their affairs in his hands. Then there were such important cases as 'the mission which he had accomplished so delicately and successfully for the reigning family of Holland', the 'summons to Odessa in the case of the Trepoff murder', the 'question of the

Netherland-Sumatra Company and of the colossal schemes of Baron Maupertuis' and 'the Arnsworth Castle business'. All these were commissions in which Holmes might ask, and expect to receive, fees on a princely scale.

It was also at about this time that he was consulted by the British Premier, Lord Bellinger, and the Right Honourable Trelawney Hope, Secretary for European Affairs, in *The Second Stain*, in which the interests at stake were no less than peace or war. 'Any reward which it lies in our power to bestow' was dangled before Holmes as the prize for successfully recovering the missing letter. Holmes appreciated the power of having 'the British Treasury behind me' should he be able to purchase the document, even 'if it means another penny on the income tax'. But it seems unlikely that the government would have paid him anything more than a refund of his out-of-pocket expenses. The reward which the Prime Minister had in mind was probably an honour, which Holmes surely refused, just as he later refused a knighthood. Lord Bellinger was not hoodwinked, as Holmes clearly perceived as he 'turned away smiling from the keen scrutiny of those wonderful eyes'. The next Cabinet reshuffle probably saw Trelawney Hope stripped of office and sent to occupy a back bench in the Lords. In time he may even have guessed that his wife was branded as a security risk. Bellinger's twinkle of mystification was not to be satisfied by Holmes' disarming remark about diplomatic secrets. And Holmes knew it; or why the hurried exit?

If *The Second Stain* was an adventure of national importance for which Holmes got no monetary reward, there was a nearly contemporaneous adventure with important personages involved for which he was exceedingly well paid. Alexander Holder, the client in *The Beryl Coronet*, told Holmes that he might go to any expense which he thought necessary, and that a £1,000 reward had already been offered. Nevertheless, Holmes was still careful to ensure that there was no mistake about his instructions: 'I understand that you give me *carte blanche* to act for you, provided only that I get back the gems, and that you place no limit on the sum I may draw.'

Holmes recovers the lost beryls, but only at a price. 'Three thousand will cover the matter,' he explains to the City banker. 'And there is the little reward, I fancy. Have you your cheque-book? Here is the pen. Better make it out for four thousand pounds.' Presumably there was more to come for Holmes than the £1,000 reward; 'you shall not find me ungrateful', Holder added, when the detective explained what had happened.

The Beryl Coronet is of great interest not only in showing what huge figures Holmes was able to command when at the height of his fame but also in demonstrating that within a few short years of settling down in Baker Street in rooms which he had to share for reasons of expense he was able to produce £3,000 of his own money to buy back the gems from the receiver. Other adventures had already made him a rich man.

We have now reached 1886, the year preceding that of *The Sign of Four* and Watson's courtship and marriage to Mary Morstan. For this period—roughly from 1886 to 1891—Watson has fortunately published many more of Holmes' cases, and a pattern of the fees for those adventures in which Holmes was remunerated begins to emerge.

Leaving aside those cases already mentioned in which Holmes was paid nothing, either because he was helping the police or because of the peculiar circumstances of the matter, and ignoring those casually mentioned adventures which lack any positive suggestion of a fee having been required, we can begin the inquiry by examining a series of cases in which Holmes must presumably have bargained for some remuneration, though the fee itself would have been only small.

The smallness of the fee would not necessarily reflect the simplicity of the case, but rather the limited circumstances of the client. Some clients, notably Hall Pycroft in *The Stockbroker's Clerk* and Violet Hunter in *The Copper Beeches*, were probably unable to afford much more than the expenses incurred by Holmes and Watson upon their journeyings, to Birmingham in the one case, to Winchester in the other. Mrs Neville St Clair and her husband, facing a drastic revision of their living standards following the exposure of *The Man with the Twisted Lip*,[14] may have paid little more than expenses. Jabez Wilson, in *The Red-Headed League*, was probably charged something, but one's impression is that the City and Suburban Bank contributed to Holmes' coffers with some generosity upon that occasion. As for Mary

Sutherland, for all her 'coquettish Duchess-of-Devonshire' manner of tilting her hat and her expectation from Uncle Ned's legacy, we believe that Holmes tactfully forgot to send in a bill, just as he never troubled to tell her the result of his investigation, knowing she would not believe it even if he did. So far as the client was concerned, *A Case of Identity* had to be abandoned as a failure.

We now come to a group of cases for which Holmes undoubtedly must have charged full fees, some of them possibly a good deal larger than the average. *The Noble Bachelor*, Lord Robert St Simon, would probably have expected to receive a bill computed in accordance with his exalted rank. Watson may well have encouraged Holmes, in this case and in others, to keep his charges high. He it was who had been dazzled initially by 'the huge crest and monogram' on the envelope containing Lord Robert's 'very fashionable epistle'. It was, to the doctor, a distinct improvement on the morning letters which, if Watson remembered rightly, 'were from a fishmonger and a tide-waiter'. The lower orders of society were a good deal less interesting so far as Watson was concerned. Holmes, who was neither snobbish nor mercenary, clearly preferred to deal with the proletariat; at least they were less likely to inflict him with 'one of those unwelcome social summonses which call upon a man either to be bored or to lie'.

The Resident Patient, which was undoubtedly one of the earlier cases and may have taken place as early as October 1882, would also have involved a fee of some substance. The client, Dr Percy Trevelyan, the Brook Street specialist, was a man of means who became a man of greater means by reason of the timely death of his benefactor. The net result of the case, so far as Trevelyan was concerned, was to relieve him for the future of being obliged to share his fees with the ailing Sutton, alias Blessington.

The curious incident which presents itself in this adventure is that Holmes and the two doctors did nothing, until it was far too late, to attempt to resuscitate the body. When this is contrasted with a similar situation in *The Stockbroker's Clerk*, where Holmes and Watson rushed into an inner room to cut down and revive the managing director of the Franco-Midland Hardware Company, one may be pardoned for wondering why Sutton was not given the same sort of attention. The answer must be that he was already quite dead and that any aid had arrived far too late. But despite Watson's opinion that the corpse had been dead three hours, some suspicion must remain that Trevelyan's lack of effort to revive Blessington—even to cut him down when the tragedy was discovered—may have been the consequence of a wish to make absolutely sure he was really dead and no longer in a position to claim three-quarters of the specialist's earnings.

If Sherlock Holmes suspected any such motive he never voiced it. Possibly he regarded the dead man as too much of a scoundrel to deserve any sympathy. Or perhaps the fee for his services was big enough to justify him in not asking the client any awkward questions.

Alice Turner, the client in *The Boscombe Valley Mystery*, sent for Holmes despite having already been provided with the services of Inspector Lestrade. And it was as well that she did, for Holmes, with his customary thoroughness, was able not only to detect the criminal and obtain his confession but also, without disclosing the real murderer's identity, to draw up 'a number of objections' to the case against James McCarthy which enabled his defending counsel to secure an acquittal at the assizes. The lady client, kept in ignorance of the fact that the killer was her own father, must have been delighted at the result and more than willing to pay Holmes whatever fee he chose to ask.

In *The Crooked Man* it was Major Murphy of the Royal Mallows who was the client. Holmes dealt with the matter so efficiently that the major was left under the impression that 'it was quite a simple case after all'. The detective's bill, for his charges and expenses, may have persuaded Major Murphy that there was more in it than met the eye.

However, there was another major who, far from depreciating the value of the detective's services, was convinced that Holmes 'could solve anything'. This was Major Prendergast, of the Tankerville Club Scandal, who was to send John Openshaw to consult Holmes over the mystery of *The Five Orange Pips*. Prendergast was the client who had been 'wrongfully accused of cheating at cards', and had his reputation saved by Holmes. The investigation was probably a difficult one, and the major had clearly formed the opinion that Holmes was unbeatable. We may feel certain that for so completely vindicating the gallant soldier's honour Holmes would have been richly rewarded.

There follows a touch of pathos. For the trusting young Openshaw, filled with Prendergast's confidence in the detective's infallibility, is sent out by Holmes to face death and disaster.[15]

A more senior officer, successful racehorse-owner and recipient of 'each of the prizes of the turf', Colonel Ross, was the client in *Silver Blaze*. One cannot doubt but that the colonel's winnings and prize money on the Wessex Plate (or was it the Wessex Cup?) yielded a handsome figure, and that Holmes himself was more than adequately rewarded for so successfully restoring the missing horse to its true owner. It may also have been one of those rare occasions upon which Dr Watson made a profit out of his bookmaker!

To continue with the line of cases of the late eighteen-eighties in which Holmes was generously remunerated, we come to *The Naval Treaty* and *A Scandal in Bohemia*. Percy Phelps voiced a pathetic plea: 'I turn to you, Mr. Holmes, as absolutely my last hope.' It may be confidently conjectured that he soon forgave Holmes his 'touch of the dramatic' which caused him to faint when he raised the cover of the breakfast-dish. He could then concentrate on showing his appreciation in a more practical way for having, at last, had his honour saved. The King of Bohemia, too, was full of admiration: 'Nothing could be more successful.' And then he continued: 'I am immensely indebted to you. Pray tell me in what way I can reward you.' Holmes, having already been paid £1,000 for 'expenses', may have thought that this was sufficient. But he was yet to receive one valuable present, described later as 'a little souvenir', the 'snuff-box of old gold, with a great amethyst in the centre of the lid'. And there was another little prize as well, which Holmes may have valued for its humorous associations even more highly, the tip of a golden sovereign from Irene Adler for witnessing her wedding to Godfrey Norton. 'I mean to wear it on my watch-chain in memory of the occasion,' remarked Sherlock Holmes.

In *The Blue Carbuncle*, the clients (if so they may be called), Peterson the commissionaire and Henry Baker, frequenter of the Alpha Inn, came from a very different class of society. But there was money in the case for Holmes nevertheless. The carbuncle was 'absolutely unique, and its value can only be conjectured, but the reward offered of a thousand pounds is certainly not within a twentieth part of the market price', said Holmes. Peterson was staggered at the figure. Holmes, however, had other ideas, and mentioned the 'sentimental considerations in the background which would induce the countess to part with half of her fortune if she could but recover the gem'.

Holmes went on to trace the thief and then to let him go. His views on penology were rather in advance of their time in 1889: 'I suppose that I am commuting[16] a felony, but it is just possible that I am saving a soul. This fellow will not go wrong again. He is too terribly frightened. Send him to gaol now, and you make him a gaolbird for life.'

It seems almost out of character for someone holding such modern ideas about the humane treatment of criminals to have been less than frank about his own profits. We wonder whether even Watson was fooled by the statement that the 'solution is its own reward'. For restoring the priceless stone and saving the insurers from full liability there must have been rewards enough. Holmes would surely have claimed them and shared out the proceeds with Peterson 'who, as you know, is a very honest fellow'. Holmes' expenses on *The Blue Carbuncle* were only few, the lost £1 bet, cab fares, a fresh goose for Henry Baker and at least seven newspaper advertisements. His net profit from this case must have worked out at a very encouraging figure.

Holmes' last case before *The Final Problem* involved his having 'been engaged by the French Government upon a matter of supreme importance', which took him to Narbonne and Nîmes, and doubtless to other places as well. Watson does not mention, and probably never knew, what this weighty matter was, but from the notes he received from Holmes he 'gathered that his stay in France was likely to be a long one'. It was a very well-paid inquiry, possibly concerned with the safety of the Republic or with some threatened scandal which might have toppled the government of the day. It was not so secret that the press remained unaware of it, for Watson had seen in the papers some account of his friend's doings in France during the winter of 1890 and the early spring of the following year. However, Holmes was to tell the doctor, in the early stages of *The Final Problem*, that 'the recent cases in which I have been of assistance to the Royal Family of Scandinavia, and to the French Republic, have left me in such a position that I could continue to live in the quiet fashion which is most congenial to me, and to concentrate my attention upon my chemical researches'.

If this was a statement intended to be taken literally, as presumably it was, the assumption must be that his earnings from these cases vastly exceeded the £6,000 which he was later to extract from the Duke of Holdernesse. What *is* plain is this, that by the time of Reichenbach in 1891 Holmes was financially independent and in the position of being able to choose whether he continued in practice or not. Thus, within less than ten years, since joining up with Watson, Holmes had advanced in fortune from being a man who had to share lodgings for reasons of expense to having achieved sufficient means to live as he pleased without worrying about money at all.

WATSON AS PARTNER

On his return to England in 1894 Holmes was able to carry on as he had left off three years previously. Brother Mycroft had preserved his rooms in Baker Street and his papers exactly as they had always been, and Mrs Hudson, quickly recovered from the violent hysterics into which the shock of the detective's unheralded return had thrown her, was ready to resume her duties as landlady and housekeeper.

The consulting detective's practice was soon busy and thriving once again. Watson was to comment, when recounting the adventure of *The Golden Pince-Nez*, that 'when I look at the three massive manuscript volumes which contain our work for the year 1894 I confess that it is very difficult for me, out of such a wealth of material, to select the cases which are most interesting in themselves and at the same time most conducive to a display of those peculiar powers for which my friend was famous'.

So Watson rejoined Holmes in the Baker Street rooms, having first sold his small Kensington medical practice to a young doctor named Verner, who gave, wrote the delighted Watson in *The Norwood Builder*, 'with astonishingly little demur the highest price that I ventured to ask—an incident which only explained itself some years later, when I found that Verner was a distant relation of Holmes', and that it was my friend who had really found the money'. Thus, Holmes' first financial transaction of any substance after the *Return* was to pay out a sufficient sum to ensure that he would not be long alone, without his friend.

And how very different was their relationship from what it had been in the early days. Then it was simply a matter of business, in order that by pooling their resources they could afford to rent Mrs Hudson's rooms. Now we find Holmes, having been back for some months, realising that he could not work happily without his old friend, and requesting him to return. And returning, what is more, as a partner in the practice.

For Watson was still the only friend Holmes had, a fact which he had acknowledged as long ago as 1887, in *The Five Orange Pips*. The scene is the memorable one of Holmes and Watson spending the evening in the sitting-room at Baker Street, a fierce gale howling outside and the driving rain beating against the windows. The front bell rings. 'Who could come tonight? Some friend of yours, perhaps?' asked Watson. 'Except yourself I have none,' was Holmes' immediate reply.

As was only to be expected, the busy life of 1894 continued into the 'memorable year' of 1895. Watson noted, in *Black Peter*, that he had never known Holmes to be in better form.

> His increasing fame had brought with it an immense practice, and I should be guilty of an indiscretion if I were even to hint at the identity of some of the illustrious clients who crossed our humble threshold in Baker Street. Holmes, however, like all great artists, lived for his art's sake, and, save in the case of the Duke of Holdernesse, I have never known him claim any large reward for his inestimable services. So unworldly was he—or so capricious—that he frequently refused his help to the powerful and wealthy where the problem made no appeal to his sympathies, while he would devote weeks of most intense application to the affairs of some humble client whose case presented those strange and dramatic qualities which appealed to his imagination and challenged his ingenuity.

But Holmes was still making money, and plenty of it. The manager and clerks of the Oxford Street branch of the Capital and Counties

Bank would have watched a steadily increasing credit balance and the acquisition by Holmes of a variety of securities and investments.

One has only to draw reasonable inferences from the many cases referred to by Watson in *The Golden Pince-Nez*, *The Norwood Builder* and *Black Peter* to appreciate how remunerative some at least of them must have been. The best paid were possibly 'the case of the papers of ex-President Murillo', the 'Smith-Mortimer succession case', the 'famous investigation of the sudden death of Cardinal Tosca'[17] and, for really good measure, the 'very abstruse and complicated problem concerning the peculiar persecution to which John Vincent Harden, the well-known tobacco millionaire, had been subjected', a case in which Holmes was immersed at the very moment he first heard of *The Solitary Cyclist*, Miss Violet Smith.

Holmes' attitude to professional fees was very little altered after the *Return*, though under the new arrangements with Watson he would properly have charged clients also with fees and expenses to cover the work done by his partner. A partnership proper, or any definite sharing arrangement, seems unlikely, but there is no doubt that after 1894 Watson was part of the business and entitled to some share of the profits. It was probably for the first time in his life that Watson was ever able to accumulate any savings. And by now he must have been earning a good deal of money from the frequent reprintings of the Sherlock Holmes adventures.

The published adventures covering the mid-nineties give a fairly clear indication that, despite Holmes' secure financial position, there were many clients who were only too willing to pay high fees to secure his services. John Scott Eccles, in *Wisteria Lodge*, was explicit: 'I retain your services, Mr. Holmes. I desire you to spare no expense and no pains to get at the truth.' John Mason, of *Shoscombe Old Place*, must presumably have promised a fee, and Holmes was probably rewarded still more generously by Sir Robert Norberton after his horse had won the Derby. In *The Norwood Builder* Holmes tells Inspector Lestrade that he does not want his name to appear in the papers, and then goes on to make one of his typical remarks about his work being its own reward. But we feel sure that the junior partner of the city law firm of Graham & McFarlane was able and willing to pay, and did in fact pay, a substantial fee to Holmes for establishing his innocence and saving him from being hanged for a murder that never was.

In *The Disappearance of Lady Frances Carfax*, the rich clients were only too pleased to produce whatever funds were required. As Holmes explained to Watson, before sending him abroad with 'first-class tickets and all expenses paid on a princely scale', the missing lady's 'family are anxious, and as they are exceedingly wealthy, no sum will be spared if we can clear the matter up'. And the lady herself, having had her life saved by Holmes in the nick of time, presumably rewarded him with unbounded generosity. A similar recompense was assuredly paid by Sir Henry Baskerville after his escape from the fiendish hound.

Violet Smith, in *The Solitary Cyclist*, was also well able to pay; but perhaps not out of her earnings as a music teacher, despite her 'splendid' salary of £100 a year. However, she inherited a large fortune, some of which would have found its way into Holmes' pockets after he had opportunely saved her 'from the worst fate that can befall a woman'. Mrs Mary Maberley, in *The Three Gables*, obtained £5,000 through Holmes' efforts, in order that she might 'go round the world in first-class style'. This huge sum would have been more than enough for her needs, and presumably she paid the detective's bill out of it. And in *The Sussex Vampire* Holmes would have charged Robert Ferguson, the tea broker, his proper fees for professional services rendered. The business correspondence between Holmes and Messrs Morrison, Morrison & Dodd '*Re* Vampires' proclaims the formality of the introduction.

Coming now to *The Blanched Soldier*, it must be fair to assume that Holmes collected a fee from James Dodd and may indeed also have received some memento from the peppery Colonel Emsworth or his son Godfrey. The detective would also have collected for himself the literary fees for having written the story himself instead of Watson.

Holmes the writer seems to have been less punctilious about detail than Holmes the detective. He slipped up twice, firstly by forgetting the correct title of the Duke of Holdernesse and secondly by confusing the Priory School with 'the Abbey School'. It is a far cry from his proud rejoinder in *The Lion's Mane* (another of Holmes' excursions into the literature of his own cases) to an admiring comment from Inspector Bardle of the Sussex constabulary. 'You certainly do things thoroughly, Mr. Holmes,' said the inspector. 'I should hardly be what I am if I did not,' replied Holmes, doubtless betraying a trace of acidity in his voice.

The Blanched Soldier also contains a reference to another case of national importance. At the time of Dodd's visit to the Baker Street rooms Holmes wrote that he 'had also a commission from the Sultan of Turkey which called for immediate action, as political consequences of the gravest kind might arise from its neglect'. Holmes was probably wise enough to collect his fees from the sultan in advance. This was one imperial potentate who would not have been allowed to settle his obligations condescendingly with a piece of jewellery or some petty hand-out of baksheesh.

The largest cheque of which Watson has left any specific record is, of course, the one for £6,000 which Holmes extracted—there is no other word for it—from that unprincipled nobleman, His Grace the Duke of Holdernesse. The duke was not, however, the client in the adventure of *The Priory School.* That was a privilege reserved to the school's headmaster, Dr Thorneycroft Huxtable, that pompous classicist whose card 'seemed too small to carry the weight of his academic distinctions'. Whether Holmes possessed the temerity afterwards to send him a note of his charges is something which Watson has failed to record.

It is probable that Huxtable's opening gambit of mentioning the detective's 'very high line in professional matters', coupled with a reference to the duke's offer, was meant to imply that Holmes was expected to work for the work's sake, unless of course he could satisfy the conditions for claiming the reward. Holmes was at first reluctant to leave London, but the princely offer was enough to lure him to the north of England to commence his investigation. And the pleasure he took in claiming the reward was a surprise, even to Watson. 'My friend rubbed his thin hands together with an appearance of avidity,' noticed the doctor. Even so, Holmes was not to be tempted by his grace's suggestion of doubling the reward for keeping quiet about the murder. Six thousand was enough. Holmes carefully folded the cheque into his notebook, 'patted it affectionately, and thrust it into the depths of his inner pocket'.

Holmes must have felt more than satisfied. It had been a good day's work. A huge sum earned, and taken from a rogue who could well afford to pay in full. His remark to the duke, 'I am a poor man', was obviously not intended to be taken literally; it was, rather, a reminder that the nobleman was far richer than Holmes and eminently deserved to be deprived of a substantial sum as some retribution for his misdeeds.

There were other cases, too, in which Holmes was able to enhance his personal fortune by the addition of fat rewards. One such episode was *The Mazarin Stone*, involving the theft of a notable crown diamond in a 'hundred-thousand-pound burglary'. The concern of the Prime Minister was to recover the stone, which Holmes succeeded in doing, celebrating his achievement by bewildering the stuffy Lord Cantlemere with a mischievous example of his 'impish habit of practical joking'. It would be far-fetched to assume that the British government would have considered paying Holmes a fee for his professional endeavours, but the gem was presumably covered by insurance. The usual 5 per cent commission would have amounted to a cool £5,000, which Holmes must have regarded with almost as much affection as the Duke of Holdernesse's cheque.

The insurance reward in *The Abbey Grange* would have been much smaller, but here again Holmes, this time having been called in by Stanley Hopkins of the police, was fully justified in claiming the normal percentage on the articles of plate which Captain Croker had dropped into the pond.

Turning now to *Thor Bridge*, there is a good deal more to discover about Holmes' financial affairs and his attitude to money. J. Neil Gibson, 'the greatest gold-mining magnate in the world', was a client to whom Holmes took an immediate dislike. This was hardly surprising, since Gibson seemed to think that a big enough pile of dollars could buy anything or anyone.

The American ex-senator offers Holmes a rich reward for getting Miss Dunbar cleared of the murder charge: 'all I know and all I have and all I am are for your use if only you can save her'. He then tells Holmes to name his figure!

But Holmes was singularly unimpressed. The time had come for putting this annoying client firmly in his place. 'My professional charges are upon a fixed scale,' said Holmes coldly. 'I do not vary them, save when I remit them altogether.'

Gibson changes his tack. Perhaps Holmes can be induced to take the case through an appeal to his reputation: 'If you pull this off every paper in England and America will be booming you. You'll be the talk of two continents.'

Holmes' reply is a classic: 'Thank you, Mr. Gibson, I do not think that I am in need of booming.'

The financial puzzle of *Thor Bridge*, however, does not so much concern Holmes' fees as the employment of counsel to defend Miss Dunbar at the Winchester Assizes. Gibson, the man to whom 'money is nothing'—he even told Holmes he might 'burn it'—has apparently not even secured the services of a leader, for Watson records that it was a 'Mr. Joyce Cummings, the rising young barrister, who was entrusted with the defence'. Is this a clue, perhaps, to the gold-king's real attitude, that even in the case of a capital charge he was willing to economise on the legal fees?

There is a subsidiary problem, namely that, contrary to all the rules of legal etiquette, we hear nothing about the solicitor, and even Holmes is proposing to communicate with counsel direct. 'You will hear from me, Mr. Cummings,' he says.

All of this sounds so improbable that we are left wondering whether perhaps Watson got it wrong, and that Mr Cummings was not a 'rising young barrister', but the solicitor who was preparing the case and who had not yet got round to instructing counsel. Any other explanation makes Gibson sound far more parsimonious than he surely was, and makes nonsense of the accepted and well-regulated manner of conducting criminal litigation.

In *The Three Garridebs* Holmes finds himself in trouble with another subject of Uncle Sam, no less a malefactor than James Winter, otherwise Killer Evans, masquerading now as a Kansas lawyer. He does at the outset remark that 'I guess your time is of value', but this was said not in the context of fees but in an effort to get Holmes down to the business at hand rather than engage in the small-talk which was raising the detective's suspicions about the visitor's genuineness. For the spurious John Garrideb was not the client, but his namesake Nathan, who was so puzzled by the American's approaches that he thought it sensible to get in touch with Holmes in the first place. It is likely that after the adventure was over Holmes had some correspondence with Nathan Garrideb about his fees, for how else was Holmes likely to hear that the eccentric archaeologist 'never got over the shock of his dissipated dreams' and 'was last heard of at a nursing-home in Brixton'?

Mention of *The Three Garridebs* prompts the question of whether Holmes was prescient. Understandably, and for more than adequate reasons, he was from the start very suspicious of the credentials of John Garrideb, the pretended Kansas counsellor at law. 'Touch him where you would he was false.' But the mystery remained to be solved and Holmes set out to discover whether the other Mr Garrideb was a fraud also. Not until the following morning did Holmes manage to 'get on the track of our American friend' through the good offices of Lestrade at the Yard, which revealed him as James Winter, having past connections with one 'Rodger Prescott, famous as forger and coiner in Chicago'.

Prior to having these revelations imparted to him, however, Holmes had been testing the veracity of the impostor. One of his ploys was to claim a mutual acquaintance from Topeka. 'I used to have a correspondent—he is dead now—old Dr. Lysander Starr, who was Mayor in 1890,' said Holmes. 'Good old Dr. Starr!' rejoined the visitor. 'His name is still honoured.'

Now why should Holmes, inventing a name on the spur of the moment, choose Dr Lysander Starr?[18] The probability must be that, from the depths of his subconscious, he was reminded of the much earlier adventure of *The Engineer's Thumb*, in which the trusting hydraulic engineer, Victor Hatherley, had been lured to the 'great widespread whitewashed building' at Eyford by a counterfeiter who had used the very similar alias of Colonel Lysander Stark. And if that is so, was there something more, deep down within the being of Sherlock Holmes, which led him to associate that particular name with the problem of the Garridebs, the nature of which was then

' "PRETTY SORT O' TREATMENT THIS!" HE CRIED, STAMPING HIS STICK.'
By F. H. Townsend, from the Newnes edition of *The Sign of Four*, 1903. A fine study of Inspector Athelney Jones, his back up against the door, barring the exit of the old seafarer, who is none other than Holmes in disguise. The 'thick oaken cudgel' of the text has become a very poor little stick in the picture.

'PATTERED OFF UPON THE TRAIL.'

By F. H. Townsend, from the Newnes edition of *The Sign of Four*, 1903. Holmes and Watson being led by the dog Toby through the grounds of Pondicherry Lodge, pitted by the treasure-seekers. Compare Paget's treatment of a similar subject in *The Missing Three-Quarter* (see page 83).

completely unknown to him? For he could have had at that stage no notion that it would also concern the counterfeiting of money.

It is a nice question. The parallel seems too close for coincidence. Did Holmes perhaps possess some singular gift of prophecy, a skill of which possibly even he was unaware? Or was it just a rather dramatic example of his well-known ability to turn the opaque into the transparent?

WHY HOLMES REFUSED A KNIGHTHOOD

It was in *The Three Garridebs*, too, that Watson disclosed that 'it was in the same month that Holmes refused a knighthood for services which may perhaps some day be described'. It was shortly after the end of the South African War at the end of June 1902. There had been many cases in which Holmes' services had been invaluable to the state and which must have served to found his reputation as the sort of person who might be considered for inclusion in an honours list. But the special action which led directly to the knighthood being offered is hidden in the mists of confidentiality. Watson merely hints that it may have been not unconnected with the Boer War. Possibly Holmes found time to serve the government in some intelligence capacity or upon counter-espionage, as he was later to do with such signal success against the Kaiser's spy-ring. If it was something to do with the South African conflict it affords an interesting parallel with the career of Watson's editor, Arthur Conan Doyle, who received his own knighthood in 1902 in similar circumstances.

Conan Doyle, however, accepted his knighthood (even if the public of the time was inclined to believe that it was earned more for his work on the Sherlock Holmes adventures than for anything he did in the war), whereas Holmes did not. Why should Holmes have been so reluctant—some would even say ungrateful—to become Sir Sherlock? He had already, as recounted in *The Golden Pince-Nez*, had the French Republic's Legion of Honour bestowed upon him, and it appears he had not made any fuss about that. Why should he have been so unwilling to be knighted by his own country?

The answer may be that this was his way of asserting his continued independence. Holmes was not, and never could be, identified with the establishment. He was ready enough to answer the nation's call when his country needed him, but he reserved the right to poke fun at authority, even to act occasionally as a one-man court of appeal, when he thought it justified. To have accepted the accolade, even towards the end of his career, might have impaired his image among those ordinary folk who, in their times of trouble, became his best-loved clients. The power of Holmes lay in his eccentric individuality. A knighthood might have altered all that.

Possibly there were financial reasons as well. He had often enough been fobbed off with jewelled souvenirs. As has already been remarked, the government seldom dangled pecuniary carrots before the eyes of those who served it. The expectation of eventually earning an honour was considered sufficient recompense. Sherlock Holmes was just not the kind of person to allow himself to be influenced by blandishments of that sort. This he had made perfectly clear to his brother Mycroft in the adventure of *The Bruce-Partington Plans*, smiling and shaking his head when told that 'if you fancy to see your name in the next honours list——' The inducement was lost on Holmes. 'I play the game for the game's own sake,' said he.

Holmes had no need to worry. Already his name was indelibly engraved upon the history of his time. Knighthoods could mean nothing. World-famous and well-off, his reputation secure, and happy in his work which had made the lives of so many people more abundant; what more did he want? Watson probably chided him for rejecting the knighthood, but then Watson possessed a keener sense of the established social order. The crest on the envelope of *The Noble Bachelor*, the 'many exalted quarters'[19] from which clients came, represented to him the imprint of success, for which a knighthood would be no less than fitting recognition.

But it did not bother Holmes. He was about to retire to a life of comparative comfort, devoting his declining years to his *magnum opus*, the publication of a *Practical Handbook of Bee Culture, with some Observations upon the Segregation of the Queen.* His prudently invested capital assured him a life of 'leisured ease'.

How much did Holmes earn? One cannot say for certain. But his income must have been counted in thousands a year when he was at the summit of fame. Recognising that his services were often provided gratis, he received, as we have seen, many fees and rewards of exceedingly high amounts. Yet his tastes were simple, almost frugal, and he must have found it difficult to spend even a small proportion of what he earned.

There were very few things he did which could possibly be regarded as extravagant. Only very occasionally did he need to employ anyone other than Watson on his professional work, and he kept no servants, unless one includes Billy the page or Mrs Hudson in that category. He had no chemical laboratory of his own, only a table in the sitting-room at Baker Street, which sufficed for most of his experiments, though there were always the facilities of Barts to which he had access when he needed them.

We never hear of his betting except when he actually attended the races, and on those rare occasions he was probably shrewd enough or sufficiently well informed to back the right horse more often than not. His self-confidence at the end of *Silver Blaze*—'I stand to win a little on this next race'—speaks for itself. His bouts of drug-taking would have been indulged in without vast expense, and smoking was also a cheap enough pastime in his day.

He had cultivated tastes in food and wine, and enjoyed being served with his favourite specialities, but, as already suggested, they were not his regular diet. As a man who carefully kept himself in training for his very exacting professional duties, he was keenly aware of the perils of gluttony. The 'faculties become refined when you starve them', he said to Watson in *The Mazarin Stone*, and it was only as a celebration or upon some special occasion that he treated himself to a gourmet's fare. And when he did visit a restaurant he could sit with Watson 'for an hour over a bottle of claret'.

Nor did Holmes spend much money on the pastimes of leisure. When he travelled abroad it was most often when investigating a case, and at the client's expense. His holidays were modest enough, even upon these infrequent occasions when he could tear himself away from London. His fondness for concerts and the opera could be catered for well within his means. And his Stradivarius, though 'worth at least five hundred guineas', as Watson tells us in *The Cardboard Box*, had been purchased 'at a Jew broker's in Tottenham Court Road for fifty-five shillings'.

Certainly Holmes never spent money on social entertaining. Invitations would normally be refused—the choice lay between lying about a previous appointment or being bored by the company if he attended—so there was no hospitality to return. He hated society with his whole Bohemian soul.

Fine art may have involved Holmes in some financial outlay, but here again he was probably clever enough to sniff out the bargains and turn his purchases into profitable investments. He frequently dropped in at picture galleries, and it may be supposed that he sometimes bought a painting. Ownership of anything so marvellous or valuable as a Greuze was, however, reserved for his arch-enemy, Professor Moriarty.

But one of Holmes' little artistic weaknesses was to have himself modelled in wax. Firstly, there was the bust by Monsieur Oscar Meunier, of Grenoble, which Colonel Moran shattered with a soft revolver bullet, fired from his famous air-gun in *The Empty House*; and secondly there was the effigy of Holmes by Tavernier, the French modeller, which so confused Count Sylvius and Sam Merton, the boxer, in *The Mazarin Stone*.

It was probably a streak of vanity in Holmes, rather than any premeditation to use them in the detection of crime, which led him to have the figures made. The Meunier bust presumably dates from the period of Holmes' travels abroad between 1891 and 1894. The date of the Tavernier facsimile is likely to have been very little earlier than the adventure of *The Mazarin Stone* itself, for 'Watson could not restrain a cry of amazement' when he saw it. He had been away from Baker Street for a while, but not for very long, so if the model had been in existence for a year or more he would undoubtedly have known of it.

The link between the two models is that both were made at times when Holmes and Watson had parted. Do they show, perhaps, that Holmes so missed his friend and companion that on each occasion his mind was fastening on a means of preserving some record of himself for the benefit of posterity? Well-known modellers like Meunier and Tavernier would not have worked for nothing, and both effigies must have cost Holmes a fairly large sum of money. But they were little extravagances which Holmes must have immensely enjoyed.

Holmes had one other petty extravagance, and it was one which entirely suited his character. Watson mentioned it in *The Devil's Foot*—'he has never been known to write where a telegram would serve'.

It is fitting to conclude this survey of the financial Holmes by referring to his last case, that epic of counter-espionage which drew him out of his well-earned, if rather early, retirement in the vital interests of England, *His Last Bow*. 'It has cost me two years, Watson,' confided Holmes after the capture of Von Bork, 'but assuredly it was worth it.'

The greatest satisfaction for Holmes must have been experienced on the day when the Premier himself deigned to visit his humble roof to ensure his co-operation. But he seemed to derive at least as much pleasure from outwitting the German and taking his money. Indeed, the very last words of Holmes that the good Dr Watson ever recorded were on the subject of money. And Holmes, sensing the challenge, was as keen as ever to get his hands on it: 'I have a cheque for five hundred pounds which should be cashed early, for the drawer is quite capable of stopping it, if he can.'

CHAPTER TWO

THE SIGN OF FOUR

Sherlock Holmes said it:

'*How often have I said to you that when you have eliminated the impossible, whatever remains*, however improbable, *must be the truth?*'

In *The Sign of Four* (or *The Sign of the Four*, as it became in the American editions) we come face to face with a series of chronological problems. Some are almost baffling in their complexity; none is immune from attack. Confronting us as the main inquiry is the dating of Dr Watson's marriage to Mary Morstan, the heroine of the adventure. Students of the Holmesian writings have probably spent more time trying to discover Watson's wedding date than on any other investigation, so the presentation of the evidence and some of the arguments necessarily involves going over some old ground. But this dating is so crucial in arriving at a proper understanding of other, and hardly less important, problems, that our quest for the truth of the matter must begin at the beginning and not half-way along someone else's trail of reasoning.

THE DATE OF WATSON'S WEDDING

The most convenient starting-point is not in *The Sign of Four* itself, but in one of the short stories from the *Adventures*, *The Noble Bachelor*. Watson states categorically that 'this remarkable episode' took place 'a few weeks before my own marriage, during the days when I was still sharing rooms with Holmes in Baker Street'. The case is not dated by reference to any specific year, though Watson does indicate that it was a 'four-year-old drama'. The first edition appeared in *The Strand* for April 1892, so if we allow a period of around six months between the writing of the story and its publication the doctor's marriage must have taken place towards the end of 1887.

Let us see, as a preliminary, whether an 1887 date for *The Noble Bachelor* fits the internal evidence of that investigation. According to the red-covered volume which Holmes consulted for information about his new client, Lord Robert St Simon was born in 1846. The detective then remarks, 'He's forty-one years of age, which is mature for marriage.' This coincides nicely with the proposed dating of the adventure because, in addition to having Holmes' word for it, it is more likely than not that a person born during 1846 would have attained the age of forty-one by the autumn of 1887.

There is other supporting evidence for this particular year when the days of the week are considered. The wedding at St George's, Hanover Square, took place on a Tuesday. Watson makes this clear in his explanation to Holmes about the reports appearing in the press. On Wednesday the *Morning Post* had carried 'a curt announcement that the wedding had taken place', and this was followed by a longer report explaining that 'the ceremony, as shortly announced in the papers of yesterday, occurred on the previous morning'. Moulton's bill from the Northumberland Avenue hotel, which he left on the same day as the wedding, was dated 4 October, so that day must have been a Tuesday. The only possible year for *The Noble Bachelor* in which 4 October did fall on a Tuesday is 1887.

This would seem to be the clearest proof that Watson and Mary Morstan married towards the end of October or in early November in the Golden Jubilee year; it follows that *The Sign of Four* cannot possibly have been later than the autumn of 1887, for otherwise we should be facing the spectacle of a bride wedded to a man whom she had not yet met. (See note 2 of Chapter 1 for the dates chosen by the major chronologists. Those who postulate 1888 as the date of *The Sign of Four* have naturally accepted that Watson's marriage could not have been earlier than the latter part of 1888. Zeisler, in fact, gave it as January 1889.)

There is also an element of possible corroboration for 1887 in the adventure of *The Crooked Man*, when Watson was undoubtedly married. He dates the case only by reference to the fact that it was 'a few months after my marriage' when Holmes called at his home on a 'summer night'. It must have been, therefore, the summer immediately after the marriage.

The case concerns the supposed murder of Colonel Barclay, of the Royal Mallows, who had been commissioned for his bravery at the time of the Mutiny. The colonel 'had married at the time when he was a sergeant'. Holmes remarks that his wife 'was a woman of great beauty, and that even now, when she has been married for upwards of thirty years, she is still of striking appearance'.

Now the Indian Mutiny, which was the immediate cause of enabling Barclay to rise from the ranks, broke out in May 1857. Ex-Corporal Harry Wood, describing his part in the events to Holmes, speaks of being besieged 'at a place we'll call Bhurtee', and of being sent out by Sergeant Barclay to communicate with General Neill's column, 'which was moving up-country' from Calcutta. Bhurtee sounds rather like Allahabad which, in June 1857, was garrisoned by a few artillery invalids and some Sikhs and was relieved by Colonel J. G. S. Neill and his Madras fusiliers, who then advanced to Cawnpore. It seems likely that Barclay got married soon after the relief column arrived, Nancy Devoy having accepted him when it appeared certain that Wood had been either killed or captured.

The Barclay marriage can thus be placed with some confidence during the late summer or autumn of 1857—even if Bhurtee is meant to represent Cawnpore or Lucknow it could scarcely be much later—and it would therefore be precisely accurate, in the summer of 1888, for Holmes to refer to the colonel's lady as having been 'married for upwards of thirty years'. If a slightly later year for Watson's marriage had suggested itself we should not cavil, but *The Crooked Man* undeniably offers some modicum of support for our thesis that the wedding between Watson and Mary Morstan took place in the early winter of 1887.

The Sign of Four could, of course, have taken place much earlier than the autumn of 1887. Watson does not tell us, for instance, whether he and Mary had a short engagement or a long one. At first sight, bearing in mind the staid respectability of both participants, one is inclined to doubt that they would have hastily taken such a serious step. The doctor was about thirty-five—the evidence of *A Study in Scarlet* indicates that 1852 was probably the year of his birth—and his fiancée twenty-seven, that 'sweet age', mused Watson, 'when youth has lost its self-consciousness and become a little sobered by experience'. Neither was in the first flush of youth, neither seems to have been an impulsive character; surely neither would have rushed into a marriage upon such short acquaintance, especially remembering Watson's lack of employment, his 'weak leg', and his weaker banking account. Allowing, as seems logical, a minimum of six months between the first meeting and the actual wedding, the latest realistic date for *The Sign of Four* would be late April 1887.

Yet this is so much at variance with the chronology of the adventure itself, and with the evidence of other cases to be examined later, that it may be worthwhile at this stage to see whether our assessment can reasonably be revised. There are two possible arguments. Firstly, it may have seemed best to the two of them that, both being mature persons alone in the world, there was nothing to be gained by waiting. Watson had 'neither kith nor kin in England' and we do not believe (for reasons that will appear subsequently) that Miss Morstan had an aunt any more than she had a living mother. Secondly, Watson was completely infatuated, and Mary, who may until then have regarded her marriage prospects as insignificant, was probably wise enough to want to make sure of her man while she had the chance. It does seem to have been a case of love at first sight, and the intensity of their feelings for each other may have prompted them to dispense with more than a brief engagement. Watson may even have feared the possibility that any delay might have presented Holmes with the opportunity of trying to talk him out of it.

We are, therefore, at least prepared to admit that the marriage ceremony might plausibly have been held only a very short time after the first introduction. Assuming a November date for the wedding, *The Sign of Four* could have occurred as late as September. It is now time to examine the textual evidence of *The Sign of Four* itself.

1887 OR 1888?

Miss Morstan consults Holmes and draws his attention to *The Times* advertisement 'stating that it would be to her advantage to come forward'. According to her, this had appeared 'about six years ago—to be exact upon the 4th of May, 1882'. At first sight, therefore, the case appears to have started in or about May 1888. Watson quotes himself similarly when asking Holmes why the 'unknown friend' should 'write a letter now, rather than six years ago?' We thus continue to find, with regard to an 1887 dating, that, as Holmes himself remarked concerning the letter, 'there are certainly difficulties'. Furthermore, Miss Morstan mentions that her father, Captain Arthur Morstan, 'disappeared upon the 3rd of December, 1878—nearly ten years ago'. This again supports a mid-1888 date. But this, as we have seen, is impossible.

If we are prepared to accept that 'nearly ten years ago' may genuinely indicate an event which happened eight and a half years previously—and it is submitted that such an interpretation is by no means impossible—the reference to the captain's disappearance 'nearly ten years ago' could still have been made in 1887. The apparently more difficult questions of the newspaper advertisement and the anonymous letter become more easily resolved when we remember that Miss Morstan produced six pearls, one for every year since they started to arrive. When Watson was writing up the case from his notes he probably included the expression 'six years ago' by reference to the number of pearls, rather than by any specific record or recollection of the actual words used, and failed to observe that this disagreed with the date of the newspaper and Major Sholto's death.

As the late Sir Desmond MacCarthy pointed out as long ago as 1929, the sending of six pearls in the circumstances described by Miss Morstan would, of course, have taken only five years, from May 1882 to May 1887 inclusive. When the problem is examined in this way it can be demonstrated that there is nothing inherently improbable in claiming that 1887 was the actual year of *The Sign of Four*. Watson had so completely convinced himself that six pearls meant six years that he repeated it throughout the narrative, and even went to the extent of misquoting Holmes himself in connection with the length of time the treasure-seekers had spent hunting for the chest and the fortune it contained.

We are, in any case, somewhat unimpressed by datings which can be fixed only by reliance upon a statement that something happened six or ten years ago. At least one such assertion in *The Sign of Four* is patently wrong. Major Sholto returned to England in about 1876 'and came to live at Pondicherry Lodge, in Upper Norwood'. The visit of Arthur Morstan, which resulted in his death, took place at the beginning of December 1878. It was not until over three years later, early in 1882, that the major 'received a letter from India which was a great shock to him', so that he nearly fainted at the breakfast-table when he opened it. This was the letter, of which we shall have something more to say later, 'written in a scrawling hand', and supposedly warning him of Small's escape. 'Towards the end of April' in the same year, the major died. And yet Jonathan Small, for it was he whose face was pressed against the window as Major Sholto breathed his last, told Holmes after his arrest that it was 'some three or four years ago', which, if taken literally from an account given in the latter half of 1887, must have meant the April of 1884, two whole years after the villain's death. In so far as Small's rough estimate of time is of the remotest assistance in compiling and checking the chronological sequences, it suggests a fairly early date for *The Sign of Four*; 1887, rather than 1888.

Additional support for the proposition that *The Sign of Four* is an 1887 case, rather than 1888, comes from *A Scandal in Bohemia*. The start of this adventure is specifically dated 20 March 1888 and Watson, having 'now returned to civil practice', has already been married for some months, for he writes that he 'had seen little of Holmes lately' because his 'marriage had drifted us away from each other'.[1] That night, Watson 'passed the well-remembered door' of the Baker Street rooms he had formerly shared with Holmes and took the opportunity of calling in. Their friendly chat was then interrupted by the king's arrival to consult Holmes on a matter 'of such weight that it may have an influence upon European history'.

However, the difficulties are not yet entirely resolved. One point which springs to mind at once is that in the very first chapter of *The Sign of Four* Holmes mentions his 'methods of work in the Jefferson Hope case', which Watson has embodied 'in a small brochure, with the somewhat fantastic title of *A Study in Scarlet*'. Since it was not until the publication of *Beeton's Christmas Annual* for 1887 that this adventure was given to the world, it is open to comment that the two friends are unlikely to have been discussing it during the summer or early autumn of that very year.

But this is not conclusive, for *A Study in Scarlet* was, in all probability, written very much earlier and Watson must be assumed to have shown his manuscript—his very first literary effort—to Holmes before it was hawked around the publishing houses; Watson had, after all, 'specially designed to please him' by writing it. Doubtless he intended at first to have it printed as a small brochure, rather than as part of a Christmas annual.

There are, nevertheless, examples of inaccurate dating in *The Sign of Four* that can still cast doubt on the case for 1887. The most direct contradiction is between the postmark on the envelope from London, SW, which was 7 July, the day on which Miss Morstan first called at Baker Street, and Watson's comment about the later events of the same day, which he describes as 'a September evening'. Obviously they cannot both be right. Watson and his editor were astonishingly careless about dates; perhaps they thought the story was the only thing that mattered. As Holmes once remarked, in the introductory episode of *The Copper Beeches*, 'You have degraded what should have been a course of lectures into a series of tales.'

We shall return in a moment to the probabilities favouring July or September, but first let us see whether any help can be derived from the dates by reference to the days of the week. When Holmes drafted his advertisement for the agony column of the *Standard* he was at pains to give any details which might assist in discovering the missing launch, which he describes as having 'left Smith's Wharf at or about three o'clock last Tuesday morning'. The evidence of the discoveries made by Holmes and Watson on their first visit to Pondicherry Lodge and of 'The Strange Story of Jonathan Small' confirms that the *Aurora* was hired in the early hours of the morning of the same day that Miss Morstan received the letter and sought Holmes' advice. In other words, 7 July was a Tuesday. Unfortunately for our projected argument, if 7 July was a Tuesday, *The Sign of Four* cannot have occurred in 1887. The nearest year in which 7 July did fall on a Tuesday was 1885, which is much too early on any showing; not until 1891, by which time Holmes was travelling abroad following his fight with Moriarty in *The Final Problem*, did 7 July reappear in the calendar as a Tuesday.

There are no useful deductions to be drawn from a study of probable or improbable days of the week, because none of the relevant days in *The Sign of Four* can have been a Sunday. If the reprinting of Holmes' advertisement is accepted as accurate—and there is not the slightest excuse for entitling us to think of rejecting it—the case began with Miss Morstan consulting Holmes on a Tuesday and ended with the pursuit of the *Aurora* and the capture of the one-legged man on the following Friday. One ingenious commentator, H. W. Bell, in *Baker Street Studies*, has proposed 27 September as the date on the postmark, relying upon a misreading of 'S27' in Watson's crabbed handwriting as 'Ju7'. This is pure supposition, but it would be doing scant justice to his learned thesis to dismiss it out of hand. It does at least possess the not inconsiderable merit of postulating a date which did in fact fall on a Tuesday in 1887.

There is further corroboration for a September, rather than a July, dating in other unconnected circumstances related in *The Sign of Four*. Before setting out to capture the criminals Holmes insists upon Inspector Athelney Jones, who 'proved to be a sociable soul in his hours of relaxation', joining them for a dinner of 'oysters and a brace of grouse, with something a little choice in white wines'. Neither gathering oysters nor shooting grouse would be appropriate to early July, though both would be acceptable in September.

The meeting outside the Lyceum Theatre took place in conditions also favouring September. Though it was not yet seven o'clock, 'a dense drizzly fog lay low upon the great city and the lamps were but misty splotches of diffused light, which threw a feeble circular glimmer upon the slimy pavement'. If that is meant to be a description of the Strand in early July, Watson's narrative is sadly at fault, for it would still be broad daylight at that hour and the lamps would remain unlit whatever the state of the weather.

On the evening of the chase Holmes and his party reached the river at Westminster at 'a little past seven'. This time there was no fog, but it was twilight before they reached the Tower and Jonathan Small had ordered the *Aurora* to be ready at eight o'clock so as to be ready for flight under cover of darkness. Watson remarks that 'the last rays of the sun were gilding the cross upon the summit of St. Paul's' as they steamed downstream in the police-boat to await the appearance of the fugitives; although it cannot be literally true that he observed the rays of the sun, he probably noticed some twilight reflections, while dreaming, perhaps, of his lady-love. The conditions described do fit Septem-

'WE WERE CLEAR OF THE TOWN AND HASTENING DOWN A COUNTRY ROAD.'
By Sidney Paget, from *The Adventure of the Missing Three-Quarter*, August 1904. This time Holmes and Watson are in Cambridgeshire, following Pompey, 'the pride of the local draghounds'.

'LOOK AT THAT WITH YOUR MAGNIFYING GLASS, MR. HOLMES.'
By Sidney Paget, from *The Norwood Builder*, November 1903. Holmes, Watson and Lestrade are again examining marks on a wall, but Paget depicts the inspector as a more distinguished-looking figure than the text warrants. No longer does he appear small, sallow and rat-faced!

ber, but would be absurd for early July, when the *Aurora* would have sped away with the setting sun illuminating her stern as she steamed eastwards.

Establishing September 1887 as the month of *The Sign of Four* is open to the slight objection that it leaves very little time for Watson and Mary Morstan to get married by November, as suggested in *The Noble Bachelor*. But, as we have seen, a speedy marriage is a distinct possibility, and our doubts about it are not sufficiently strong to justify ignoring the many statements and inferences which point the other way. Before leaving the subject, however, we must examine some of the other cases. There are other problems and inconsistencies to explore before we can consider ourselves entitled to put reasonably certain dates on *The Sign of Four* and Watson's marriage.

Turning back for a moment to *The Noble Bachelor*, an adventure which may now be fairly confidently dated within a month, possibly even within a week, after *The Sign of Four*, and certainly only 'a few weeks' before Watson's marriage, we find the doctor spending the whole of a stormy day indoors and alone. He was feeling unwell, for the old wound, the relic of his Afghan campaign, 'throbbed with dull persistency'. Yet he fails to mention his fiancée, makes only a passing reference to his fast-approaching marriage, and appears quite careless of the plans he ought sensibly to be making for entering medical practice and arranging for his future life as a married man. He seems to have nothing special to do except surround himself 'with a cloud of newspapers' until he eventually became 'saturated with the news of the day'. Presumably he was still feeling much as he did during his conversation with Holmes on the afternoon Miss Morstan arrived with the pearls when, offered a jab of cocaine, he brusquely told Holmes, 'My constitution has not got over the Afghan campaign yet. I cannot afford to throw any extra strain upon it.'

The wound was much on his mind during *The Sign of Four*. He speaks of the 'dangerous thoughts' of matrimony for 'an Army Surgeon with a weak leg', and of the strange surprises of the night which have 'shaken my nerve completely', later admitting, after the long trudge with Toby, that he 'was limp and weary, befogged in mind and fatigued in body'. At the end of the case it was Holmes who expected himself to be as limp as a rag for a week. In fact it seems to have been Watson who succumbed. The engagement apparently failed to give him the mental and physical lift that might have been expected.

Whilst there are other cases, notably *Silver Blaze*, *The Resident Patient* and *The Five Orange Pips*, which may have taken place between *The Sign of Four* and the doctor's marriage, *The Noble Bachelor* is the only one in which we may be absolutely sure that Watson was an engaged man. In no other case does Watson mention his engagement or his bride-to-be, so possibly this is a factor which may be indicative of a very short engagement, rather than a long one.

Silver Blaze may have been an autumn case of 1887, during Watson's engagement, and probably was. The racehorse was 'from the Isonomy stock', held as brilliant a record as his famous ancestor, and was then in his fifth year. As his sire did not go to stud until 1881, Silver Blaze could not have been bred and reached his fifth year before 1887 at the earliest. Holmes and Watson were still together at Baker Street—suggesting that this was at a time prior to the marriage—and the events occurred when Dartmoor was 'bronze-coloured from the fading ferns', and the landscape 'tinged with gold, deepening into rich, ruddy brown'. It sounds rather like late September or early October.

The two friends went to Devonshire on a Thursday and, after a full programme of investigations, must have returned to London very tired. Thursday 29 September is a possible date for *Silver Blaze*, though this would conflict with *The Sign of Four* if 27 September, the previous Tuesday, is accepted for the start of that adventure. Thursday 6 October is possible for *Silver Blaze*, perhaps likely, because the following day, 7 October, was marked by Watson burying himself under the cloud of newspapers and nursing his throbbing wound; for that was also the day on which Holmes was consulted by Lord Robert St Simon in *The Noble Bachelor* and solved the mystery of the disappearing bride. Possibly his exertions on Dartmoor on the Thursday afford some further explanation of Watson's idleness on that particular Friday. However, it is only fair to add that the next Thursday, 13 October, is also a plausible date for the opening day of *Silver Blaze*.

The 'curious incident' of *Silver Blaze* is not so much that 'the dog did nothing in the night-time' but that Watson did nothing about his dear Mary. There need be no surprise at her absence from the journey to King's Pyland, but the following Tuesday was the day of the Wessex Plate; Holmes and Watson went to Winchester to watch the race, but poor Mary Morstan was left behind in London and probably forgotten. We feel reasonably certain that neither Mrs Cecil Forrester's requirements nor an appointment with the dressmaker detained Miss Morstan in town; the conclusion must be that Watson ignored her—a foretaste of what was to come during the marriage, when the doctor would come and go as he pleased with little or no consideration for his wife's convenience—and that he and Holmes never troubled to invite her to accompany them for a pleasant day out. Or perhaps Watson was frightened of Holmes falling into some error, such as backing the wrong horse, and then blaming Mary for having biased his judgement.

It is now time to examine two more of Holmes' cases, *The Five Orange Pips* and *The Cardboard Box*, which may, at first sight, cast some doubts both upon the proposed September 1887 dating for *The Sign of Four* and upon the suggestion that Watson and Miss Morstan were married about two months afterwards.

The Five Orange Pips, which is the subject of a special note below, following the chapter on *The Hound of the Baskervilles*, is dated late September 1887. Its opening is reminiscent of *The Noble Bachelor*, whose almost exact contemporary it purports to be. In the preamble Watson records that 'the equinoctial gales had set in with exceptional violence. All day the wind had screamed and the rain had beaten against the windows'. It sounds very much like the same period of bad weather which characterises the beginning of *The Noble Bachelor*, in which Watson writes of the weather having 'taken a sudden turn to rain, with high autumnal winds'. The only point of slight difficulty is that if—as it would appear—*The Five Orange Pips* preceded *The Noble Bachelor* by a week or so it is hardly accurate for Watson to speak of the less vile weather in the latter case having taken a sudden turn for the worse. Be that as it may, it could have been the same autumn, if the tempestuous conditions of wind and rain are anything to go by.

The trouble about accepting *The Five Orange Pips* in this chronological sequence is the statement by Watson that he was 'a dweller once more in my old quarters at Baker Street' because his 'wife was on a visit to her aunt's'. The situation becomes more confused, as some earlier students have pointed out, by the first appearance of the story in *The Strand* for November 1891. Here Watson writes of his wife being away on a visit to her mother's.

MARY MORSTAN'S MYTHICAL AUNT

Let us say here and now that we no more believe in the existence of Mary Watson's aunt than we do in the orphan-girl's mother. Both were figments of Conan Doyle's imagination, erroneously inserted in the manuscript while he was editing Watson's notes for publication. We suppose what happened was that Watson's notes showed that he was living at Baker Street and that Conan Doyle, misled into assuming that Watson was already married, invented the visit to Mary's mother as being the most plausible explanation he could think of to account for the doctor's absence from home. Conan Doyle's mistake may have emanated from Watson's final note, recording the news 'that is all which we shall ever know of the fate of the *Lone Star*', by which time Watson would actually have been married.

There is a reference to Watson's 'professional work' on the day following Openshaw's call; this accords more appropriately with the married Watson, but the date is so close to the wedding—though admittedly close also to the engagement earlier the same month—that the doctor had probably taken up a busy locum for a few days with the object of bringing his practical medical knowledge a little more up to date.

We wonder what Watson thought upon discovering that he had suddenly become saddled with a mysterious mother-in-law. Obviously he never bothered to read the proofs; probably he was going through bouts of depression at that time, as he thought of his old friend, dead at the bottom of the Reichenbach abyss. When the story was published Conan Doyle and Watson agreed, in all likelihood, not to make any drastic textual amendments when the adventure was reprinted, but to mention his wife's aunt instead of her mother.

However, as we have said, we think the aunt is as fictional as the mother. The whole basis of Miss Morstan's appearance in *The Sign of Four* is that she was entirely alone in the world. At the time of being sent home from India for schooling at 'a comfortable boarding establishment at Edinburgh' she 'had no relative in England'. And we do not believe that any aunt subsequently arrived. When Miss Morstan speaks of her father's disappearance we hear that she consulted the manager of the hotel, communicated with the police and advertised in all the papers. It sounds as though there was no aunt to visit at that time. Then, after the arrival of the letter, it is Mrs Forrester who is consulted, and then, on her recommendation, Holmes. Again, there is no suggestion of an aunt. Had there actually been such a lady in existence, surely somebody would have asked her at some stage whether she had heard anything which could throw some light upon the matter.

Having, as we hope, effectively disposed not only of the aunt but also of any serious suggestion that Watson had graduated from bachelorhood by the time of *The Five Orange Pips*, we may now ignore the apparent contradiction and accept the dating in the text without demur. Holmes and Watson had a very busy autumn in that eventful year of 1887, but *The Five Orange Pips* did not take up much of Holmes' time. Perhaps it was because of overwork and heavy commitments elsewhere that he was so negligent in protecting his client and allowing John Openshaw to expose himself to a fatal attack. The dating in Watson's narrative is explicit and could scarcely be questioned at all, were it not for the mention of the doctor being already a married man. When that assertion is explained, as we have endeavoured to do, the difficulties vanish and these other small indications, all of them consistent with the autumn of 1887, become apparent.

'THE CARDBOARD BOX'

The Cardboard Box is an adventure likely to create some chronological problems almost regardless of the dates selected for *The Sign of Four* and the Watson-Morstan marriage. Some students of the Holmes saga have been so seriously led astray by it that they have propounded theories that are not merely untenable by ordinary logical or deductive reasoning, but involve acceptance of practical impossibilities. Consider the facts. *The Cardboard Box* was first published in *The Strand* for April 1893 while Holmes was away from active London practice during his travels abroad which followed *The Final Problem.* It must therefore have taken place before 25 April 1891, the unquestioned and unquestionable date of Holmes' departure from England pursued by Moriarty. 'It was a blazing hot day in August' when, in the Baker Street sitting-room, Holmes was reading and re-reading a letter which he had received by the morning post and Watson was thinking of his postponed holiday and the preposterousness of war. Holmes then produces a note from 'our friend Lestrade' about the gruesome packet which has been delivered to Miss Cushing. Watson is not in practice and admits to Holmes that he is 'longing for something to do'.

Initially, this situation points to the time prior to Watson's marriage, when he is living permanently with Holmes at Baker Street and has not yet returned to medical practice. While they are chatting about the case Holmes reminds Watson of 'the investigations which you have chronicled under the names of *A Study in Scarlet* and of *The Sign of Four*'.

It is obvious, therefore, that the date of *The Cardboard Box* must be an August after the publication of these earlier adventures. *The Sign of Four* was the later of the two to be published, the first edition having been brought out in February 1890. It follows that the only possible August for *The Cardboard Box* is August 1890, and at that time Watson was married and living away from Baker Street.

It is this apparent contradiction which has misled some commentators, but the most reasonable and likely explanation is simple enough. Watson has allowed Mary to spend August at the seaside, himself remaining in London until later in the month when he had a locum engaged for his practice and intending to join her for the end of their vacation. The locum has arrived, but Watson, regretting that a 'depleted bank account' has caused him to postpone his own holiday, sends his excuses to his wife and moves in with Holmes.

As Watson touchingly puts it at the commencement of the narrative, 'Everybody was out of town, and I yearned for the glades of the New Forest or the shingle of Southsea.' (He may have been yearning for Mary, too. An alternative explanation, to be examined subsequently, is that Watson and his wife had quarrelled and were living apart. Watson's 'longing for something to do' may refer to the practice being particularly quiet; several times he refers to the summer being the slackest time of the year.) So, in fact, there is nothing so contradictory about *The Cardboard Box* as to lead us even to consider having to revise the 1887 dates already proposed for *The Sign of Four* and the doctor's marriage.

CONCLUSION

To sum up the evidence, it now seems safe beyond peradventure to declare as proven that Watson's marriage was in the early winter, probably November, of 1887 and that *The Sign of Four* occurred between a Tuesday and a Friday of September, earlier in the same year. The precise date of the wedding is anyone's guess; but some speculation, though it is no more than pure guesswork, about the date of *The Sign of Four* may be worthwhile. If the latter part of September is selected, *The Five Orange Pips* presents less difficulty because it would not then be one of the adventures of Watson's engagement period in which Mary Morstan is nowhere mentioned. Specifically, 27–30 September has its attractions, particularly on account of the scholarly deductions drawn from Watson's supposedly crabbed handwriting. Furthermore, the later the date the darker it would be for the eight o'clock departure of the *Aurora* and the efforts of her hirers to elude the police in the evening gloom. On the other hand, if *The Sign of Four* can be placed earlier in the month, it is no longer so close to *The Noble Bachelor* and there is no possibility of a clash of dates with *Silver Blaze*; Watson and Mary Morstan are given a little longer to get to know each other before embarking on matrimony, and the daylight would be better able to illuminate the early morning trudge along the trail of creosote and, on the final evening, the gilded cross on the dome of St Paul's.

And what of Watson's marriage? It was probably a very quiet affair at the parish church near Mrs Cecil Forrester's, for presumably Mary was married from there. Few, if any, guests can have been invited. Holmes may have been persuaded to act as best man; or possibly he gave away the bride and left it to Percy Phelps, or even Athelney Jones, to look after Watson. If there was a reception afterwards, the bridegroom may have been encouraged, over a glass of champagne, to recount the anecdote about how he 'fired a double-barrelled tiger cub' at the musket which had looked into his tent during his service days in Afghanistan.

WATSON'S MEDICAL PRACTICE

The marriage started off well enough. Within just a few short months, in March 1888, Watson refers, in *A Scandal in Bohemia*, to his 'complete happiness, and the home-centred interests which rise up around the man who first finds himself master of his own establishment'. The only troublesome feature at that time was their 'most clumsy and careless servant girl' who had been given notice. Holmes observed that Watson had put on weight and remarked that wedlock suited him.

Although he must have realised that the wound pension was unlikely to provide a very solid basis for the expenses of married life, Watson appears not to have intended to acquire a practice immediately on getting married. The idea must surely have been in the back of his mind, though it seems he neglected to tell Holmes anything about it. 'Shortly after my marriage', Watson wrote in *The Stockbroker's Clerk*, 'I had bought a connection in the Paddington district.' One wonders how he managed to pay for it, modest as the price undoubtedly was. Funds were very low at the time of *The Sign of Four*, for Watson is regretting the weakness of his bank account when the first thoughts of a courtship are entering his mind, and it must have become still weaker by the time he and his wife had set up their home. Possibly his bankers obliged him with a loan; or maybe Mary was able to realise some money on her pearls.

The practice kept him very busy at first, and it was 'one morning in June', which, we are told, was 'three months after taking over the practice', that Holmes arrived and they went off together to Birmingham with Hall Pycroft. This accords with *A Scandal in Bohemia* when Watson called on Holmes one night ('it was on the 20th of March, 1888'), 'while returning from a journey to a patient', and

Holmes deduced that Watson had, as he put it, 'returned to civil practice'. Work must then have been a novelty for the doctor, for Holmes is heard to say, 'And in practice again, I observe. You didn't tell me that you intended to go into harness.'

There are, in *The Stockbroker's Clerk*, some suggestions as to the relative lightness of Watson's professional duties at this time. Despite his protestations of being 'kept very closely at work', it sounds as if this was the case only when he looked after his neighbour's practice as well as his own. He had been confined to the house with a severe chill for three days of the previous week, but raised not the slightest demur to Holmes' proposal to depart immediately for a day in Birmingham. By the summer, 'the slackest time of the year' according to Watson in *The Naval Treaty*, the 'practice could get along very well for a day or two' while he assisted Holmes in saving the reputation of 'Tadpole' Phelps.

In *The Crooked Man*, another case which probably engaged Holmes' attention during the summer of 1888, and which we shall examine in more detail later, Watson was ready to hand over his practice to Jackson and set off to Aldershot with Holmes 'by the 11.10 from Waterloo'. By the following summer in 1889, he records that his 'practice had steadily increased' and that he had 'got a few patients from among the officials' at Paddington station. Yet, in that case, *The Engineer's Thumb*, Watson was quite prepared to take the day off and accompany Holmes and his patient Hatherley to Berkshire. And in the slightly earlier case of *The Boscombe Valley Mystery*, Watson, despite his 'fairly long list', adopts his wife's suggestion of letting Anstruther do his work for him so that he may be free to join Holmes in the west of England. This was in early June 1889 and involved an absence from home and work of two whole days.

Despite these absences, Watson's practice continued to prosper. By late 1889 or early 1890 he was able to move to a more pleasant home in Kensington. It may have been at Christmas 1889 that the doctor was kept fully occupied with the business of moving because, as he says in *The Blue Carbuncle*, it was not until 'the second morning after Christmas' that he found time to call on Holmes to wish him the compliments of the season.

There is no certainty about what happened to the Paddington practice, but surmise has it that Watson retained his consulting-rooms there and sublet the remainder of the house. He also put up his plate at his new residence in Kensington.

These assumptions are based on a number of pieces of evidence. Watson was still at Paddington in the summer of 1889 at the time of *The Engineer's Thumb*, but by the following year, in the account of *The Red-Headed League*, Watson refers to his home in Kensington. And when he goes from his house to join Holmes in the hunt for John Clay he makes his way 'across the Park, and so through Oxford Street to Baker Street'. There was a consulting-room at the Kensington property, for this is where Holmes called in April 1891 when he sought Watson's aid against Moriarty in *The Final Problem.* Mrs Watson was then, according to her husband, 'away upon a visit'.

It is unlikely that Watson would have abandoned his Paddington connection when he moved his home to Kensington. After all, he had spent considerable effort working it up from the decline in which the afflicted old Dr Farquhar had left it. To start afresh in a more fashionable area without the backing of his established Paddington practice would have been rather foolhardy.

Admittedly there is only slight evidence of Watson's retention of the Paddington practice, which comes from *The Dying Detective.* Mrs Hudson has at last obtained Holmes' grudging permission to call in Watson, who writes: 'I listened earnestly to her story when she came to my rooms in the second year of my married life and told me of the sad condition to which my poor friend was reduced.' The reference to 'my rooms' presumably means Watson's consulting-rooms; and it is likely that these were the rooms at Paddington because there was so little conversation in the cab on the way back to Baker Street that a fairly short journey is indicated. The point is by no means more than suggestive, for it was 'a foggy November day' and so, being in the second year of Watson's married life, could equally well have been 1888 or 1889; and, even if the later year, it could have been before the Watsons moved to Kensington. Nevertheless, it is surely not impossible that the doctor had, for a time at least, two practices.

SHADOWS OVER THE MARRIAGE?

Was there, perhaps, another reason for moving to Kensington? Was the marriage possibly not as happy as it might have been? In the early days, as one would expect, the picture is of domestic bliss. *A Scandal in Bohemia* finds Watson putting on weight and tacitly acknowledging that wedlock suits him. But, having called upon Holmes on impulse, he spends the whole evening at Baker Street despite his wife having not the slightest notion of his whereabouts; and the following night he sleeps at Baker Street—again, presumably, without any prior arrangement—stays for breakfast in the morning, and then goes out with Holmes and the king to Briony Lodge, having sent no word whatever to his waiting wife.

Two and a half months later, in *The Stockbroker's Clerk*, Watson tells Holmes that he and Mary 'are both very well'. But he entirely omits to consult her about the hurried trip to Birmingham; he merely 'rushed upstairs to explain the matter' and then joined Holmes on the doorstep. It must have been very late at night when the two men returned. Similarly, in *The Naval Treaty*, a case during 'the July which immediately succeeded' Watson's marriage, and again a year later, in *The Engineer's Thumb*, Mary is just given the briefest of explanations before Watson rushes off to Holmes with, respectively, the letter from his old schoolfellow and his injured patient.

In *The Man with the Twisted Lip* Mary, who must have expected her husband to return in the cab with Isa Whitney, has to be content with a note brought by the cabman saying that he has thrown in his lot with Holmes. And at the end of the Christmas 1889 adventure of *The Blue Carbuncle*, Holmes and Watson settle down contentedly to their goose supper, neither of them having even thought of inviting Mary Watson to join them; indeed, she is not mentioned at all. It would be out of character for Holmes, despite his mysogynist tendencies, so completely to have forgotten his manners as to be deliberately discourteous to his colleague's wife, but she is ignored throughout the whole case and Watson has even failed to mention her when wishing Holmes 'the compliments of the season'.

Mary Watson must have got more and more disheartened at being left alone. Watson describes her making 'a little face of disappointment', in *The Man with the Twisted Lip*, when she thought that a patient had arrived unexpectedly during the evening. It was more probably a gesture of annoyance on her part. This was in June 1889, when the Paddington practice was at its most prosperous, and the doctor 'newly back from a weary day'.

The Crooked Man opens at a quarter to twelve at night. Watson has just knocked out the ashes of his last pipe and nodded over a novel. As for Mrs Watson, 'My wife had already gone upstairs, and the sound of the locking of the hall door some time before told me that the servants had also retired,' the doctor explains. Watson there and then promises Holmes to join him on the train to Aldershot the next morning. But this was only 'a few months' after the wedding and Watson appears to be neither very attentive nor considerate towards his wife. The years of bachelorhood may have made him very self-centred as a husband.

As for Mary, she was quite willing, in June 1889, at a time when she had been married for little over eighteen months, to pack her husband off to bed so that she might have a private girlish chat with her old schoolfriend Kate Whitney, concerning the supposed madness or infidelity of Isa Whitney, in *The Man with the Twisted Lip*. The conclusion must be that the Watson marriage produced some strained situations. There is no evidence anywhere of much satisfaction on the sexual side, nor the barest clue that they ever thought of producing a family.

At the start of *The Boscombe Valley Mystery*, however, all is sweetness and harmony. Watson asks Mary for her opinion about his going with Holmes, she thinks the change would do him good as he has been looking rather pale lately, and he alludes to *The Sign of Four*, in which he gained a wife. Are these outward expressions of conjugal bliss meant to be taken at their face value? Is it possible that Watson is behaving so politely in this exchange because of some recent quarrel in which Mary has let him know that his conduct leaves a lot to be desired? Mary may have approved so readily of the Boscombe Valley trip not so much on account of Watson's pallid looks, but in order that she might have a day or two of peace and quiet without him. When she remarks 'you are always so interested in Mr. Sherlock Holmes' cases', could she have meant it sarcastically, implying that her husband took more interest in Holmes' doings than in hers? If so, the doctor's rejoinder, 'I should be ungrateful if I were not, seeing what I gained through one of them' takes on a new meaning. Possibly he hoped that the adventure in the west of England might put him in touch with some rather more congenial female company.

Watson was not averse to looking at other women with obvious approval. Violet Hunter, of *The Copper Beeches*, would undoubtedly have come within that category. As the 'young lady entered the room' Watson recorded, and with no lack of relish, that 'she was plainly but neatly dressed, with a bright, quick face, freckled like a plover's egg, and with the brisk manner of a woman who has had her own way to make in the world'. He may have thought the quick face, covered in freckles, a decided improvement on the 'little face of disappointment'. He seems even more elated as he and Holmes are on their way to Winchester a fortnight later to see Miss Hunter. 'The sun was shining very brightly, and yet there was an exhilarating nip in the air, which set an edge to a man's energy.' He then describes the rolling hills on this sunny spring day, with the little red and grey roofs peeping out from amidst the light green of the new foliage. ' "Are they not fresh and beautiful?" I cried,' writes Watson. Spring fever? Or elation at the prospect of meeting Miss Hunter? At the end of the case Watson expresses disappointment that Holmes 'manifested no further interest in her', but the doctor took the trouble at least to follow her future career with some care and was able to report that 'she is now the head of a private school at Walsall'.

Before discounting this episode as far-fetched or over-imaginative, be it remembered that *The Copper Beeches* took place in the early spring of 1890. Though no specific date is given in the text—and Watson had good reason for omitting it—it cannot have been earlier than 1890, on account of *The Blue Carbuncle* being mentioned, or later, because it cannot possibly have occurred in the same spring as *The Final Problem.* However, in *The Copper Beeches*, Watson is spending over two weeks at Baker Street with Holmes and nothing is heard of Mary. Had she gone off somewhere on her own to get away from Watson, or had he deserted her with the object of gaining some respite from their marital stress? If Watson ever had cause to look at another woman during his marriage, this was the moment when opportunity coincided with likely inclination.

By the summer of the same year, August 1890, Watson is staying with Holmes again, this time yearning for his postponed holiday, and going with his friend to unravel the puzzle of *The Cardboard Box*. At first sight, it would seem from the text that, for reasons of economy, Mary had gone away without him. Were the reasons for their not being together other than financial? Holmes was wise enough in the ways of women to be able to remark, in *The Second Stain*, that 'their most trivial action may mean volumes'. Did Mary Watson take her holiday alone because she was becoming disgruntled with her husband and had been suffering more than she could stand from his 'natural Bohemianism of disposition'? The move to Kensington could have been not so much an attempt to better himself professionally as a second try to make the marriage work, away from the house at Paddington which may have harboured unhappy associations.

The Final Problem opens with Holmes inquiring whether Watson's wife is at home and being told that she is 'away upon a visit'. Visiting who? Mrs Cecil Forrester, perhaps; surely not the fictitious aunt from *The Five Orange Pips*. It sounds like the same old excuse, the simplest way Watson knew of covering up for Mary's absence. Holmes found him in 1891 quite alone and perfectly willing to leave England for a week on the Continent. Actually Watson was away from 25 April until at least 5 May, ten days at the absolute minimum. If, as has been suggested by some commentators, Mary had gone away to take treatment for an illness from which she subsequently died, why did not Watson say so when Holmes asked? And, if his wife really had been ill, Watson would surely have preferred to remain in England so that he could visit her; he was not anchored to London by the claims of his practice.

Watson's practice, or practices, cannot have been very flourishing during 1890 and 1891; it was easy enough for him to leave them at almost a moment's notice, and there is no mention of his calling upon the assistance of some accommodating neighbour. Perhaps he did eventually dispose of the Paddington connection without first effectively establishing himself in Kensington. He was forced to admit to Holmes, during the adventure of *The Red-Headed League* in 1890: 'I have nothing to do to-day. My practice is never very absorbing.' And in the early spring of the same year, during the affair of *The Copper Beeches*, the doctor is living at Baker Street and the narrative contains no reference whatever to his practice, nor, incidentally, to his wife. Why had Watson so reduced his professional activity?

At the time of *The Final Problem* Holmes and Watson had seen very little of each other for many months. To be sure, Holmes had been heavily engaged 'upon a matter of supreme importance' for the French government, but the two friends had drifted apart and Holmes had not visited Watson for a long while. Was Holmes unaware of the doctor's domestic situation? Or had he tactfully kept away for fear of embarrassment?

There may be a common answer to all these questions; that the relationship between Watson and his wife had steadily deteriorated and she had finally left him. The parting would in all probability have made Watson careless of his medical duties. He had 'another set of vices' beyond the peccadilloes he had confessed to Holmes at the time of their first meeting in *A Study in Scarlet.* Gambling was one of them. He was to admit somewhat ruefully in *Shoscombe Old Place* that he paid for racing 'with about half my wound pension'. He must have been a difficult man to live with. Even Holmes, who was not exactly faultless himself, was heard to complain, in *The Three Students*, of the doctor's 'eternal tobacco' and 'irregularity at meals'. At times of mental pressure and stress Watson's propensities for gambling and drink probably came to the fore, though whether they contributed to the broken marriage or were resorted to by Watson in his loneliness is unknown.

We suspect that Watson was probably cruel, perhaps even violent at times, to Mary, especially when he was in drink. It was a family failing. *The Sign of Four* begins with a deductive demonstration by Holmes, when he described the doctor's 'unhappy brother' by reference to an examination of his watch. 'He was a man of untidy habits—very untidy and careless. He was left with good prospects, but he threw away his chances, lived for some time in poverty with occasional short intervals of prosperity, and, finally, taking to drink, he died.' So

Holmes summed up his findings, which Watson confirmed were 'absolutely correct in every particular'. Is it not reasonably likely that Watson had also succumbed to a similar, but fortunately not fatal, downfall? He had good prospects in the medical profession, periods of poverty through idleness and betting, intervals of prosperity when he troubled to work hard in his practice, and was at all times liable to take excesses of alcohol. He needed Beaune, for example, to stimulate him to tackle Holmes about the latter's drug-taking on the afternoon Miss Morstan arrived with her pearls. He may have become more and more reliant upon the bottle as his marriage started to break down.

Holmes probably distrusted Watson's discretion at this period. During the three years abroad after *The Final Problem* Holmes several times took up his pen to write, but finally decided to keep his old friend in ignorance of the fact that he was still alive. Though his explanation in *The Empty House* is considerate and polite, Holmes probably feared, during his years of incognito, that Watson might unwittingly betray him through some indiscretion committed while under the influence of drink.

The breakdown of Watson's marriage may not have been entirely his fault. With his great 'experience of women which extends over many nations and three separate continents', Watson may have found the former governess too frigid a female for his sexual palate and have sought solace elsewhere. But whatever the prime cause may have been, the marriage failed, and Watson's once flourishing practice declined.

Mary enters no more into Watson's life. In *The Empty House* the doctor comments that in some manner, during his absence, Holmes had learned 'of my own sad bereavement', and his sympathy was shown in his manner rather than by his words. 'Work is the best antidote to sorrow, my dear Watson,' said he. The bereavement and sorrow are supposedly meant to refer to Mary's death, but of course they could have been bereavement and sorrow of other kinds; the late Christopher Morley, one of the founders of the Baker Street Irregulars, of New York, once suggested that the 'bereavement' meant that Watson and his wife had separated but came together later. But Watson's sadness might, for instance, signify remorse for his own

'WE ALL THREE SHOOK HANDS.'

By Sidney Paget, from *The Hound of the Baskervilles*, March 1902. Holmes and Watson greet Inspector Lestrade on the platform of Coombe Tracey station. Lestrade is now 'a small, wiry bulldog of a man'. The years have changed him from the original description in *A Study in Scarlet*.

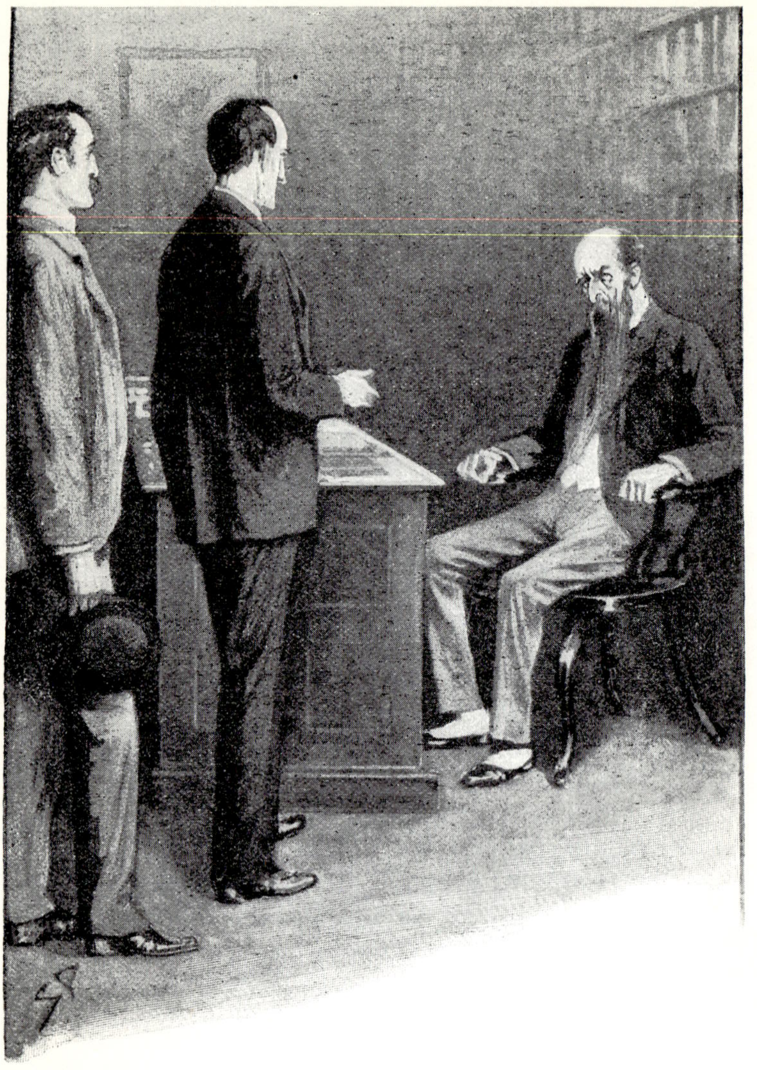

'THE MURDERER HAS ESCAPED.'

By Sidney Paget, from *The Adventure of the Priory School,* February 1904. Holmes explains to the Duke of Holdernesse how he solved the mystery of young Lord Saltire's disappearance, having just collected the largest professional fee of his career. a cheque for £6,000.

misbehaviour. On the night of Small's arrest in *The Sign of Four* he knew he had gained a treasure; perhaps his dejection in *The Empty House* was an expression of regret at having lost her love.

Watson saw the publication of *The Musgrave Ritual* in 1893, before *The Return*; in it he records Holmes explaining just this sort of situation: 'A man always finds it hard to realize that he may have finally lost a woman's love, however badly he may have treated her.' We can only be sorry for Watson that a marriage which began with such happy promise should have ended in tragedy. The doctor's boast about his familiarity with the fair sex, which he must have deliberately included in the manuscript while writing up *The Sign of Four* in 1890, may point to his realisation that the marriage was even then already tottering; perhaps he kept it in as a measure of self-assurance, audaciously believing that he could still manage his wife and attract other women as well.

There are two other questions. Why did Mary Watson call her husband James and when did she die? The riddle of the first and the answer to the second both come from adjacent paragraphs of *The Man with the Twisted Lip*.

In conversation with Kate Whitney, reported by Watson as having taken place 'in June '89', Mary offers their visitor wine and water and shows her to a comfortable seat, from where she can 'tell us all about it'. She then continues, 'Or should you rather that I sent James off to bed?' This can only be meant to refer to Watson, but the doctor's first name was, of course, John. Miss Dorothy Sayers conjectured that James was a 'pet-name' for Watson, invented by Mary and derived from his second name, which she supposed must be Hamish, the Scottish form of James. It is an attractive theory, and the learned lady expressed it with undoubted charm, but there exists not one shred of evidence that the doctor bore the name Hamish at all. The most we can be sure of is that the initial was H, for so it appears beneath the title of Part I of *A Study in Scarlet*, being 'a reprint from the Reminiscences of JOHN H. WATSON, M.D., Late of the Army Medical Department'.

It seems far more likely that James was a printer's error or merely a mistake made by Conan Doyle when editing Watson's notes for publication in *The Strand.* A blunder like this in the printing of a man's name would normally have been noticed in the proofs, or at least corrected in later editions, just as 'mother' was amended to the equally inaccurate 'aunt' in *The Five Orange Pips.* But the reference to Mary Morstan's mother would have shocked Conan Doyle, and it was presumably he who arranged for the subsequent alteration; the appellation James could have offended only Watson, and he was probably in no mood to be bothered about it. *The Man with the Twisted Lip* first appeared in December 1891, at a time when Watson must have been very miserable indeed. His great friend Holmes was lying dead at the bottom of the abyss, his medical practice had failed, his marriage had collapsed. And, as we shall see in a moment, it was now too late for any attempt to be made to patch it up with Mary. Work being the best antidote to sorrow, as the wretched doctor realised already, Watson threw himself into the task of writing up his notes in order that the readers of *The Strand*, and successive generations, might enjoy his continued reminiscences of Sherlock Holmes. Even if he noticed it at all, the erroneous printing of his name would hardly have worried him; he had far too much on his mind already.

CLUE TO WATSON'S BEREAVEMENT

And what of Mary's death? As we have hinted in the previous passage, Mary Watson had breathed her last by the time *The Man with the Twisted Lip* came to be written. She had died earlier in 1891, probably during the summer or autumn. We do not know whether it was illness or accident. She was only thirty. And how do we know? The clue is contained in the paragraph which precedes the reference to the doctor as James. It begins with quoted speech from Kate Whitney, talking to Mary, and ends with a comment from Watson. Here it is in full:

> 'I didn't know what to do, so I came straight to you.' That was always the way. Folk who were in grief came to my wife like birds to a lighthouse.

Clearly, if Watson had been referring to a wife who was then still living he would have written in the present tense, and not the past. Of the living Mary, certainly of the Mary who was his real and actual wife, he could only have said: 'That is always the way. Folk who are in grief *come* to my wife like birds to a lighthouse.' Watson's tragedy, as he must have fully understood by then, was that he had no lighthouse to which to fly with his own grief; the lamp in the beacon had gone out.

We admit to some feelings of disloyalty in propounding the theories here stated and challenging the traditionally held view of Watson's utter steadfastness and sturdy respectability. To portray him as a pathetic figure, standing alone amid the ruin of his little world, will not, we hope, be branded as heresy or libel. For, though we regret to have to say it, there does appear to be greater evidence of an unhappy marriage than of a happy one, cut short, as we think it was, by Mary Watson's untimely decease. The weight of authority, as presented in these pages, is convincing enough. Watson's neglect of his wife, which some women with less sheltered backgrounds might have endured or even accepted, was too much for Mary. We are reminded, as Holmes reminded Watson in *A Case of Identity*, of the old Persian saying, 'There is danger for him who taketh the tiger cub, and danger also for whoso snatches a delusion from a woman.' And who can ever forget that Watson's tiger cub was double-barrelled?

MYSTERY OF THE MAJOR'S LETTER

As a pendant to this adventure, an interesting speculation is raised by the letter which Major Sholto received from India. If any credence can be placed in Small's account, here is an example of one of Holmes' deductions being proved wrong. While he and Watson are following the creosote trail behind the dog Toby the detective explains 'the only hypothesis which fits the facts'. He tests it by seeing 'how it fits in with the sequel'. Here is the conversation:

> '. . . Major Sholto remains at peace for some years, happy in the possession of his treasure. Then he receives a letter from India which gives him a great fright. What was that?'
>
> 'A letter to say that the men whom he had wronged had been set free.'
>
> 'Or had escaped. That is much more likely, for he would have known what their term of imprisonment was. It would not have been a surprise to him. What does he do then? He guards himself against a wooden-legged

> man—a white man, mark you, for he mistakes a white tradesman for him, and actually fires a pistol at him . . .'

In fairness to Holmes it must be admitted that the initial error of reasoning about the contents of the letter was Watson's, but the detective does at once adopt it, and it is logical to suppose that his mind was working along similar lines. It is plain, however, that Holmes was quite wrong in assuming that the letter from India, which the major had received early in 1882, referred to Small's escape or release. It is not unlikely that Small had escaped from the Andamans even before Morstan left India; indeed, it may have been Morstan who told Sholto of it and thus precipitated a more violent quarrel about the treasure than would have transpired if only the two British officers had been at liberty.

Consider what Small and his faithful Tonga did after getting away from the convict settlement. They sailed to Jiddah, settled down among the Malay pilgrims, went through a lengthy series of adventures, drifting here and there about the world, something always turning up to keep them from London. And, after reaching England, Small had, as he describes, to make his preparations for achieving his objective, preparations which must have taken at least two or three months.

Therefore, the letter must have been written from India long after Small had gained his freedom. It is most improbable that Sholto would have remained for long in ignorance of an event of such vital importance to him; in fact he must have known of it, because his 'marked aversion to men with wooden legs' was a feature of his eccentricity before the letter arrived. So the letter contained not news of Small's escape, something of which the major was already well aware, but the far more terrible news that vengeance was at hand.

It is worth speculating on who wrote the letter and how it came to be sent. Remember, first of all, that it was 'short and written in a scrawling hand'. The same expression is used by both Thaddeus Sholto and Jonathan Small in describing 'the sign of the four' which was pinned on the major's chest. To scrawl his handwriting may have been one of Small's more characteristic habits. Was he not, perhaps, himself the writer of the letter from India, posting it just before his departure for England, so that both travelled on the same ship? To Sholto, the arrival of the letter would confirm also the arrival of his sworn enemy. The period from 'early in 1882' until 'the end of April' gave Small exactly the length of time he needed to reconnoitre his adversary's heavily defended position and plan his attack. How nearly he succeeded; and how wrong was Holmes' deduction about that letter.

SECOND INTERVAL

SOME CHRONOLOGICAL PROBLEMS OF THE MARRIAGE PERIOD

Sherlock Holmes said it:

'I have to let you see my little difficulties, if you are to understand the situation.'

The inaccuracy of many of the dates given in the Sherlock Holmes adventures is particularly apparent in the cases which occurred between the time of Doctor Watson's marriage to Mary Morstan and the end of April 1891, when Holmes and Watson went to the Continent, pursuing, or being pursued by, the infamous Professor Moriarty. Whoever was responsible was very careless indeed; perhaps he thought it didn't matter.

At whose door should the blame be laid? It is tempting to accuse Watson of being the culprit, but there is reason as well to regard Conan Doyle as having been at least implicated. The clue to Conan Doyle's involvement is that, in his capacity as editor, he wrote a brief preface to the collected volume of *Short Stories* which was published by John Murray in October 1928. There he included some of the most glaring errors of all.

Writing about the 'series of stories concerning Sherlock Holmes apart from the four novels', he explains that it begins with the detective's 'first appearance in this form in "A Scandal in Bohemia" which came out in 1892, until he made his final exit in the "Adventure of Shoscombe Abbey" in 1925'. In a piece consisting of two short paragraphs and containing only two dates, Conan Doyle managed to get both years wrong. *A Scandal in Bohemia* will be found in *The Strand* for July 1891 and *Shoscombe Old Place* in the April 1927 issue of the same magazine. And the idea of referring to the 'Adventure of Shoscombe Abbey' at the front of a volume which actually contains the adventure of *Shoscombe Old Place* suggests either a flagrant disregard for accuracy or a playful attempt to poke fun at the serious students who were scrutinising Conan Doyle's texts more closely than he ever intended they should. Careless errors or deliberate mistakes, they may have been just the latest of a long series, to which the editor himself had substantially contributed. Perhaps it wasn't all Watson!

'A SCANDAL IN BOHEMIA'

A Scandal in Bohemia was the first adventure to be published in short-story form, so let it be the first of the marriage-period cases to be considered here. There is no problem about the year, which is specifically 1888. But there is a difficulty about accepting 20 March as the date of the evening when Watson and the King of Bohemia both called upon Holmes. The whole purpose of the king's visit was to prevent Irene Adler from carrying out her threat to send the compromising photograph to the King of Scandinavia 'on the day when the betrothal was publicly proclaimed', and that day would be 'next Monday'. Holmes replies, in a yawn, that 'we have three days yet'. The consultation would therefore seem to have taken place on a Friday (possibly on a Thursday, if Holmes meant three *clear* days), but 20 March 1888 was a Tuesday.

Before attempting to conjecture where the error in the narrative lies, it is worth asking whether there is an explanation of the apparent inconsistency which still fits all the given facts. Holmes might well have reasoned along these lines: 'Today 20 March is Tuesday; the betrothal is to be publicly proclaimed next Monday; the announcement will be made in Scandinavia by the Princess Clotilde's father; if Miss Adler is to stop the engagement she must arrange for the photograph to reach the Court of the King of Scandinavia by Monday at the latest; for this to be achieved, she must dispatch it from London by

Friday evening at the latest; my client must also leave London by then in order to reach Scandinavia in time for the public announcement; therefore, we have three days yet.'

When the facts as presented in the narrative are capable of a perfectly plausible explanation like this, is it necessary to think further of disputing the text? Some commentators have been so sadly misled into assuming that the three days which were left to Holmes for carrying out his client's commission expired on the Monday—no doubt because of the king's stating, somewhat ambiguously, that Miss Adler intended to *send* the photograph on the day of the proclamation—that they have insisted on changing not only the month but the year as well.

The solution presented here is, in fact, supported by Holmes in a question he asked just before he spoke of the three days being available. Told by the king that there were 'no lengths to which Miss Adler would not go' in order to ruin him, Holmes asked whether he was 'sure that she has not sent it yet'. The *sending* of the photograph was therefore in Holmes' mind at that very moment; he clearly appreciated that some period of time must elapse while the photograph was being transported from London to Scandinavia. Thus, when the client says that Monday is to be the day of the promulgation of the engagement, Holmes is already thinking about the time it would necessarily take for the photograph to be delivered.

Accordingly, there is no need to consider here in any detail how the alleged inconsistency should be interpreted. To postulate another year yields no useful result, for the case is then set at variance with Watson's acquisition of a civil practice soon after his marriage, and the nearest years when 20 March fell on a Thursday or Friday were 1884 and 1890, which are both impossible upon any sensible view being taken of the datings of *The Sign of Four* and the doctor's marriage. To propose a different month is no more helpful, though it is fair to record that the 20th of January, April and July fell on Fridays in 1888. To suggest that the king made a mistake about the day—saying, for instance, that Monday was to be the day of the betrothal while meaning Friday or Saturday—can have no foundation whatever and is equally unavailing. Should anyone still insist on altering the text, it seems just as likely that Holmes said something like 'we have a few days yet', which Watson misheard and noted down as 'three' instead of 'few'.

But exercises of this sort in the context of *A Scandal in Bohemia*, however entertaining, are quite irrelevant when one bears in mind, as Holmes himself did, the length of time it would take for the photograph to travel from England to Scandinavia.

'A CASE OF IDENTITY'

Following *A Scandal in Bohemia* comes *A Case of Identity*, in which Holmes proudly shows Watson 'his snuff-box of old gold, with a great amethyst in the centre of the lid', which was his 'little souvenir from the King of Bohemia', and the ring which had been presented to him by 'the reigning family of Holland'.[1] The year of Hosmer Angel's disappearance is not mentioned in the text, but presumably it must have been 1888 still. There is also the clue that Miss Sutherland was supposed to have been married on Friday the 14th, for that was the date mentioned in the *Chronicle* advertisement. The earliest month of 1888 in which the 14th fell on a Friday was September, so it is likely that the case took place during the early part of the week commencing 17 September.

A Case of Identity is not an episode which involves any real chronological difficulty, but it is convenient to include it here, because some critics have been tempted to place it in months and years to which, in my view, it could not possibly belong. In case it should be objected that September is impossible on account of Holmes and Watson sitting 'on either side of the fire in his lodgings at Baker Street', let it be remembered that a conscientious landlady, as Mrs Hudson undoubtedly was, would have ensured that supplies of coal were available for her lodger's comfort during the colder days of the so-called English summer. And even if no fire was actually lit, is there anything wrong in the two friends sitting where the best chairs would usually be found whatever the time of year, on either side of the fire?

'THE MAN WITH THE TWISTED LIP'

It is now time to turn to *The Man with the Twisted Lip*, which contains a fundamental error of date, and to see whether this can be resolved in a sensible way. Watson observes at the outset that 'it was in June '89' that his wife's friend, Kate Whitney, called at his house during the evening, 'about the time when a man gives his first yawn, and glances at the clock'. Watson then goes to the opium den in Upper Swandam Lane to rescue Isa Whitney and bring him home. As soon as he is aroused, Whitney asks to be told the day, to which Watson replies that 'it is Friday, June 19'. There is some discussion between them on this subject, because Whitney thinks it is still Wednesday, but Watson proceeds to assure him that 'it is Friday'. But 19 June 1889 was a Wednesday.

The approximate year is confirmed by Watson being a married man living at home with his wife. The actual year of 1889 is supported by other internal evidence, namely Holmes' synopsis of the affairs of Neville St Clair, who came to Lee 'some years ago—to be definite, in May, 1884', was married in 1887 and already had two children. It can hardly have been earlier than 1889. 19 June would not fall on a Friday until 1891, when Holmes was assuredly out of England; and the previous year in which 19 June fell on Friday was 1885, when Watson was still a bachelor. So there is no need to think of disturbing the year.

The explanation is probably very simple; in fact, there is a choice of three solutions: 1. the printer mistook a handwritten 14 for 19—for 14 June *was* a Friday in 1889; 2. Watson, as Martin Dakin has suggested, had noted Ju.19 in his records and transcribed the month as June, when it should have been July—for 19 July was also a Friday in 1889; 3. Watson recollected his argument with Isa Whitney about 'Wednesday' but was at fault in thinking that that was the day Whitney had left home, when actually it could have been on Wednesday 19 June 1889 that Watson drove to the 'vile alley' and threw in his lot with Holmes.

None of these choices involves any drastic amendment and none is inconsistent with the other stories of the same period. Nothing so serious is required as, for instance, turning a mother into an aunt! If the reader is undecided which solution he prefers, we suggest he should adopt the well-tested and time-honoured method of 'sitting upon five pillows and consuming an ounce of shag'.

'THE RED-HEADED LEAGUE'

Advancing one further year, to 1890, we are confronted with an error or errors of dating that are far less capable of rational explanation. As one wag put it, '*The Red-Headed League* makes lead-headed fatigue!' Were it not for conjuring up the amusing prospect of Fleet Street jam-packed with red-headed men rushing hither and thither like a crowd of pixies among the seven dwarfs we should cry quits and sit this one out. For it is a problem worthy of Holmes at his best, and we have a sneaking suspicion that he, too, would have been baffled by it. *The Red-Headed League* is one of those cases which were published in *The Strand* and reprinted in the collected *Adventures* while Holmes was away from England after Reichenbach; had he been given the chance of casting an eye over the proofs before it came out we might have been presented with something very different.

The adventure took place on a Saturday. It had to be a Saturday because the essence of John Clay's plot was to break into the bank vaults on a Saturday night, so as to leave the rest of the weekend free for the criminals to get away with the bullion before its loss was discovered. As Holmes pointed out, 'Saturday would suit them better than any other day, as it would give them two days for their escape'. Saturday was also pay day at the league's office in Pope's Court, where 'the manager came in and plonked down four golden sovereigns' for Wilson's week's work. Wilson was left unremunerated for his final week in the office, for on the morning of his consultation with Holmes he had found the 'little square of cardboard' proclaiming the league's dissolution fastened to the office door.

The first point of apparent conflict concerns the date on 'this curt announcement', 9 October 1890, since that day was not a Saturday, but a Thursday. There is no virtue in postulating some other year for the adventure; 1890 appears twice in the narrative, and it is hardly likely that an account written no later than July 1891 (it first appeared in *The Strand* that August) would contain a repeated mistake involving the immediately previous year. Furthermore, the nearest year in which 9 October did fall on a Saturday was 1886, when Watson was living with Holmes in Baker Street before his marriage to Miss Morstan, and

The Red-Headed League commences with the categorical statement by Watson that 'I had called upon my friend, Mr. Sherlock Holmes, one day in the autumn of last year', which must indubitably have been 1890.

To suggest September or November, the other autumn months, is unavailing because the 9th was not a Saturday in either case, and to propose another day in the given month of October has no particular merit, despite H. W. Bell, Dorothy Sayers and W. S. Baring-Gould having opted for 4 October and Dr Christ for 18 October. In fact it is unnecessary to tamper with the text at all.

The date on 'the piece of white cardboard' was presumably that of the day on which the notice was written, and there are no grounds for objecting to its having been made out on the Thursday and posted at the league's premises between then and Wilson's arrival for work on the morning of Saturday 11 October. It seems safe enough, therefore, to proceed to the more difficult aspects of this problematical case upon the hypothesis that Holmes was visited on Saturday 11 October 1890.

Wilson's impression was that he had been the victim of a practical joke. He was none too pleased about it and had to be reassured by Holmes that he could take comfort in having become 'richer by some thirty pounds'. The client rejoined by mentioning the precise amount. 'It was a pretty expensive joke for them,' he asserted, 'for it cost them two-and-thirty pounds.' This means that Wilson received four pounds on each of eight Saturdays, 16 August to 4 October, inclusive. He would have become engaged by the league on Monday 11 August, and have started on copying the *Encyclopaedia Britannica* the following day.

But now the difficulties emerge. The newspaper advertising the vacancy in the league was '*The Morning Chronicle*, of April 27, 1890' which, as Watson remarked, was 'just two months ago'. This cannot be dismissed as a slip of the tongue, for Wilson had produced the journal, explaining that his assistant, Vincent Spalding, 'came down into the office just this day eight weeks with this very paper in his hand'. Ostensibly, this sounds like a reference to Saturday 16 August, but that is impossible; the pawnbroker presumably meant to indicate the same date, two months previously, which would have been the correct Monday for his visit to Pope's Court with Spalding, 11 August.

Be that as it may, we are still faced with the problem of the date on the newspaper itself. 27 April appears to have no relevance whatever, and one's initial reaction is to reject it as a printer's error or as a mistake on Watson's part in compiling his notes. The trouble is that Holmes had specially requested Watson to make a note of the paper and the date, which Watson then quotes himself as saying was 'just two months ago'. Any attempt to explain such an apparently obvious impossibility may sound rather far-fetched, but we suggest it is not as strange as would appear at first sight.

Watson's comment about its having been 'just two months ago' may well have been made and noted elsewhere during the conversation, in the context of the length of time Wilson had been employed on his 'purely nominal' services. And there is no need to assume that the date of the paper was necessarily incorrect, since Clay and his companion Archie (alias Duncan Ross) had presumably inserted the advertisement some time previously in connection with plans which had then failed to materialise. Clay had then entered Wilson's employment about the middle of July and used the same newspaper as his excuse for getting a free run of the pawnbroking premises for his tunnelling into the cellars of the bank. There was a mean streak in Clay's character—why else did he dissolve the league before the robbery, merely in order to save one week's wage of four pounds?—and he would hardly have wasted unnecessary shillings on a second insertion of the advertisement. No doubt he showed Wilson the paper carefully folded over so that the date of issue was invisible and rushed him off to Fleet Street before he had a chance to check it. There is a slight discrepancy involved in adopting this theory, namely that 27 April was a Sunday, but this is scarcely sufficient reason for disregarding such a definite statement in the text.

If 'the fourth smartest man in London' was foolish enough to risk spoiling his well-laid scheme for the sake of a few paltry pounds, it may not be so surprising that Watson, who would never have aspired to such a reputation for intelligence, failed to appreciate the puzzle that his lack of precision had created. But we may be wrong ourselves; we claim no greater credibility for the solution presented here than for the reasoning of others which leads along different trails. Of wholly solving the problems of *The Red-Headed League* we have, as Holmes blandly warned Clay in the vaults of the City and Suburban Bank, 'no chance at all'.

The adventure possesses the additional interest of containing short pen-pictures of the official police view of Holmes, and vice versa. The Scotland Yard agent, speaking of Holmes, voiced his opinion thus: 'He has his own little methods, which are, if he won't mind my saying so, just a little too theoretical and fantastic, but he has the makings of a detective in him. It is not too much to say that once or twice . . . he has been more nearly correct than the official force.' Holmes, as he 'lay back in the cab' with Watson, described Inspector Peter Jones in this way: 'He is not a bad fellow, though an absolute imbecile in his profession. He has one positive virtue. He is as brave as a bulldog, and as tenacious as a lobster if he gets his claws upon anyone.' At the *dénouement* Holmes is paid handsome compliments by the criminal Clay and the bank director Merryweather; Jones was probably too embarrassed to comment.

Having effectively disposed of the 'murderer, thief, smasher, and forger', who was by common consent 'at the head of his profession', Holmes diverted his attention towards the most dangerous criminal in London, 'the Napoleon of crime', Professor Moriarty himself. And so emerge two subsidiary, yet relevant questions; was there some connection between Clay and the professor, and why were the police, as late as 1890, so ignorant of Moriarty?

The second of these questions is conveniently dealt with first. It arises from a remark by Inspector Peter Jones in *The Red-Headed League*, informing Mr Merryweather that he would rather have his bracelets on Clay than on any criminal in London. Jones then continues on the subject of Clay, using the kind of language Holmes might well have reserved for describing Moriarty. 'His brain is as cunning as his fingers, and though we meet signs of him at every turn, we never know where to find the man himself.'

Holmes had little choice but to agree about Clay's criminal standing.

He had, after all, been outwitted by Clay on one or two previous encounters—'little turns', Holmes called them. And Clay had kept the police at bay despite their having 'been on his track for years'. Despite this, it seems strange that Jones should have used the superlative in relation to Clay if he was aware at this time of the menace of Moriarty. Perhaps he didn't know; or perhaps he had heard, but forgotten. Perhaps he only wanted to impress Mr Merryweather. To be fair to Peter Jones, the police may have remained in complete ignorance of the professor until Holmes chose to disclose his hand in the spring of 1891; for, at the opening of *The Final Problem*, Watson is informed that 'no one has heard of him', which 'puts him on a pinnacle in the records of crime'.

Was there some connection between Clay and Moriarty? The professor was 'of good birth and excellent education', Clay the grandson of a royal duke and educated at Eton and Oxford. And the professor's involvement in the catalogue of crime bore a striking resemblance to Clay's. Holmes has been made conscious of his 'deep organizing power . . . in cases of the most varying sorts—forgery cases, robberies, murders'. Surely it is not illogical to infer that they knew each other, and possibly also collaborated from time to time in their nefarious activities. The chief difference between them seems to have been that Moriarty confined himself to planning—he was 'the spider in the centre of its web'—while Clay was prepared not only to plan but to carry out the crimes as well. It can only be pure speculation, but perhaps the capture of Clay, in the tunnel beneath the bank vaults, constituted the warning to Moriarty that his position of security as leader of the underworld was in jeopardy, thus forcing him to come more and more into the open, to make that 'little, little trip', which enabled Holmes to cast his net and come at last face to face with his quarry.

'THE FINAL PROBLEM'

It is now appropriate to consider those early months of 1891, when Holmes appears to have been performing the miraculous feat of being in two places at once. The evidence is in *The Final Problem*. Holmes tells Watson at great length about the professor and about his own efforts to break up and expose the organisation of 'the higher criminal world of London'. To Holmes it has become a crusade, a matter of pride and personal honour. 'You know my powers, my dear Watson, and yet at the end of three months I was forced to confess that I had at last met an antagonist who was my intellectual equal.' Which three months is Holmes talking about?

At first sight he seems to be referring to the early months of that very year, to very recent history, in fact. But then we remember that during the winter of 1890 and the early spring of 1891 Holmes had been 'engaged by the French Government upon a matter of supreme importance', and was writing to Watson, from Narbonne and from Nîmes, indicating 'that his stay in France was likely to be a long one'. Presumably Holmes returned about the middle of April, for Watson was surprised to see him when he walked into the doctor's consulting-room 'upon the evening of the 24th of April'.

Holmes comes straight to the point, mentioning his fear of air-guns and the contest with Moriarty; his life is in peril and a climax is about to be reached. At this particular moment, towards the end of April, Moriarty is clearly the only business in hand. So which were the three months during which Holmes devoted his whole energy to breaking up the professor's organisation? They can hardly have been between November 1890 and March 1891, because Holmes was then away in France. He served the Republic so well that his reward was handsome enough to figure substantially in enabling him to make plans for retirement, so that he might 'continue to live in the quiet fashion which is most congenial to me, and to concentrate my attention upon my chemical researches'. To be true, Holmes may have visited London occasionally during his mission for the French government, but the whole tenor of the 'matter of supreme importance' is suggestive of a long, arduous investigation, which had to be tackled in isolation, to the exclusion of any outside distraction.

We are therefore half-inclined to place the three months of the Moriarty investigation back in the summer or autumn of 1890—*The Red-Headed League* being either an interlude or a component part—after which Holmes had to contain himself in patience until Moriarty made his little mistake and enabled Holmes to lay his plans for trap-

'IT PASSED WITH A RATTLE AND A ROAR.'
By Sidney Paget, from *The Adventure of the Final Problem*, December 1893. Holmes and Watson, concealed behind a pile of luggage on the platform of Canterbury railway station, as Professor Moriarty's special speeds away towards Dover, Saturday 25 April 1891.

'HIS BODY WAS DISCOVERED.'

By Sidney Paget, from *The Hound of the Baskervilles*, August 1901. Barrymore, the butler at Baskerville Hall, finds the body of Sir Charles at the far end of 'the famous Yew Alley'. Paget presumably drew this illustration before reading the next-but-one episode of the serial, in which Barrymore is described as 'a remarkable-looking man, tall, handsome, with a square black beard, and pale, distinguished features'.

ping the whole gang. The professor's 'little, little trip' may have coincided with Holmes' return from the Continent; perhaps it was encouraged by increased self-confidence on Moriarty's part while Holmes was absent from London. Plausible though this hypothesis may sound, it just will not do, because Moriarty, in his interview with Holmes at Baker Street, specifically names the days on which his path was crossed.

The professor was nothing if not tidy and methodical. In his memorandum-book were recorded the dates on which Holmes had given him cause for complaint.

> 'You crossed my path on the 4th of January,' said he. 'On the 23rd you incommoded me; by the middle of February I was seriously inconvenienced by you; at the end of March I was absolutely hampered in my plans; and now, at the close of April, I find myself placed in such a position through your continual persecution that I am in positive danger of losing my liberty. The situation is becoming an impossible one.'

It is plain beyond peradventure that Holmes was keenly and actively pursuing Moriarty and his minions from the very start of 1891. It is also plain that Holmes was at the same time away in France, his time wholly occupied upon the inquiry which both he and the French government regarded as being of such supreme importance. It would seem as if there must be added to Holmes' many and undoubted powers the ability to be on both sides of the Channel simultaneously. Quite an accomplishment!

IN PURSUIT OF THE PROFESSOR

And now, towards the end of April, it is almost time for Holmes to be crossing the Channel again. But time is short; the plotting gains in urgency; the climax approaches. On the morning of Friday 24 April, Professor Moriarty, 'not a man who lets the grass grow under his feet', calls upon Holmes. The detective's schemes are nearly complete, but a few things remain to be done. 'I can only spare you five minutes,' he informs his adversary.

By the evening, when Holmes pays his visit to Watson, his plans are laid. But, as Moriarty realises only too well, Holmes 'can do nothing before Monday'. In the circumstances, Holmes wisely decides that he 'cannot do better than get away for the few days which remain before the police are at liberty to act'. So Holmes and Watson propose to leave for the Continent.

Now follows the mutual pursuit which ends in that famous encounter upon the narrow path above the fall of Reichenbach. But first we must pause to consider the curious events of Saturday 25 April—remembering only this, that just as Holmes was fleeing for motives of self-preservation from the professor's promised vengeance, Moriarty himself had to take good care for his own safety in readiness for the arrests which, as he well knew, the police were about to make on the Monday.

Holmes decides to take the continental express from Victoria to Dover. An elaborate scheme is devised for the purpose of contriving his escape from London incognito. The detective even goes to the length of disguising himself as a venerable Italian priest. Moriarty has not been idle. Despite Holmes' precautions (perhaps it would have been better for Watson to have travelled in disguise as well), he only just misses catching him at the station. Watson tells how, glancing back, he 'saw a tall man pushing his way furiously through the crowd and waving his hand as if he desired to have the train stopped'.

Then comes the chase. Moriarty, as Holmes deduces, hires a special in an effort to head him off at Dover. Holmes eludes his pursuer by alighting from the boat-train at Canterbury, while the professor speeds through towards the coast. As Holmes explains to Watson: 'There are limits, you see, to our friend's intelligence. It would have been a *coup-de-maître*[2] had he deduced what I would deduce and acted accordingly.'

It is here that Holmes seems to have underestimated the skill of his opponent. Remember what Holmes wanted to achieve. As he had explained to Moriarty the previous morning, if he could be assured of placing the professor in the dock he would, 'in the interests of the public, cheerfully accept' the eventuality of his own destruction. What Holmes failed to appreciate that Saturday morning was Moriarty's own wish to escape from the consequences of his crimes. The professor, also, was in flight. This same lack of understanding has misled a number of commentators, who have relied exclusively on the argument that Holmes was in mortal danger and had to elude Moriarty at all costs. See, for instance, the chapter 'The Strategy of Winning' in *How to Take a Chance* by Darrell Huff.

They have projected their theories upon the basis that Holmes is doomed if Moriarty catches him, but that Holmes achieves only a draw unless he succeeds in making his escape from England. For two such brilliant brains to endeavour to outreason each other—ie, 'he will deduce that I shall deduce that he will decide . . .' and so on—would reduce the problem to sheer chance, for both must be assumed capable of outreasoning the other to the point of mutual bafflement. Therefore it must be assumed, so it is argued, that both decide on the best mathematical chance, which is to make a random choice on a basis that will make Canterbury a 60 per cent probability for Holmes and Dover a 60 per cent probability for Moriarty.

This is all very well, but the argument is a valid one only if the premises are correct and if the two enemies are engaging in a series of battles in which each is attempting to achieve the best possible long-term result upon the reckoning of theoretical mathematical probability. It will be seen at once that on both counts such a contention must fail.

Immediately apparent is the undoubted fact that the choice between stopping at Canterbury and going on to Dover is a once-for-all decision which each man in his turn must make, without any knowledge of what the other has decided. There can be no consolation, after losing the first encounter, in the hope of being able to retrieve fortune by winning the succeeding throws. The argument supporting the original premise fares no better. After all, upon what grounds is one entitled to assume that if Moriarty catches Holmes he kills him, or that if Holmes eludes his adversary the chances for the future remain equal?

If Moriarty had wanted to close with Holmes at all costs he made a serious error in not ordering his special to stop at Canterbury to see whether Holmes and Watson had got off the boat-train there. Even if his inquiries had proved negative, indicating that Holmes had proceeded to Dover, Moriarty could have reboarded his own train with still a fair prospect of catching up with the detective at Dover. Possibly Moriarty was unaware, or had forgotten, that the continental express stopped at Canterbury on its way to Dover. His own special was obviously capable of greater speed than the boat-train, so the time lost in stopping at Canterbury to ask whether Holmes had alighted there would probably have made no significant difference in the haste of his pursuit.

Had Moriarty got down from his special at the same station as Holmes from his express, the detective, being the first to arrive, would be armed at the very least with the knowledge that the master criminal was hot on his trail; he would have been able to take precautions accordingly, however murderous Moriarty's intentions may have been. Holmes was so much more the man of action that his chances of success must have been enhanced in any fight against 'an abstract thinker' who usually 'sits motionless'. As in fact happened later at Reichenbach, when the two protagonists did come face to face, Holmes proved the stronger despite the presence, as we learn from *The Empty House*, of the professor's dangerous confederate who 'had been a witness of his friend's death' and of Holmes' escape.

Holmes, therefore, had relatively little to fear from an attack by Moriarty alone; it was in London, where danger lurked in the most unexpected places, that Holmes was in real peril, and from London Holmes had already managed to escape. Is it not entirely plausible to assert that, having got himself away from London, where Moriarty and his associates were strongest, Holmes was the more likely winner if the lone Moriarty should venture to attack him?

The professor's position was anything but satisfactory. Compelled to forsake the comparative safety of the metropolis, where his subordinates were standing by, ready to carry out his instructions, he was setting forth into the unknown against the brain and brawn of Sherlock Holmes, for both of which he can hardly have lacked a measure of respect. In addition, he was himself in flight; hunting, yet hunted as well. Holmes, through the agency of the official police, would strike, as the professor was only too well aware, on the following Monday, a matter of two days ahead. The small fry, in the outer threads of the spider's web, would have to take their chance and fend for themselves; Moriarty, the leader, must run away and save himself if he can.

Such, surely, must have been Moriarty's view of the matter when he engaged the special; to catch and kill Holmes if he could, but to keep one eye steadily fixed on the aim of effecting his own escape. The professor, as we know, was activated by the former consideration alone when, early in May, he inveigled Holmes on to the narrow pathway above the yawning abyss. By then, as Holmes explained to Watson at the *Return*, 'He knew that his own game was up, and was only anxious to revenge himself upon me.' But on 25 April Moriarty was not equipped with such single-mindedness of purpose. So far as he was concerned, his first thoughts must have been for his own safety, and there still remained the possibility that the police might bungle the matter of the arrests.

Why, then, did Holmes get off at Canterbury? And why did Moriarty decide to head straight for Dover? Perhaps it was pure chance. Perhaps, on the other hand, there were reasons, not of brilliant deductions, but of mutual misunderstanding of the other's position.

No sooner had the boat-train drawn out of Victoria than Holmes must have realised that he was now relatively safe. He had, at least, evaded pursuit in London, where his enemies were strongest and most dangerous. He could now breathe more freely and perhaps even relax his precautions a little. Judging from Paget's drawing, the priest's disguise was certainly abandoned before the train reached Canterbury. The important thing, once Moriarty was known to be aware of his escape, was to keep him occupied—'an arrest is inadmissible' and would 'ruin the work of three months', as Watson was told when he suggested that the professor might be apprehended—for the two days remaining until the police were ready to pounce. What is strange is that Holmes, who must have perceived this from the outset, should have been so surprised upon hearing, two days later, that Moriarty had avoided arrest. Had he really expected him to return to London? The professor must have been presumed fully occupied, up to the Monday, either saving his own skin or pursuing Holmes, perhaps both. From the Monday onwards, Holmes knew only too well that Moriarty would 'devote his whole energies to revenging himself'. And so it proved. After Brussels and Strasburg it was a fight to the death, which Holmes eventually won; at the outset, however, there were other considerations clouding the issues and making it less important than even Holmes realised which station they went to.

Bearing this in mind, ought not Holmes to have decided on Dover? Had Moriarty followed him there, as would actually have happened, Holmes still had the chance, with Watson to help him, of getting away from his pursuer or of pretending that he had given up the unequal struggle and was retiring abroad. After all, the whole object of Moriarty visiting Baker Street the previous morning was to try to persuade Holmes that he should drop his investigations: 'You must stand clear, Mr. Holmes, or be trodden under foot.' By contrast, if Moriarty had decided on Canterbury and failed to continue to Dover, Holmes would have made good his escape and shown the professor a very clean pair of heels. The master criminal might, in either event, have abandoned his plans for flight and returned to London, thinking himself safe and risking the arrest which was awaiting him on the Monday. By selecting Canterbury, Holmes made it inevitable that if Moriarty should catch him he would have to abandon any possibility of convincing the professor that he had heeded the warning and was running away. If Moriarty missed him the confrontation was only deferred, leaving Holmes with the immediate problem of finding an alternative route abroad and the inconvenience of losing his luggage. It seems likely that Moriarty also reasoned in this way, namely that however much Holmes might play the game of bluff and counterbluff, his balance of advantage depended upon continuing with the original plan and proceeding to Dover. Therefore, Moriarty logically, and most sensibly, went to Dover, where his own options remained open and whence he could, if necessary, more propitiously tread the path of the fugitive.

CHAPTER THREE

THE HOUND OF THE BASKERVILLES

Sherlock Holmes said it:

'*Some people without possessing genius have a remarkable power of stimulating it.*'

Of all the stories in the Holmes saga it is *The Hound of the Baskervilles* which raises the most difficult problems—even, we venture to suggest, some which must remain insoluble. Even its authorship (editorship, if you prefer) has been called in question. The circumstances attending its publication were curious and the work itself, including the preparation of its illustrations, carelessly done. The ostensible date of the adventure, the autumn of 1889, is open to a number of objections, but so is every other possible date. Indeed, a case can be presented for the events having occurred in almost any year between about 1885 and 1900, excluding, of course, the years of Holmes' disappearance and travels abroad following the fight with Moriarty at the Reichenbach Falls.

Let us examine first of all a few of the facts which are beyond dispute. The adventure appeared in serial form in *The Strand* between August 1901 and April 1902, both months inclusive. The normal procedure was followed of the story being in the form of an account by Watson written in the first person. We know that by the turn of the century there was considerable pressure placed upon Conan Doyle to revive his accounts of the exploits of the famous detective, and some vilification had been directed at him for having dared to be the mouthpiece whereby the avid public was forced to accept the death of its hero in *The Final Problem*, which appeared in the pages of *The Strand* for December 1893. Even as late as 1901 Conan Doyle seemed reluctant to disclose to the world a fact of which he must have been well aware, namely that Holmes was still alive and engaging in active and successful practice. *The Hound of the Baskervilles* seems to have been a sort of compromise between Conan Doyle and the public, another adventure of Sherlock Holmes but without as yet any admission that the detective had survived his encounter with Moriarty.[1] We therefore have the situation of a disinterested editor responding half-heartedly to public clamour by bringing out a piece in which he apparently had little interest except perhaps the not inconsiderable financial reward.

But how much of the writing was Conan Doyle's? Claim has been made, and by no less a person than an octogenarian called Baskerville, that one Fletcher Robinson was responsible for compiling the story and that he allowed Conan Doyle to bring it out under his own name. The allegation seems to be that Conan Doyle was so little interested in working up Watson's notes of the case that he employed Robinson, a young man already known as an author of thrillers, to act as a kind of ghost-writer. Some support for this suggestion is afforded by the book's dedicatory letter. 'My dear Robinson,' it reads, 'It was to your account of a West-Country legend that this tale owes its inception. For this and for your help in the details all thanks.' Conan Doyle was more explicit in his acknowledgement to Robinson in a footnote to the title of the adventure as it originally appeared in *The Strand* for August 1901: 'This story owes its inception to my friend, Mr. Fletcher Robinson, who has helped me both in the general plot and in the local details.' Undoubtedly there was some measure of collaboration between the two men, but most probably Conan Doyle's version, namely that Robinson first mentioned the spectral dog (and possibly also provided some ideas for local colour), is the correct one.

It is noteworthy that Holmes himself plays only a limited part in the narrative; the story is much more an account of the adventures of Watson. And it is a case in which Holmes did not enjoy his accustomed complete success. To be sure, his deductions were proved correct and the criminal was tracked down, but Stapleton still escaped the justice of the law. Had he been arrested and tried one can fairly speculate whether a murder conviction would necessarily have followed. Mrs Stapleton, as the accused man's wife, could not have been called by the prosecution. So far as the death of Sir Charles is concerned, sufficient medical evidence may well have been wanting, and Mrs Lyons might not have proved a very convincing witness in view of her complicity. Holmes did indeed admit to Watson in retrospect that 'it would be almost impossible to make a case against the real murderer'. Possibly the best verdict to be hoped for would have been one of attempting to murder Sir Henry.

Furthermore, in this case Holmes nearly lost his client, and not once but twice. Upon the discovery of Selden's body dressed in Sir

Henry's 'peculiar ruddy tweed suit' Holmes believed it was the baronet who had been killed and at once reproached himself. 'In order to have my case well rounded and complete', he groaned, 'I have thrown away the life of my client. It is the greatest blow which has befallen me in my career.' Despite this warning of the magnitude of the danger from the hound, Holmes again miscalculated at the climax, putting Sir Henry in great personal peril and allowing time for the hound to 'spring upon its victim, hurl him to the ground and worry at his throat'—this after a chase which was so frightening to the client that Holmes and Watson 'heard scream after scream from Sir Henry'. In addition, all the delay and confusion allowed the criminal to make his escape. Lestrade, having missed what Holmes had promised was 'the biggest thing for years', may not have been too pleased at having to return to London without making an arrest.

It is quite possible that Stapleton got clean away. Certainly he managed to escape that night along the pathway through the mire, and he may well have reached the safety of 'the bog-girt island where he had hid his savage ally'. Holmes assumed from the lack of footprints on the 'firmer ground beyond the morass' that Stapleton had perished in the swamp, but this can be neither proved nor disproved. If the firm ground was capable of disclosing footmarks, why were none found to confirm Stapleton's departure as he set out with his dog for Merripit House the previous afternoon? The only evidence upon which Holmes based his assumption was the absence of the 'slightest sign' of footsteps. If Holmes thought it of such importance he must confidently have expected to discover traces of Stapleton's arrival if he really had reached safety. But if that is the case he must also have expected to see footsteps going the other way which the murderer must have made only a few hours earlier when he collected the hound in readiness for the attack upon Sir Henry. And yet there was not the slightest sign.

Holmes surely had no firm basis for his expressed certainty that Stapleton had been driven to destruction. Quite probably he was right in claiming that the 'cold and cruel-hearted man is for ever buried' in the foul slime, but he may deliberately have pretended to be more certain about it than he actually was in order to reassure Sir Henry and to retrieve some measure of credit for himself. Mrs Stapleton told

Holmes that her husband was prepared for failure and 'had made preparations so that he might have a refuge' in the old mine. Yet Holmes and Watson made no very thorough search when they went there the following morning. It is not inconceivable that Stapleton was crouching nearby in some carefully concealed hiding-place while the two friends briefly explored the island, and that he later made his escape when the coast was clear.

Holmes was by no means at his efficient best during the Dartmoor adventure. He was above all anxious to capture the criminal, and risked his client's life in the attempt. In the end he still failed to catch his man. Holmes expressed the right priority when advising his client in another case which is discussed more fully later. 'The first consideration,' he declared, 'is to remove the pressing danger which threatens you. The second is to clear up the mystery, and to punish the guilty parties.' This quotation comes from *The Five Orange Pips*, a case which closely resembles *The Hound of the Baskervilles* in that, although Holmes cleared up the mystery, the client was not sufficiently guarded and the guilty parties were never punished. Sir Henry, driven through Holmes' negligence to a state in which he 'lay delirious in a high fever', seems to have been induced to believe that Holmes had achieved a brilliant success, and probably rewarded him handsomely for his services.

After the case is over we find Holmes starting to excuse himself for his blunders. On the November evening after Sir Henry and Mortimer have called while 'on their way to that long voyage' which had been prescribed for the restoration of Sir Henry's shattered nerves, Holmes discussed the affair with Watson, explaining that 'at the cost of a severe shock to our client we succeeded in completing our case and driving Stapleton to his destruction. That Sir Henry should have been exposed to this is, I must confess, a reproach to my management of the case, but we had no means of foreseeing the terrible and paralysing spectacle which the beast presented, nor could we predict the fog which enabled him to burst upon us at such short notice.'

Were these excuses really justified? As for 'foreseeing the terrible and paralysing spectacle which the beast presented', surely Holmes must have been expecting something pretty devilish; after all, two men already, first the old baronet and then the escaped convict, had died of fright. Had Holmes been more careful of his client's wellbeing and less keen on compiling 'a case which could go to a jury' he would surely have considered the risk and made some approach to Stapleton to warn him that the game was up. Even if that had led to Stapleton's flight Holmes would still have achieved a success as far as his client was concerned without putting his life in peril.

In the passage quoted above Holmes claims that he could not have predicted the fog's coming down at such short notice. Surely Holmes knew enough about the moor to have at least considered the possibility of weather conditions interfering with his scheme. The whole plan depended entirely on Holmes, Watson and Lestrade being able to keep Sir Henry under close observation as the hound was released and then to rescue him quickly as he walked 'alone and apparently unprotected' across the moor. The chance of sudden fog was not such a remote contingency as to entitle Holmes to shrug off his failure to take adequate precautions. If Holmes felt that to act as he did was the only realistic way of achieving his ends he might also have thought of arranging for other help to be standing by and for a posse of local policemen to be surrounding the house.

To put it bluntly, it does seem possible that Conan Doyle was so irritated at being pestered to recount more adventures of Sherlock Holmes that he selected *The Hound of the Baskervilles* as a case which contained only a limited characterisation of the detective and failed to show him at his best. Perhaps it is not so unlikely that in these circumstances use was made of Robinson as a sort of additional sub-editor to write in, or at least to draft, those parts of the book which were not taken directly from Watson's notes. (Against the charge of possible disinterest, we must record that Conan Doyle described the story in a letter to his mother as 'A real Creeper!' and in another letter wrote: 'Holmes is at his very best, and it is a highly dramatic idea which I owe to Robinson.')

The writing and publication of the story were carelessly done. Several examples of such lack of care can be cited. Probably the most obvious textual error appears in the first edition of Chapter XIV, in *The Strand* for March 1902. At page 250 we are told how Holmes,

Watson and Lestrade alighted from the hired wagonette near the gates of the avenue leading to Baskerville Hall, where 'the wagonette was paid off and ordered to return to Temple Coombe forthwith'. It is clear beyond peradventure that Temple Coombe, that railway junction village miles away in Somerset, had nothing whatever to do with the Dartmoor adventure, and indeed when the complete book was published in a single volume later the same year the correction to Coombe Tracey was duly made. But even if we allow an understandable slip of the pen in the manuscript, why was the proof so cursorily read that the magazine was printed and distributed before anyone noticed the mistake? Was it an error made by Watson which the transcriber failed to observe, or had Conan Doyle spent so long waiting on Temple Coombe station, where trains connected only fortuitously, that its name was indelibly imprinted on his mind and thus slipped accidentally into the text?

Another oddity in the case is the 'unsigned warrant' which Lestrade brought with him from London when he came to join Holmes and Watson in their efforts to trap the mysterious hound. One assumes that this was requested by Holmes in his wire to Lestrade, for the latter's answering telegram refers to it, and although the unsigned warrant is not mentioned again we are led to believe that the inspector duly arrived with it in his possession. But what was the purpose of this manoeuvre? If a warrant was needed at all for what Holmes expected the police to be doing, why have it unsigned? Presumably Lestrade meant a warrant for the arrest of Stapleton, but no such authority would be required for an arrest on a serious charge such as murder, and a warrant without signature would have no validity in any case. It is strange that both Holmes, with his 'good practical knowledge of British law', and Lestrade, an experienced police officer, should have been unaware of this.

How Lestrade figures in the story at all is a bit of a mystery. We are told that Holmes sent for him as an officer who could be relied on in the emergency that was expected (though in actual fact he behaved like a coward at the critical moment when danger threatened), but we hear nothing about the local Devonshire constabulary who would ordinarily have been consulted. Holmes would have been guilty of a gross breach of etiquette and normal police procedure if he sent for Lestrade on his own initiative without the knowledge and consent of the local force. That Holmes did in fact break the rules in this regard seems to be borne out by two otherwise startling omissions, namely that when Lestrade arrives at the railway station no local policemen but only Holmes and Watson are there to meet him, and that when the climax is reached Lestrade is unaccompanied by any Devonshire detective, which one would have expected if the London man's participation had been arranged with the county force.

Holmes did, of course, intend to 'communicate with the police' about Selden's death, but he changed his mind about that and instead 'sent a report from Grimpen to Princetown' informing the prison authorities rather than the local constabulary. Was this a final attempt to prevent the Devonshire police from knowing that he was conducting a murder inquiry in their area? As previously mentioned, it would have been far more sensible of Holmes to have taken the local police into his confidence, so that they might provide some extra protection when Sir Henry was eventually attacked and also assist in preventing Stapleton's escape.

While on the subject of Lestrade, it seems as though he was a very peculiar policeman. Holmes and Watson both carried guns and Lestrade, though supposed to be armed as well, was most evasive when Holmes asked him about it. 'The little detective smiled,' and then declared, 'As long as I have my trousers, I have a hip-pocket, and as long as I have my hip-pocket I have something in it.' Only later, when Holmes has killed the hound after having 'emptied five barrels of his revolver into the creature's flank', do we discover what Lestrade really had in his hip-pocket. As the insensible Sir Henry 'made a feeble effort to move', Lestrade 'thrust his brandy-flask between the baronet's teeth'.

Incidentally, poor Sir Henry was not the only client who had to be revived with brandy after experiencing the shock of a Holmesian finale. Percy Phelps, in *The Naval Treaty*, had to have it poured down his throat to stop him fainting when Holmes, not satisfied with merely reporting his success (which was, after all, the only thing the client was really interested in hearing), served up the missing document under the cover of a breakfast dish. Whether by exposure to physical peril or untimely practical-joking, to be a client of Sherlock Holmes was not always a tranquil business. Possibly Lestrade knew Holmes well enough to realise the wisdom of arming himself with spirits rather than firearms. The late Bill McGowran, of the London *Evening News*, maintained that Lestrade's production of the hip-flask confirmed his theory that the little detective was a tippler and that this failing explained why promotion eluded him. He made his debut as an inspector and was still in the same grade twenty years later.

Consider also the references to the cigarettes. Watson, we are told, always smoked cigarettes from Bradley of Oxford Street. A stub printed with the tobacconist's name which Holmes found outside the hut on the moor enabled him to confirm his suspicion that Watson was waiting inside. Holmes himself and Mortimer were also cigarette smokers; both were smoking when Mortimer was reading out Hugo Baskerville's paper about the family curse. Holmes finished smoking, 'yawned and tossed the end of his cigarette into the fire' as Mortimer finished the narrative. Mortimer had rolled and lit his soon after entering the room. It is a little curious that Holmes, being in possession of cigarettes and having already noticed that Mortimer too was a smoker, failed to offer him one; but surely it is more curious that Holmes, having waved Mortimer into a chair, purported to 'observe from your forefinger that you make your own cigarettes'.

Now we know that Holmes was an expert on distinguishing between the ashes of various tobaccos and had early in his career written a monograph on the subject, but can it really be said that he was such a skilled observer of smoking habits that he could tell by glancing at a client's forefinger that he was in the habit of making his own cigarettes, as opposed to smoking those manufactured by a tobacconist? The forefinger indication must presumably have been a nicotine stain, and this would be visible whatever kind of cigarette was smoked. Was it just a guess, or had Holmes perhaps observed a tobacco pouch rather than a cigarette case sticking out of Mortimer's pocket when he noticed the Baskerville parchment? He might then have referred to the forefinger in order to make his so-called deduction appear the more impressive. When only Watson was present Holmes hardly thought it

'WELCOME, SIR HENRY!'
By Sidney Paget, from *The Hound of the Baskervilles*, October 1901. Barrymore now appears as described in the text; hardly the same person as the man who discovered the body of Sir Charles Baskerville in the Yew Alley.

'I'LL FILL A VACANT PEG, THEN.'

By Sidney Paget, from *The Adventure of the Crooked Man*, July 1893. Holmes hangs up his bowler. Watson's hat, which is already hanging on the hall stand, is a topper.

necessary to complicate the reasoning; otherwise, we may be sure, Holmes would never have mentioned Bradley's but would have claimed instead to have recognised the ash from the cigarette thrown aside by Watson on the moor. Incidentally, we wonder where Holmes procured his own cigarettes. His 'pound of the strongest shag tobacco' came from Bradley's, so possibly he bought his cigarettes there as well.

PAGET'S DRAWINGS

Sidney Paget's illustrations for *The Hound of the Baskervilles* provide further support for the view here expressed that publication of the instalments was a careless and rather hasty matter. The well-known drawing 'And So Down Regent Street' was not printed correctly, but reversed. The most obvious indication of this is seen in the artist's name which shows up as a mirrored impression. We have heard it suggested that this was an intentional mistake by the publisher so that Holmes and Watson would be shown facing towards the text on the opposite page. However, that argument is far from convincing, because in the previous instalment the wicked Hugo Baskerville is shown riding away from the facing page of text and in the next episode the wagonette is driving away.

When it comes to depicting the Barrymores Paget draws them as he guessed they should look for the early chapters, and only later does he show them as described in the text. The butler first appears in Chapter II of the story, which was part of the first instalment published in *The Strand* for August 1901. We are told that the late Sir Charles Baskerville's 'indoor servants consisted of a married couple named Barrymore, the husband acting as butler and the wife as housekeeper'. Paget's illustration of Barrymore discovering the baronet's body in the yew alley depicts the butler as an elderly man, of stocky build and medium height, with a round, bald head and a bushy, greyish beard. Since the text of the first part of the serial contains no description of Barrymore's appearance, one assumes that Paget drew him from his own imagination.

Barrymore does not figure at all in the second instalment of the adventure, though he reappears in the next episode when we are told a lot more about him. To start with, he is described as 'a man with a full, black beard', and a little later Watson writes that Barrymore is 'a remarkable-looking man, tall, handsome, with a square black beard, and pale, distinguished features'. Paget, now called upon to draw Barrymore for two illustrations for Chapter VI, shows him as Watson indicates, firstly in his welcome to Sir Henry and secondly serving the dinner. In both illustrations the butler is tall and lean, with a well-trimmed black beard (albeit more pointed than square) and a good head of dark hair receding slightly at the temples. There is no resemblance whatsoever to the Barrymore of the first instalment. Doubtless the artist had never seen the manuscript of Chapter VI when illustrating the earlier part and was forced to alter his ideas when faced with the detailed description later on.

Presumably Paget was only supplied with the manuscript a month at a time and had to do the best he could. It is not surprising that the original Barrymore picture 'His Body was Discovered' was one of the illustrations omitted from the complete volume when it appeared in 1902. The inaccuracies of the original publication are none the less indicative of a certain lack of care in bringing out the work and ought to have been avoided.

Paget's treatment of Mrs Barrymore is not dissimilar. When Watson and Sir Henry arrive at Baskerville Hall in Chapter VI she is shown standing behind her husband as he welcomes their new master. Paget imagines her as a tall, slim woman. He is afforded no help from the text which mentions only that the 'figure of a woman was silhouetted against the yellow light of the hall'. In the seventh and eighth chapters, published in the following issue of *The Strand*, Watson describes her in some detail as 'a heavy, solid person, very limited, intensely respectable, and inclined to be puritanical', also mentioning that she was 'a large, impassive, heavy-featured woman with a stern, set expression of mouth'. Paget was thus compelled to revise his previous conception of the housekeeper's appearance, though the next drawing of Mrs Barrymore came out only with a subsequent instalment, in *The Strand* for December 1901. Now, however, her picture amply justifies Watson's description and the accompanying words: 'Her bulky figure in a shawl and skirt . . .' It is now a very different Mrs Barrymore from the thin lady who appeared briefly in the earlier portion of the serial.

The drawings of Holmes in the last four parts of the story are also unconvincing. In all the outdoor scenes (twelve altogether, including the shadow picture which is the frontispiece for January 1902) Holmes is wearing a soft hat, whereas Watson specifically noticed that 'in his tweed suit and cloth cap he looked like any other tourist upon the moor'. This description actually faces the illustration of Holmes bending over the prostrate figure of the convict. Paget may have had to draw the shadow picture without first having had the opportunity of reading the text of Chapter XII where the cloth cap is mentioned, but if that is so he would surely have realised and corrected his mistake when working on the rest of the book. It is inconceivable that Holmes had two pieces of headgear, for he makes it clear in his explanation to Watson that his only change of clothing was 'a clean collar', to which he then added the comment, 'What does a man want more?' (What, indeed?) And yet, curiously enough, Paget does make slight amends in one illustration, 'The Lady Sprang from her Chair', in which Holmes is shown facing Mrs Lyons and is holding, but not wearing, a cap. But immediately afterwards Paget falls from grace again; once more it is the hat which Holmes wears as he greets Lestrade on the station platform, and the cap is nowhere to be seen.

Even now we have not quite finished with Paget's strange habit of hat-switching. He seems, for some unaccountable reason, to have had it in mind that Holmes, Watson and Lestrade were playing some sort of game like musical chairs, amusing themselves by trying on each other's hats. Lestrade, as he alights from the train at Coombe Tracey station, is wearing a bowler, and this, with one exception, he retains throughout. The change comes in the picture of Sir Henry looking round him in surprise as the three investigators are crouching behind some boulders; here, the inspector is wearing a cap. And then, in those few tense seconds while the hound is bounding after its victim, Lestrade finds time (perhaps during his moment of cowardice when he 'gave a yell of terror and threw himself face downwards upon the ground') to don his bowler once again. The cap then makes an astonishing reappearance a little while later as Holmes retrieves the baronet's old black boot out of the slime, though this time it is on Watson's head, and the doctor is still wearing it when they reach the abandoned miner's cottage 'where the creature had been confined'.

This is not the only adventure in which there is some confusion about the headgear shown in the illustrations. In *The Crooked Man* Holmes, carrying a stick, calls on Watson and fills a vacant peg on the doctor's hat-stand. Holmes' hat is a bowler. Watson's, the only other hat on the stand, is a shiny black topper. When the two friends call on Henry Wood, Watson is holding the bowler in his right hand; Holmes does not appear to be in possession of hat or stick. In the last picture, with Major Murphy, Holmes and Watson both have sticks. Watson is wearing the bowler, and Holmes a top hat. We wonder when Holmes picked up his top hat. Or did he and Watson exchange hats? There is another example of a quite unexplained switching of hats in *The Greek Interpreter*. Holmes and Watson return to their rooms in Baker Street to find Mycroft waiting for them. Holmes walks in carrying a top hat. After hearing that Melas is once again in the hands of the criminals, Holmes rushes off to go to the rescue. Yet when, a short while later, Holmes is shown emerging from the charcoal-filled room of the house at Beckenham, he is wearing a soft, felt hat.

Reverting to the illustrations in *The Hound of the Baskervilles*, Paget's imagination is at variance with the text when he is depicting Holmes and Watson spending the evening with Sir Henry at Baskerville Hall. Holmes, who has come to Dartmoor with his tweed suit as his only main attire, is shown both at table and afterwards wearing formal dinner dress, while Watson, who presumably came to Devonshire well equipped with plenty of clothing, appears in a very ordinary suit which looks as though it requires some attention from a valet. The answer may be that Holmes borrowed an evening suit, possibly Watson's, but it fits him perfectly and he wears it with no lack of assurance. Some other commentators have referred to errors in Paget's drawings. In particular, Martin Dakin has drawn attention to the fact that the illustrations of the wicked Hugo Baskerville depict the figures in eighteenth-century costume instead of the seventeenth-century required by the text.

'THE DATE BEING. . . ?'

We now turn to the most confusing aspect of *The Hound of the Baskervilles*, namely the dating of the adventure. It may be helpful at the outset to attempt a reconstruction of the events in days and not to worry about the particular year at this stage. The early days of the case may be tabulated for convenience as follows:

A. The first day of the story. Mortimer calls upon Holmes. This was presumably a weekday. It was a day when *The Times* was published. The shipping-office was open, because Mortimer thought he might have left his stick there. Bradley's the tobacconists and Stanford's the stationers were also open for business, because Holmes was able to procure his tobacco and Ordnance Survey map. Other shops were open too, as Sir Henry was able to buy boots and other articles upon his arrival. For reasons which will be explained later, it would seem that this particular weekday was a Tuesday.

B. The second day of the story. Sir Henry, accompanied by Mortimer, calls upon Holmes, and the bearded man watches from his cab. This day again would have to be a weekday. There was a 'stream of traffic' in Regent Street and 'the tide of vehicles' in the roadway is also mentioned. Arrangements were made for Sir Henry and Watson to go to Dartmoor 'at the end of the week . . . on Saturday'. It is unrealistic to suggest that this day could have been a Sunday; we believe it was in fact a Wednesday. This was also the day on which Selden escaped from prison, for he had been 'out three days now' when Perkins mentioned it on the Saturday evening.

C. The third day of the story. Mortimer spends the day looking after Sir Henry.

D. The fourth day of the story. Mortimer is still guarding Sir Henry but neglects his duty to the extent of visiting the Museum of the Royal College of Surgeons during the afternoon.

E. The fifth day of the story. Watson goes to Baskerville Hall with Mortimer and Sir Henry 'upon the appointed day . . . as arranged'. This must therefore be a Saturday. On the railway platform Mortimer swears 'that we have not been shadowed during the last two days'. It seems reasonable to assume that if Mortimer and Sir Henry had been followed on any other intervening day they would have said so. Accordingly there were two clear days only between the cab episode and the Saturday of the train journey. We can thus establish that no days have been omitted from our tabulation and therefore the days we have lettered *A–D* were actually Tuesday to Friday inclusive.

F. The sixth day of the story, which must have been a Sunday. Watson inquires of the local postmaster about Holmes' telegram to Barrymore. There is no real inconsistency in the availability of the postmaster on a Sunday, because post offices were commonly open for a few hours on Sundays at the end of the nineteenth century. Even if Watson had called at a time when the office was closed he would have experienced little difficulty in tracing the postmaster at his private house, which was probably situated over the village grocery.

There is now a break in the narrative which is partly filled in with copies of some of Watson's letters to Holmes. The earliest of these to be printed is dated 13 October at which time Watson writes of Selden that 'a fortnight has passed since his flight'. Watson mentions to Holmes the 'previous letters and telegrams' which he has dispatched during the intervening period, but they are not reproduced. The reference to a fortnight having passed since Selden's escape seems to indicate at first sight that 13 October was a Wednesday, two weeks after day *B*. But 'a fortnight' may never have been intended as a precise measure of time. A couple of days either way, probably in colloquial English usage a day or two longer than an exact fortnight, seems reasonable.

However, there is a difficulty over Watson's commencing words in the ninth paragraph of the letter: 'The other day—Thursday, to be more exact—Dr. Mortimer lunched with us.' This statement is best considered in conjunction with a remark in Watson's next letter, dated two days later, 15 October, that he and Sir Henry 'are to dine at Merripit House next Friday'. These quotations, taken together, make no sense except upon the basis that the Friday of the proposed dinner belongs in the week following the Thursday of the Mortimer luncheon. Watson can hardly mean 'yesterday' when he writes 'the other day', so the letter of 13 October cannot have been written earlier than the Saturday after Mortimer's visit. This extends Selden's 'fortnight' of liberty to a period of seventeen days, so let us assume for the moment that 13 October was a Saturday. This necessarily involves a corresponding assumption that the letter of 15 October was written on a Monday. On the present hypothesis this fits in quite nicely with the expression 'next Friday' (which would be the 19th) for the dinner engagement with the Stapletons.

We now come to Watson's two diary entries of 16 and 17 October, followed by his journey to Coombe Tracey to interview Mrs Lyons on the 18th, after which he met Frankland and was reunited with Holmes. If our tentative suggestions about these October days are right, then the 18th of the month would be a Thursday. This is in fact confirmed when Holmes and Watson are discussing the case after the death of Seldon, for Holmes refers to the ordeal which Sir Henry 'will have to undergo tomorrow, when he is engaged, if I remember your report aright, to dine with these people'. This now enables us to establish Friday 19 October as the date of the dinner at Merripit House and the attempt upon Sir Henry's life.

We are now in the position of being able to complete the tabulation of the known days:

Thursday 11 October. Mortimer lunches at Baskerville Hall and the Stapletons come in afterwards.

Friday 12 October. Possibly the day of Watson's first meeting with Frankland.

Saturday 13 October. In the early hours of the morning Watson and Sir Henry observe Barrymore signalling at the window to the escaped convict. Sir Henry has a dispute with Stapleton about the lady and one assumes that the Stapletons did not dine at Baskerville Hall as arranged previously.

Sunday 14 October. Watson and Sir Henry fall asleep in the early hours while keeping their 'most lonely vigil'.

Monday 15 October. The abortive chase of the convict.

Tuesday 16 October. The 'dull, foggy day'.

Wednesday 17 October. Watson meets Mortimer who tells him about Mrs Lyons being Frankland's daughter.

Thursday 18 October. Watson visits Mrs Lyons and afterwards discovers Holmes on the moor.

Friday 19 October. Lestrade arrives and the adventure reaches its climax.

We are now able to assign dates to the early days of the adventure which have so far only been tabulated by letter:

A. Tuesday 25 September. Mortimer calls on Holmes.

B. Wednesday 26 September. Sir Henry meets Holmes and Selden escapes from gaol.

C. Thursday 27 September. Mortimer and Sir Henry remain together all day.

D. Friday 28 September. Mortimer spends the afternoon at the College of Surgeons Museum.

E. Saturday 29 September. Watson goes to Devonshire.

F. Sunday 30 September. Watson visits the village postmaster.

EVIDENCE FOR AN EARLY CASE

Consideration must now be given to deducing the actual year of these happenings. If the datings given above are correct, we have to choose a year in which 30 September fell on a Sunday. The outside limits of time for Holmes' active practice in association with Watson may be stated as 1882–1903, and in this period there are four years which satisfy that requirement. These are 1883, 1888, 1894 and 1900. On any showing 1900 must be the latest possible year for *The Hound of the Baskervilles*, because by August 1901 publication of the story had already commenced in the pages of *The Strand*. However, other years in addition to these will have to be considered as possibilities, so perhaps we should first of all discuss whether this is a late case or an early one. The indications are numerous but, unfortunately, contradictory.

To begin with, there is the very specific evidence in the text that 1889 is the year, and, accordingly, that it is a fairly early case. Mortimer's presentation 'Penang lawyer' walking-stick had the date 1884 engraved on a broad silver band just under the bulbous head, and

Holmes remarked to Watson that this was 'five years ago'. The accuracy of the 1884 date is supported by the full entry of Mortimer's particulars in the *Medical Directory*. This 1889 dating for the adventure directly conflicts with the conclusion previously drawn from other textual references that the case must have occurred in a year in which 30 September fell on a Sunday. It therefore follows that any dating which may be adopted as a working hypothesis must be at variance with at least one of the solutions presented above, despite the fact that either of these, taken in isolation, would appear to be conclusive. There is really no alternative but to admit at the outset of our inquiry that precise dating of this case, so as to be absolutely sure about it, is impossible. It is a measure of the difficulty of dating the adventure that only Blakeney accepts the evidence of Dr Mortimer's walking-stick and opts for 1889. The other chronologists choose the following years: 1886 Bell; 1888 Baring-Gould; 1897 Christ; 1899 Brend; 1900 Zeisler, Folsom, Dakin.

It is now time to turn to other evidence that is suggestive of *The Hound of the Baskervilles* being an early case.

1. Holmes and Watson are both in fit physical condition, and presumably fairly young. When Baskerville and Watson were chasing the convict—'we ran and ran until we were completely blown', wrote Watson—they are both described as 'fair runners and in good condition'. We know that the baronet was 'about thirty years of age', and unless Watson was attempting to cover up for his physical deficiencies in some way, his statement seems to indicate that he himself at the time was not a great deal older. Watson's assessment of his own ability as a runner is confirmed in a passage which refers also to the speed of Holmes. In the description of his friend rushing to Sir Henry's aid as the hound attacks, Watson writes: 'Never have I seen a man run as Holmes ran that night. I am reckoned fleet of foot, but he outpaced me.' This must mean that, at the time of *The Hound of the Baskervilles*, Holmes, addicted as he was to habits like heavy smoking and drug-taking, which are hardly calculated to improve a man's ability as a runner, was still a capable sprinter.

If Holmes and Watson were young, as these passages suggest, then the case must have been an earlier one. Nevertheless, one wonders quite how early it can have been. In *The Sign of Four*, which took place in 1887, Watson is complaining that his 'constitution has not got over the Afghan campaign yet', though this must have been some seven years after he had been wounded in battle. We also know that during his hospital days Watson had played rugby for Blackheath, so he could reasonably be expected to possess considerable athletic prowess even when less than 100 per cent fit. But in *The Hound of the Baskervilles* the good doctor gives no hint of continued infirmity, which is at least suggestive of *The Sign of Four* having been the earlier case.

Conclusions can be drawn from other accounts in the canon that both Holmes and Watson were born in or around 1852 (the year 1854 being generally accepted as Holmes' birth year, with that of Watson a year or two earlier), so if *The Hound of the Baskervilles* was after the *Return*, that is to say in 1894 or later, both of them would be over forty. If the latest possible year, 1900, is right (and, as we shall see, this is by no means entirely ruled out when other evidence is taken into account), they would be nearly fifty. Although at that age they might have retained some of their youthful vigour, the remarks we have quoted, with the possible exception of Watson's confession of being 'completely blown', are more in accord with the view that they must have been fairly young at the time.

2. A similar conclusion can be deduced from certain references to Holmes' state of health. To put it briefly, Holmes seems to have deteriorated rapidly after the *Return*, yet in *The Hound of the Baskervilles* he was apparently perfectly well. Therefore it seems reasonable to suggest that the case was probably an early one. The fact of Holmes being so fleet of foot that he outpaced Watson has already been mentioned. But observe, too, that Holmes, who had been busy all day and had been living a Spartan kind of existence on the moor without complaint or ill-effect, showed no signs of fatigue.

Notwithstanding Watson's assertion in *Black Peter*, an 1895 case, that Holmes had never been 'in better form, both mental and physical', the position had dramatically changed for the worse two years later. His iron constitution showed symptoms of giving way and his holiday to Cornwall in *The Devil's Foot* was taken on the orders of a Harley

Street doctor so that he might 'surrender himself to complete rest' in an effort 'to avert a complete breakdown'. Though under fifty years of age, Holmes was far from well. The illness, though what it was is not disclosed, may have caused Holmes discomfort or pain, which would explain why he became so bad-tempered on occasion.

By 1902, as Watson explained in *The Three Garridebs*, it was his habit to spend several days in bed from time to time, and he retired soon afterwards, when still only about fifty years old. A voluntary retirement at that sort of age hardly sounds consonant with the true character of Holmes, a man so completely engulfed in the affairs of his specially chosen profession. An enforced retirement on medical advice may have been unavoidable.

Whatever the real position may have been, we have said enough to demonstrate that if *The Hound of the Baskervilles* was a very late case it must have occurred while Holmes was experiencing some relief from the disease which dogged him during middle age. Bearing that in mind, the probability must be that the case was an earlier one, when Holmes' health was unimpaired.

3. When Mortimer calls for his consultation with Holmes the invitation to Watson to remain is given in a most formal way. This indicates that the case was probably quite early, at a time when Watson was certainly associating with Holmes but not necessarily collaborating with him regularly. Consider Holmes' exact words: 'Don't move, I beg you, Watson. He is a professional brother of yours and your presence may be of assistance to me.' Does it not sound as though Watson had already made a move towards the door when Holmes stopped him? And also, is it not clear that Holmes was asking Watson to remain not so much as a friend and colleague, but because the visitor was another doctor and Watson might later be able to help in explaining any medical problems that arose? This sounds like the procedure of a fairly early period, before Holmes and Watson had reached the stage of almost full-time partnership.

There is a similar passage in *The Sign of Four* (undoubtedly an early case prior to Watson's marriage) in which Holmes, having asked Mrs Hudson to send up Miss Morstan, says to Watson, 'Don't go, doctor. I should prefer that you remain.' Holmes may have said this to offer Watson some solace for his wounded feelings after the somewhat strained conversation they had just had concerning Watson's elder brother who had died after taking to drink, or possibly to provide Holmes with moral support as he listened to the story of an unknown lady, but it is more in keeping with the general rule then operating that new clients consulted Holmes alone unless Watson was asked to stay.

Again, in *The Noble Bachelor*, another case before Watson's marriage, the doctor was presumably on the point of leaving as the client arrived, because Holmes immediately broke in with, 'Do not dream of going, Watson, for I very much prefer having a witness, if only as a check to my own memory.'

The Beryl Coronet is perhaps an exception to the rule, but in that case Watson probably stayed in the room to hear Holder's story because of the client's distressed condition which might have required his own professional attention, though if a sedative was prescribed he failed to mention it.

Objection may also be taken that *The Five Orange Pips*, in which Watson remained while the client told his story without any specific invitation, is an early case, but there are good grounds for suggesting that *The Hound of the Baskervilles* was still earlier. The reasons in support of that assertion are presented later in this chapter.

Similarly, in *A Case of Identity*, Holmes introduced Watson to the client only in an incidental way, almost as an aside, after the interview had continued for some time; but this case, although fairly early, is later than both *A Scandal in Bohemia* and *The Five Orange Pips*.

The classic case in support of the theory that Watson was not in the habit of intruding on Holmes' affairs without cause is *A Scandal in Bohemia*. After the two friends have heard 'the sharp sound of horses' hoofs and grating wheels against the kerb, followed by a sharp pull at the bell', comes this piece of conversation:

> 'I think I had better go, Holmes.'
>
> 'Not a bit, Doctor. Stay where you are. I am lost without my Boswell. And this promises to be interesting. It would be a pity to miss it.'
>
> 'But your client——'
>
> 'Never mind him. I may want your help, and so may he.'

And how right Watson was going to be, if only he had been allowed to finish the sentence he obviously started to say, 'But your client may wish to consult you in the strictest confidence.' For it is only a few moments later that the king tells Holmes that he would 'much prefer to communicate with you alone'. This does indeed seem to establish clearly Watson's position regarding Holmes' practice in the early years.

However, when we turn to the later cases, after the *Return*, Watson no longer considers it expected of him to withdraw when clients arrive. The two colleagues are now, as explained in *The Norwood Builder*, in 'partnership'. Indeed, Holmes has paid 'the highest price that I ventured to ask' for Watson's 'small Kensington practice' so as to get the doctor to return 'to share the old quarters in Baker Street'. For example, in *The Norwood Builder*, and again in *The Solitary Cyclist*, Watson stays for the interview as a matter of course; he is a partner now, and Holmes' business is his business too.

At the turn of the century Watson's position is very firmly established. When Sir James Damery calls to consult Holmes on a 'very delicate' matter for *The Illustrious Client*, he gives the doctor 'a courteous bow' and remarks, 'Of course, I was prepared to find Dr. Watson.' That Watson had by this time lost all his former diffidence about participating in Holmes' confidential interviews is amply borne out in *The Creeping Man*. Bennett wants to speak privately, without 'any third person' being present, and Holmes dismisses the suggestion by saying quite casually that Watson 'is the very soul of discretion'. But—and observe this—in spite of his continued presence being specifically questioned by the client, Watson makes no offer to go.

To resume the main thread of our argument, Watson's near-exit when Dr Mortimer arrives is entirely in accord with the case belonging to the early years, when the association had not yet blossomed into partnership.

4. Watson records that when Holmes suggested he should go down to Dartmoor with Sir Henry and Mortimer the 'proposition took me completely by surprise'. Surely, if *The Hound of the Baskervilles* was a later case, Watson would have no justification for astonishment at being chosen for the mission. He showed no surprise, for instance,

when asked to go to the Farnham area to examine some of the problems of *The Solitary Cyclist*, which is one of the *Return* stories and dated 1895 (though this is probably an error for 1898, when 23 April fell on a Saturday), nor when Holmes sent him to Switzerland and Germany to look into *The Disappearance of Lady Frances Carfax* which, though undated except by reference to Shlessinger's ear injury, must have been towards the end of the eighteen-nineties. And, at about the same period, when Holmes requested Watson to go as his representative to investigate the troubles of *The Retired Colourman*, Watson was not in the slightest taken by surprise, but immediately consented 'to set forth to Lewisham'.

All these are fairly late cases and it may be that Holmes did not start sending Watson away on his own until after the *Return*, but if Watson was sincere in his assertion that the Devonshire suggestion took him 'completely' by surprise, there can be little doubt that *The Hound of the Baskervilles* must have taken place at a reasonably early period. If the doctor had already been sent abroad with 'first-class tickets and all expenses paid on a princely scale', as happened in *The Disappearance of Lady Frances Carfax*, when Watson did at first display some slight incredulity on being told he was to carry out his researches alone, how on earth could he possibly experience such a feeling of complete surprise when asked to take the relatively modest trip with Sir Henry Baskerville?

There is only one possible explanation if *The Hound of the Baskervilles* actually was a later case. Watson might have been taken completely by surprise not because it was a novel event to be sent off alone, but because Holmes had been so rude and dissatisfied about his conduct on previous occasions. 'You really have done remarkably badly,' Watson was told in *The Solitary Cyclist*, and then there follows a catalogue of everything he had done wrong. 'A very pretty hash you have made of it,' was Holmes' comment at Montpelier[2] in *The Disappearance of Lady Frances Carfax*. And then he added the rather cruel observation about Watson's efforts that he could not 'at the moment recall any possible blunder which you have omitted'. Poor Watson felt bitterly about it. Holmes was scarcely less ungrateful for his partner's report about Amberley's affairs following the visit to

Lewisham. He may even have told Watson that he was never again to be entrusted with a job on his own.[3] In any event, the disparaging attitude of Holmes would hardly lead Watson to expect that he was likely to be sent anywhere else, and this may account for a genuine reaction of complete surprise when Holmes made the suggestion of his accompanying Sir Henry to Devonshire. However, on balance, it does seem that Watson's complete surprise is rather more consistent with *The Hound of the Baskervilles* having been an early case, before any previous instance had arisen of Watson being sent off alone as Holmes' emissary.

5. After Selden's body has been discovered, Stapleton approaches Holmes and Watson on the moor and tries to find out whether Holmes suspects him. When Stapleton has departed Holmes declares, 'I told you in London, Watson, and I tell you now again, that we have never had a foeman more worthy of our steel.' This was no isolated, unconsidered remark. He had spoken in similar terms after the visit of Clayton, the cabman, and then he repeats his admiration for the criminal at the end of the case while he and Watson are inspecting Grimpen Mire. At that stage, Stapleton having disappeared, Holmes states that 'never yet have we helped to hunt down a more dangerous man'.

For Holmes, a man of such precise intellect, to have used those words can mean only that *The Hound of the Baskervilles* took place earlier than the encounter with Moriarty. Surely Holmes could not possibly be heard to suggest even once, let alone three times over the space of about three weeks, that Stapleton was a tougher proposition than Moriarty, 'the Napoleon of Crime', of whom Holmes was forced to confess after three months of investigation 'that I had at last met an antagonist who was my intellectual equal'. That Stapleton should be worthy of greater respect as a cleverer criminal than Moriarty just does not ring true. It would assuredly be at odds with Holmes' very serious observations in *The Final Problem*, where he describes Moriarty as occupying 'a pinnacle in the records of crime'. It follows that if we accept the eulogy of Stapleton at its face value *The Hound of the Baskervilles* must have been one of Holmes' early cases.

6. Another remark made by Holmes about his experience as a detective also points to *The Hound of the Baskervilles* being an early

case. When Selden's body is found, 'face downwards upon the ground', Holmes and Watson are both under the misapprehension that the corpse is that of Sir Henry. Holmes groans, blaming himself for the tragedy: 'I have thrown away the life of my client. It is the greatest blow which has befallen me in my career.' This sounds as though for the very first time a client has been murdered. If that is right, *The Hound of the Baskervilles* must be an earlier case than *The Dancing Men* and *The Five Orange Pips*.

In *The Dancing Men* the client Hilton Cubitt was murdered after putting his case into Holmes' hands and, although he never admitted it, the client's life could probably have been saved if Holmes had acted more promptly. *The Dancing Men* is a case in which Holmes was so anxious to produce a complete solution, presumably for the impressive effect of the denouement, that he failed to keep Cubitt informed of the suspected danger, against which he could at least have taken some precautions. The truth is that as soon as Cubitt departed from his second consultation Holmes deciphered the code. This enabled him to deduce that an American called Abe Slaney was involved and that there existed 'every cause to think that there was some criminal secret in the matter'.

But what does Holmes do? He wastes two precious days awaiting a cable from the New York Police Bureau and fails to give his client any warning of possible trouble. Holmes must have been in rather a queer mood throughout, because he mentions his hope of going to Norfolk 'to take our friend some very definite news', but refuses to confide in Watson (who, after all, might have suggested the wisdom of letting Cubitt know the peril in which he stood), despite the fact that the good doctor must have made it obvious from his demeanour that he was 'filled with curiosity'.

As it turns out, Holmes eventually decides that he can wait no longer for the expected telegram. He has 'let this affair go far enough' and must take 'a train to North Walsham tonight', if possible. By now the final 'grotesque frieze' has arrived by post from the client and Holmes is at last prodded into urgent action. When the cable from Hargreave does arrive Holmes casually remarks that the message 'is quite as I expected', so there was no excuse for his having adopted such

' "HOLMES," I CRIED, "YOU ARE TOO LATE." '
By Sidney Paget, from *The Five Orange Pips*, November 1891. Sherlock Holmes, at a moment of failure: 'That he should come to me for help, and that I should send him away to his death——!'

'THE LADY SPRANG FROM HER CHAIR.'

By Sidney Paget, from *The Hound of the Baskervilles*, March 1902. Holmes and Watson together visit Mrs Laura Lyons, who 'sprang from her chair' as Holmes explained that 'the evidence may implicate not only your friend Mr Stapleton, but his wife as well'. Holmes is seen holding his cap. We recall that Mr Grant Munro 'sprang from his chair' in *The Yellow Face*; so did Watson in *Thor Bridge*.

a lackadaisical attitude to the case if he really had his client's interests at heart. Subsequently, when Holmes arrives at the scene too late to save poor Cubitt from being killed, he admits, 'I anticipated it.' If Holmes had been honest with himself on that occasion he might have confessed with some justification that he had suffered the greatest blow to have befallen him in his career. It was unquestionably a blow for which, owing to his gross negligence, he was personally responsible.

Before leaving *The Dancing Men* and considering similar circumstances which appear in the still earlier case of *The Five Orange Pips* it is perhaps relevant to add that Inspector Martin was most concerned about the risk that Holmes was still prepared to take in his manner of apprehending the murderer. Armed with the knowledge of the name and address of the criminal, Holmes does not immediately tell the inspector, so as to enable the police to go and make the arrest, but instead sends a coded message to decoy the killer to Ridling Thorpe. Fortunately the ruse succeeds, but while waiting for Slaney to appear Martin was wise enough to 'speak freely' to Holmes about his unconventional methods. The inspector was only too well aware of the 'serious trouble' he would have to face if the murderer had made his escape during the unnecessary delay caused through Holmes' creation of an artistic ending to the adventure. There is just a hint of guilty conscience in the order in which Holmes explains the previous events to the inspector. He quotes Hargreave's cable before mentioning the final message of the dancing men, whereas it was the warning to Elsie, which he had already deciphered by the time the cable arrived, that finally stirred him into action.

Attention may now be turned to *The Five Orange Pips*, another case in which the client was murdered after putting his problem into Holmes' hands. Here again the tragedy would probably have been averted had Holmes taken sensible precautions. It was obvious to Holmes as soon as Openshaw had recounted his story that the young man was 'threatened by a very real and imminent danger'. Yet, beyond counselling the client to guard himself closely, Holmes did not apparently consider it necessary to arrange any protection. In fact Openshaw was lured to his death while on the way from Baker Street to Waterloo station. Presumably he had been watched and followed during the whole time he was in London. Did Holmes not consider accompanying him to the railway and seeing him safely on the train, or possibly sending Watson to Sussex while he himself pursued his inquiries in town? We know that Watson had a busy day ahead of him on his own professional work, but he could probably have found someone to be a substitute for him, unless he was himself at the moment acting as locum for another doctor.

The Five Orange Pips is another regrettable episode in which Holmes blundered seriously, and at a time when he was well aware of the 'deadly urgency of this new case'. As he himself explained to young Openshaw, 'the first consideration is to remove the pressing danger which threatens you'. Why, then, did he fail to suggest an escort? Sending Openshaw home alone through the dark, stormy night was an act of similar stupidity to using Sir Henry Baskerville as bait for Stapleton and his fiendish hound. Yet, when the client has set out on his last journey, Holmes, after discussing the facts with Watson, is sufficiently unworried to be able to spend half an hour playing the violin. Like Nero, fiddling while Rome burned. Was not the murder of Openshaw a disaster which could also be accurately described as 'the greatest blow which has befallen me in my career?' Holmes was rightly very ashamed of himself and deeply moved when he heard the news. 'I feared as much,' he confessed to Watson as he finished his breakfast. And then he added, '. . . it hurts my pride . . . That he should come to me for help, and that I should send him away to his death——!'

If *The Hound of the Baskervilles* took place after that, how could Holmes have forgotten his terrible mistake in advising poor Openshaw so carelessly? Surely we are not meant to believe that the superlative in disasters is reserved for a baronet, and that the deaths of mere commoners like Cubitt and Openshaw are just unfortunate accidents? It certainly seems as though *The Hound of the Baskervilles* may be earlier also than *The Five Orange Pips*, a case dated 1887 and possibly after Watson's marriage[4] but assuredly an early case before the fight to the death with Professor Moriarty.

7. At the end of the retrospection, Holmes, who has taken a box for the opera, suggests to Watson that 'we may turn our thoughts into

more pleasant channels' and hear the De Reszke brothers in *Les Huguenots*. Guy Warrack, in his admirable monograph *Sherlock Holmes and Music*, explains that the famous Polish tenors did indeed perform in the Harris production of the opera in London in 1887. If, as seems likely, this is the performance Holmes and Watson saw, here is another indication that *The Hound of the Baskervilles* adventure took place that year and is therefore one of the early cases.

This evidence, strong as it is, cannot be conclusive, because according to Warrack's careful researches this production took place in June and not 'upon a raw and foggy night' at 'the end of November'. Nevertheless, from the point of view of establishing an approximate date, the De Reszkes are of some importance, because proof does exist of their performance in London at the period in question. We can only guess—and of course it is pure conjecture—that Watson was going through his notes to make them more legible and helpful to his editor when he found he had merely recorded dinner at Marcini's, followed by the opera. Casting his mind back, he possibly recalled having heard the De Reszkes in *Les Huguenots* at about that time and noted it down from memory as being, as he thought, the performance which he and Holmes had seen that night. We know from other cases that Holmes was fond of opera, and Watson probably went with him quite often.

It may not be too surprising, therefore, if Watson made a mistake about the actual work they saw on that particular evening when trying to recall it in detail many years later. If this, or something like it, was so, then at least it is a fairly strong indication that *The Hound of the Baskervilles* was one of the earlier adventures and happened in the same year that the De Reszke brothers were singing in London.

POINTERS TO THE CONTRARY VIEW

We have now completed our survey of the main body of evidence in favour of the theory that *The Hound of the Baskervilles* is an early case. It is now time to turn to the various significant points in support of the contrary proposition.

1. On the railway journey to Devonshire Watson observes that 'young Baskerville stared eagerly out of the window and cried aloud with delight as he recognised the familiar features of the Devon

scenery'. If this happened in one of the years before *The Final Problem*—say between 1885 and 1890—Watson was still in his mid-thirties. Taking 1852 as the earliest date that can reasonably be conjectured as the year of his birth and 1890 as the latest autumn prior to the Moriarty episode, he can have been no older than thirty-eight and was probably a couple of years younger. Does a man of that sort of age refer to someone of thirty as *young* so-and-so? Surely it cannot be suggested with any confidence that Watson was using that word to distinguish *young* Sir Henry from *old* Sir Charles, whom Watson had never met and was then dead.

If *The Hound of the Baskervilles* is a case before the *Return* the only reason which can be realistically advanced for Watson's use of the description 'young' is that it was inserted when the doctor, in middle age, was revising or expanding some of his notes for the benefit of his editor. If they had not met in the meantime, Watson was perhaps still imagining Sir Henry as a man of thirty, as he had been at the time of the adventure, and mentioned him quite casually as 'young Baskerville' with all the unthinking superiority of a person approaching fifty when possessed of the mental picture of somebody nearly young enough to be his son.

It is difficult, however, to accept this as a really tenable proposition. The normal and ordinary meaning of the expression must indicate that at the date of the train journey Watson was Sir Henry's senior by a good many years. And if this is the correct interpretation then it must, as a matter of common sense, place the adventure at a late date, possibly 1899 or 1900. (One must not be too dogmatic on this point, since in *A Scandal in Bohemia* Holmes twice spoke patronisingly of Irene Adler as 'this young person' at a period when she was thirty and he around thirty-four.)

2. A similar indication is revealed in Watson's description of Mortimer, whose 'long back was already bowed' when he called for his consultation. Were this the only piece of evidence available on the subject, it would raise a presumption that Mortimer was already in middle age. It makes some sense if the adventure took place shortly before the turn of the century, for it would then follow that, provided Mortimer's *Medical Directory* dates were correctly transcribed, he had

been in practice for about fifteen to twenty years. But we are faced with the problem that Mortimer was also described as a young man, and Holmes had even concluded from the walking-stick that Mortimer would turn out to be 'a young fellow under thirty'.

It has already been mentioned that the only specific dating in the case, cogent evidence of its having been an early adventure, is the statement by Holmes that Mortimer's marriage in 1884 was 'five years ago'. However, suppose for a moment that the remark Holmes actually made was 'fifteen years ago' and that, through accident or design, the period was curtailed by a whole decade. The deductions drawn from the inscription on the walking-stick have to be amended and Mortimer can no longer be described as still being young, but this hypothesis does fit in with the doctor's already bowed back, which would be unlikely in a man under thirty.

The supposition is also afforded some support from the description of Mortimer's clothes. This is a man who, having started his career at a famous London hospital, where he had some early 'hopes of a consulting practice' and had written articles for medical journals, has come to London on an important visit dressed in 'slovenly fashion, for his frock-coat was dingy and his trousers frayed'. Is this really what one would expect in a professional man who had been only five years in the country? He was returning to the capital to meet a titled gentleman, to consult Sherlock Holmes, to visit the College of Surgeons, to stay at an hotel, and to deal with any kind of unknown eventuality. After fifteen years of rural practice he might have become so careless as to appear in the metropolis in frayed trousers; surely not after only five years' absence, even though he was, on his own admission, 'an unpractical man'.

To prefer fifteen years instead of five years may be a somewhat tenuous proposition, but not entirely unavailing. It gains in credence when Mortimer is heard, during his original interview with Holmes, speaking of the baronet as 'this lad Henry'. If Mortimer and Sir Henry were about the same age, as the narrative states, there is no excuse for Mortimer using such an expression unless, perhaps, he had picked it up from Sir Charles, who might naturally have been expected to refer to his nephew in those terms, during one of those 'charming' evenings they 'spent together discussing the comparative anatomy of the Bushman and the Hottentot'. But if Mortimer was well into his forties, and speaking as a man of that age naturally might, his reference to 'this lad Henry' takes on a new significance.

3. The *Times* leading article from which the warning message to Sir Henry was cut was on the subject of free trade. It was 'yesterday's' newspaper and therefore contemporaneous with the start of the adventure. The relevant question, which has also been raised by earlier commentators, is whether one period or another is more likely for *The Times* to be publishing such an article.

Free trade as an economic proposition was a topic closely engaging the attention of mercantile nations throughout almost the whole of the nineteenth century. To that extent, therefore, a leading article on this theme would not be inappropriate to any period. Britain's own free trade policy, for instance, wavered with the swings of politics and the expediency of the moment during the eighteen-eighties, so if the article belonged to that decade it would serve to advance the supposition that *The Hound of the Baskervilles* was one of the early cases. But free trade did not become of prime importance as a current political issue in England until the early years of the twentieth century. Even the autumn of 1900, the latest possible date for the case, does not sound too promising for such an article. Nevertheless, it is more plausible than any earlier year, and does at least provide a modicum of support for the other evidence which favours a later date for the adventure.

As against this, it is only fair to add that, in another adventure, Watson quotes himself as having read aloud to Holmes a paragraph 'in one of the society papers' which was referring to 'the present free-trade principle' as early as 1887. These passages come from *The Noble Bachelor*, undoubtedly an early case before Watson's marriage, which has already been carefully examined from the chronological viewpoint in the chapter dealing with *The Sign of Four*. The adventure concerning Lord Robert St Simon was, moreover, one of those published during 1892, so there can be no question of Watson's having misquoted from memory the substance of a columnist's paragraph which might more aptly have appeared in connection with another Anglo-

American wedding of some years later. Accordingly, whilst still favouring a later date for *The Hound of the Baskervilles*, it must be conceded that it is not impossible for the free trade reference to belong to the eighteen-eighties.

4. It is worth repeating, though it has previously been mentioned in another context, that the fact of Watson having been sent off alone to carry out an investigation indicates the later period of his association with Holmes. There is no record of Holmes having dispatched Watson anywhere as a substitute for himself until the partnership proper was brought into effect after the *Return*. Watson's mission to Devon is thus far more in accord with a late dating for *The Hound of the Baskervilles* than an early one, for it then coincides with the other cases of about the same time when he was sent on similar journeys.

There is, too, another slight clue which may be significant. In his second report, as he turns from dealing with Stapleton's brusque rejection of Sir Henry's advances to the account of his inquiries into 'the mystery of the sobs in the night', Watson suddenly interposes a plea for recognition of his efforts. 'Congratulate me, my dear Holmes,' he writes, 'and tell me that I have not disappointed you as an agent—that you do not regret the confidence which you showed in me when you sent me down.' Almost screaming for a crumb of praise, isn't he? The reason why may not be far to seek. Watson would not have forgotten the biting sarcasm and caustic comments with which Holmes belittled his endeavours in *The Disappearance of Lady Frances Carfax* and *The Retired Colourman* when he had been trying so hard to do his best. If Holmes was not going to express satisfaction with his efforts this time the hurt would be unbearable. Upon the basis that this is what that rather touching request means, it follows that this was the latest of Watson's lone missions. It has to be admitted, however, that the strength and validity of this argument are minimised by Watson's expression of surprise at being sent at all. It just depends on how you prefer to look at it.

5. In the course of his inquiries in Devonshire Watson pays a visit to Frankland's estranged daughter, Mrs Laura Lyons. Deserted by her artist husband, she has 'had a pretty bad time'. Several friends, among whom were Stapleton, Mortimer and Sir Charles Baskerville,

have taken pity upon her and 'set her up in a typewriting business'. When Watson calls at her rooms in Coombe Tracy he finds Mrs Lyons 'sitting before a Remington typewriter'. It was during the eighteen-nineties that the typewriter increased both in popularity and technical development; and to find a lady typewriting for a living in England much before the turn of the century would have been distinctly unusual. The evidence of Mrs Lyons and the typewriter therefore indicates a strong probability that the case was a late one. Certainly it is most unlikely that she would have considered taking up such employment during the eighties, or that her friends would then have backed her financially to enable her to do so.

6. There are several remarks in *The Hound of the Baskervilles* which point to the fact that Holmes and Watson had worked together for some considerable time. Firstly there is the reassurance that Holmes gives Watson when the latter, having discovered his friend living in the stone hut on the moor, is dismayed at the thought that his careful 'reports have all been wasted'. As Watson complains 'with some bitterness' about 'the deception which had been practised' upon him, Holmes begs forgiveness and encourages him by professing that 'you have been invaluable to me in this as in many other cases'. Of course there were 'many other cases' in which Watson had shown his true worth even if *The Hound of the Baskervilles* was a fairly early one (for example, *A Study in Scarlet*, *Charles Augustus Milverton* and *The Speckled Band*), but the more long-standing their association the more natural it would have been for Holmes to speak in those terms.

Previously, when proposing the arrangement with Sir Henry in London, Holmes has recommended Watson as a reliable ally with the observation that 'there is no man who is better worth having at your side when you are in a tight place'. It is necessary only to recall the tight places in which Watson had assisted Holmes in the three very early cases just mentioned to realise that the recommendation of Watson to Sir Henry could appropriately have been made before many years had passed, but it is more apposite to a later period when Holmes had accumulated a vast experience of his companion's value.

The third quotation on this question of time comes from Watson himself, in his diary entry for 17 October. Priding himself on 'developing the wisdom of the serpent', he adds, 'I have not lived for years with Sherlock Holmes for nothing'. Now the first period of their residence together, that is to say until Watson left the bachelor quarters in Baker Street upon his marriage, was for about six years at the most. Therefore, though it is by no means impossible for Watson to have put this in his diary as an accurate record towards the end of that time, it is more consistent with a later period and with *The Hound of the Baskervilles* being one of their later cases.

7. 'We all three shook hands, and I saw at once from the reverential way in which Lestrade gazed at my companion that he had learned a good deal since the days when they had first worked together. I could well remember the scorn which the theories of the reasoner used then to excite in the practical man.' Thus Watson describes Lestrade's arrival at Coombe Tracey station. So far as the police are concerned, Holmes, though sometimes irregular in some of his methods, has earned their respect and confidence through the achievement of a long series of brilliant results, in many of which he has allowed the official force to take the credit they never deserved. And, as regards Holmes, he has sent to London for Lestrade, in preference to any other officer, to come and help him in the final round of his campaign against Stapleton.

Antipathies on both sides have waned with the passing of the years. At one moment of exasperation in the past, while investigating *The Boscombe Valley Mystery*, Holmes has even referred to Lestrade as an 'imbecile'; again, after setting the police on the right track in *The Cardboard Box*, he has told Watson that the inspector was 'absolutely devoid of reason'. Holmes would not then have accepted the opinion of the *Daily Chronicle* reporter that Lestrade was 'one of the very smartest of our detective officers'. As late as 1894, after the *Return*, Watson was sufficiently fed up with Lestrade's pompous attitude to grumble that his 'insolence was maddening'. This was in *The Norwood Builder*, possibly the case Watson had in mind as Holmes welcomed Lestrade to Devonshire, for in that inquiry the inspector had freely taunted Holmes with being a theorist rather than a practical man,[5] though at the end he had graciously acknowledged Holmes' success as 'the brightest thing that you have done yet'.

Other cases could also be cited as confirmation of the rather strained relations between Holmes and the police (the latter suspicious of unorthodox procedures and Holmes despairing at their lack of intelligence), but *The Norwood Builder* is of particular importance in that it not only shows mutual feelings of distrust still persisting after the *Return* but also reveals the beginnings of a less hostile, even respectful, attitude towards Holmes on the part of the official force. It would be wholly out of context for Watson to have imagined anything 'reverential' in Lestrade's feelings for Holmes at any earlier date. This can mean only that *The Hound of the Baskervilles* belongs somewhere in the later period of Holmes' activities, at all events after 1894.

We may, however, be able to deduce an even more precise dating. The opening paragraph of *The Six Napoleons* is particularly relevant.

> It was no very unusual thing [writes Watson] for Mr. Lestrade, of Scotland Yard, to look in upon us of an evening, and his visits were welcome to Sherlock Holmes, for they enabled him to keep in touch with all that was going on at the police headquarters. In return for the news which Lestrade would bring, Holmes was always ready to listen with attention to the details of any case upon which the detective was engaged, and was able occasionally, without any active interference, to give some hint or suggestion drawn from his own vast knowledge and experience.

We are now in a period of much closer co-operation, probably a few years later than 1894. As the curious adventure of the smashed Napoleon busts unfolds, Lestrade and Holmes are sometimes working on different lines of inquiry, but always in harmony, helping each other as additional evidence is gathered together. Finally, Holmes is the recipient of a more generous tribute than he can ever have dreamed of, forcing him to turn away in order to conceal his emotions. Lestrade is now full of reverence: 'I've seen you handle a good many cases, Mr. Holmes, but I don't know that I ever knew a more workmanlike one than that. We're not jealous of you at Scotland Yard. No, sir, we are very proud of you . . .' At last, the police are convinced.

Could there be a direct connection between *The Six Napoleons* and *The Hound of the Baskervilles*? It is possible. We have already questioned the irregular procedure of Lestrade's travelling to Devonshire without any apparent liaison with the local constabulary. Is it not a possibility that Lestrade took the risk of a reprimand for circumventing normal channels in answering Holmes' appeal because of the 'reverential' sentiments he still retained from the other case?

Let us look more carefully at the dates in *The Six Napoleons*. Beppo was employed by Gelder & Co, of Stepney, until his arrest for knifing another Italian in the street, for which he was sentenced to twelve months. The firm had last paid him on 20 May the previous year. That day was presumably a Saturday. This leads to the conclusion that Beppo was arrested in the year 1899, for no other year in which 20 May fell on a Saturday will do. If it were 1882 Lestrade would be eulogising Holmes far too early, when he hardly knew him and before Holmes could have acquired his 'vast knowledge and experience' The only other possible year for Beppo's arrest, 1893, would make *The Six Napoleons* an almost exact contemporary of *The Norwood Builder*, which is ridiculous so far as Lestrade's attitude goes and quite inconsistent with his fairly regular practice of looking in on Holmes and Watson of an evening to discuss their cases, because Holmes had not been back in England long enough. On the other hand, 1899 fits perfectly. Beppo was probably convicted by about July of that year, following his arrest towards the end of May, and started his quest for the famous pearl as soon as he was released from prison. The investigation of *The Six Napoleons* may well have taken place during August or early September 1900, a year generally agreed by the majority of the Holmes chronologists.

A connection with *The Hound of the Baskervilles* may now be conjectured. If 1900, one of the more likely years on the ground of 30 September being a Sunday, is selected for the Dartmoor adventure, then *The Six Napoleons* just preceded it. What more natural than that Lestrade, having praised Holmes in such moving terms only a few weeks beforehand, should be ready to disregard regulations and take himself to Devonshire with a 'reverential' gaze gleaming upon his countenance?

To sum up, therefore, the police aspect of the case distinctly favours *The Hound of the Baskervilles* being a later case and, more specifically, there are plausible grounds for proposing that the actual year was 1900.

8. At the time of *The Hound of the Baskervilles* Watson is ordinarily resident at Baker Street with Holmes, is not engaging in medical practice, and is apparently unmarried. Although this was the position during the very early period up to his marriage to Mary Morstan, it seems far more likely when taken in conjunction with other evidence examined already that it relates to the years following the *Return.*

The story actually commences with an observation by Watson about Holmes' morning habits, and they are regularly breakfasting together. Watson exhibits a proprietory interest in the furnishings, among which is 'my small medical shelf' from which he consults the *Medical Directory*, and he refers to Mortimer as 'our' visitor, which is certainly suggestive of a date during the partnership period from 1894 onwards.

A couple of months later, when Sir Henry and Mortimer are setting out on their 'long voyage', Watson is still living at Baker Street. It is quite clear that he had no other home at the time. Furthermore, the evidence is all against Watson having any professional work to do. He spends a whole weekday at his club while Holmes passes 'hours of intense mental concentration' pondering the death of Sir Charles and the legend of the hound. When the proposition is made that Watson should accompany Sir Henry to Baskerville Hall there is no suggestion that he is otherwise than completely free to go; nothing is said about medical work and no arrangement needs to be made for any 'accommodating neighbour' to attend Watson's patients while he is away.

It follows from these circumstances that Watson was not on any temporary visit to Holmes at the time of *The Hound of the Baskervilles* and that he was unmarried. This is supported by the lack of any reference whatever in the whole book to Watson's wife. Considering his long absence from London it is really quite unthinkable that he should have omitted all mention of her if he had been married at the time. The case for the later period is thus enhanced still further because the ostensible date of the adventure, 'five years' after 1884, is absolutely impossible, for in 1889 Watson was undoubtedly married and living 'at no very great distance from Paddington Station', a fact which is plainly stated in *The Engineer's Thumb.* The next two years must be dismissed for the same reason, and probably 1887 and 1888 as well, depending upon the view taken about Watson's wedding date. All this points most strongly to *The Hound of the Baskervilles* being a later case, for otherwise only a very limited choice of years would remain, all of which are very early indeed and highly improbable.

9. As Holmes is commenting on the inferences drawn by Watson from Mortimer's walking-stick he speaks of 'all the accounts which you have been so good as to give of my own small achievements'. The remark gave the doctor 'keen pleasure, for', as he says, 'I had often been piqued by his indifference to my admiration and to the attempts which I had made to give publicity to his methods'. *The Hound of the Baskervilles* therefore belongs in a period after the publication of at least a few of Watson's narratives. This is later confirmed by Stapleton when he tries to get Watson to disclose what view Holmes is taking about the Baskerville legend. Watson is quite properly reticent and gives nothing away. It seems as though he is about to deny having any connection with Holmes, but this stratagem proves useless when Stapleton reminds him that 'the records of your detective have reached us here'. Stapleton's suspicion that Holmes is involved has been aroused immediately on hearing Watson's name, so the two friends must have been very well known by then through the adventures already published.

All these allusions are to Watson's own writings and not to publicity gained from other sources, such as newspapers. Observations of this sort would be quite inappropriate to the early period. Not until the end of 1891 at the earliest, by which time *A Study in Scarlet*, *The Sign of Four* and the first six *Adventures* had appeared, could such remarks possibly be made, and by that time Holmes had disappeared from England after the tussle with Moriarty.

CONCLUSION

Having now reviewed the textual evidence as impartially as we can, the task remains of deciding the issue. So conflicting and confusing is the evidence concerning the dating of *The Hound of the Baskervilles* that it is impossible to be sure when the adventure occurred. Since valid objections can be raised to every date which might be tentatively postulated, any attempt to settle the issue must necessarily consist of guesswork. We are to some extent impressed by the conclusions to be drawn from the day-to-day chronology, which suggest that 1888, 1894 or 1900 are the most likely years, despite the weight of authority which favours alternative dates.

Our guess is that 1900 is correct, for not only does it neatly follow *The Six Napoleons*, but also Conan Doyle and Watson may well have thought it appropriate that the new story to be submitted for publication should be a recent one. If so, they then had to face the challenge of how to achieve this without admitting to the public that Holmes was then alive and still continuing his activities as a consulting detective. It is a tenable theory that this difficulty was resolved by their deciding deliberately to falsify Mortimer's age and to insert other indications into the text as confirmation that the case belonged to an earlier period.

As so often happens in other fields of human endeavour when an intentionally false picture is painted, discrepancies emerge which cast doubts upon the accuracy of other features that are truthfully stated. And so we believe it was with *The Hound of the Baskervilles.* How well Conan Doyle and Watson succeeded in their deception may be measured by the extent to which students of the Holmes saga have been baffled ever since.[6]

THIRD INTERVAL

A NOTE ON THE FIVE ORANGE PIPS

Sherlock Holmes said it:

'A man should keep his little brain attic stocked with all the furniture that he is likely to use, and the rest he can put away in the lumber-room of his library, where he can get it if he wants it.'

The dating of *The Five Orange Pips*, though specifically 1887 in the text, has to be carefully considered in conjunction with Watson's assertion that he was once more occupying his old quarters with Holmes in Baker Street because his wife was away on a visit to her aunt's. The date of Watson's marriage is by no means certain, but 1887 (and, if the text is right, necessarily well before the September of that year) is probably too early. Watson may well have been right about the date, and also about the other years mentioned in Openshaw's story, but mistaken in thinking that the case took place after his marriage. Doubtless there were occasions when as a married man he reoccupied his former bachelor quarters with Holmes at Baker Street during Mrs Watson's absences from London, and he may have got confused about them when expanding his notes while preparing *The Five Orange Pips* for publication. We may be sure that the story was very carelessly written because, in the original publication in *The Strand*, the text has it that Watson's wife was on a visit to her mother's, and we all know, from *The Sign of Four*, that Mary Morstan was an orphan.

The explanation could be that Watson's notes, from which Conan Doyle had to draft his manuscript, just showed that the doctor was living at Baker Street with Holmes, and that Conan Doyle, wrongly assuming that Watson must have been married at the time, decided on his own initiative to cover up for the wife's absence by inserting the first thing that came into his head, namely that Mrs Watson had gone to visit her mother. As previously suggested, Watson would have been shocked on reading the adventure in *The Strand* to discover that he had suddenly acquired a phantom mother-in-law! Possibly he and Conan Doyle would have agreed, so as not to alter the text drastically, to mention his wife's aunt instead when the story was reprinted but to make no amendment about the marriage. Certainly no time was lost in rectifying the mistake about Mrs Watson's mother; the aunt took her place in the collected *Adventures* which appeared in 1892 and has remained there in subsequent editions ever since.

Should the explanation be otherwise than suggested here, we have to face the rather unlikely supposition that Watson himself was responsible. Quite apart from the reaction he might expect from his wife, amazed and possibly distressed that he should have been guilty of such a glaring error, one does expect a man to be able to remember at least the correct year of his marriage when writing a partly autos biographical piece only four years at the latest afterwards.

But if we have to revise the dating so as to fit in with Watson'-marriage it may also be convenient to question the precise dates in Openshaw's account of his unfortunate family history. He says his uncle received the letter containing the pips on 10 March 1883 and that on the very same day he sent for Fordham, the Horsham lawyer, and made his will. That day, however, was a Sunday and, even if Uncle Elias did then receive the letter with the Pondicherry postmark, it seems improbable that he would have given instructions for his will and have had it prepared and completed the same day. Elias Openshaw was obviously at his wit's end and in fear for his life when the letter reached him. In those circumstances he might well have taken urgent steps to set his personal affairs in order, but would he have done all this on a Sunday? Solicitors often have to prepare wills in a hurry, and at any time of the day or night, but even if Fordham had been found that morning he may have been somewhat reluctant to miss church (and whatever else he may have been intending to do) and dash out to make a will for somebody who was in perfect health. Perhaps we just have

'OUR VISITOR SPRANG FROM HIS CHAIR.'

By Sidney Paget, from *The Adventure of the Yellow Face*, February 1893. A picture of the sitting-room at 221B Baker Street 'one day in early spring' at about five o'clock in the afternoon. Observe that there is no fire burning in the grate; indeed, there is no fuel at all to be seen. Had the fire been alight the position taken by Holmes would have placed the tails of his frock-coat in danger of being singed. A similar illustration for *A Scandal in Bohemia* shows Holmes standing in much the same position, with the fire blazing merrily away. The point, however, is that the best chair is placed by the side of the fire, and Watson is presumably seated in another armchair opposite. We cannot claim that this illustration actually *proves* anything, unless it be that the clock on the mantelpiece has stopped for at least an hour.

'I SPRANG TO MY FEET, FOR THE EXPRESSION UPON THE MILLIONAIRE'S FACE WAS FIENDISH IN ITS INTENSITY, AND HE HAD RAISED HIS GREAT KNOTTED FIST. HOLMES SMILED LANGUIDLY AND REACHED HIS HAND OUT FOR HIS PIPE.'

By A. Gilbert, from *The Adventure of Thor Bridge*, 1922. Ex-Senator Gibson, furious at finding that Holmes is in no need of booming, displays 'a hot flame of anger'. Holmes begs him not to be noisy, for 'after breakfast, even the smallest argument is unsettling'.

to accept young Openshaw's statement about it, unlikely as it sounds.

There is another rather unsatisfactory feature in *The Five Orange Pips*, and this concerns Holmes' very odd deductions from the sight of John Openshaw's boots. Consider the conversation as Holmes hangs up his young client's waterproof coat and umbrella:

> 'You have come up from the south-west, I see.'
>
> 'Yes, from Horsham.'
>
> 'That clay and chalk mixture which I see upon your toe-caps is quite distinctive.'

Whatever Holmes may or may not have concluded from the clay and chalk mixture, how could he possibly have suggested that Openshaw came from the south-west? Openshaw would have been more accurate had he replied, 'No, from Horsham.' When a Londoner speaks of the south-west he is definitely not thinking of Sussex. Cornwall, Devon or Somerset, certainly, maybe even Dorset or Wilts; but Sussex, never. And yet here is Holmes adopting the client's misleading reply in order to create an effect for a false deduction which is impressive only for its inaccuracy. The point is rendered even more ridiculous when a map is consulted. Horsham itself is within ten miles of a line drawn due south of Baker Street, and it is actually on the same longitude as Harrow and Surbiton. If Holmes did make a mistake he was not prepared to admit it, and Openshaw said nothing to correct him.

Is there a reasonable explanation? We believe there is, though the blame is now transferred to Watson's shoulders. Holmes could quite genuinely have said not 'south-west' but 'Sussex'. Watson may then have become the culprit by writing 'SX' in his notes and later allowing this abbreviation to be transcribed as 'south-west'.

Finally, it seems not inopportune to examine the legal side of the projected murder charge against Captain Calhoun of the *Lone Star* and his two mates. If the barque had reached its home port, what would the police of Savannah have been able to do? Holmes—or perhaps he got the London police to do it—had sent a cable to America saying 'that these three gentlemen are badly wanted here on a charge of murder'.

Extradition proceedings would have been necessary, and these would have involved showing *prima facie* evidence of the substance of the allegation. And where exactly was this evidence to be found? In default of the guilty men making confessions, how could the prosecution have even begun to establish any charge? The evidence of the pips that were set on Elias and Joseph Openshaw was known only to young John, and he was already dead. What Holmes, Watson, Prendergast or anyone else may have been told about the matter was hearsay and would have been inadmissible in evidence. There was only one remaining paper which had escaped burning, and this can hardly have implicated any of the murderers. Both brothers had died in circumstances which suggested only suicide or accident, and John Openshaw's 'body exhibited no trace of violence', there being 'no doubt', according to the newspaper report, 'that the deceased had been the victim of an unfortunate accident'. The only possible evidence that might have been used in any way to connect Calhoun and his associates with John Openshaw was the envelope found in his pocket and the letter from KKK, which Holmes probably retained.

How on earth did Holmes think he could found a murder charge on such flimsy evidence? He may be considered rather lucky in that the *Lone Star* was lost, for if he had tried to get Calhoun and the two mates convicted of murder the case would assuredly have been laughed out of court.

CHAPTER FOUR

THE VALLEY OF FEAR

Sherlock Holmes said it:

'The temptation to form premature theories upon insufficient data is the bane of our profession.'

In *The Valley of Fear* Holmes is seen at his brilliant best. A thoroughly workmanlike piece of detection, unhurried and systematic, reveals the killer and brings him to justice, in this instance the justice of an acquittal. The official police, helpful if somewhat suspicious, are left floundering. They waste their energies pursuing the most obvious clue, leaving Holmes to do the serious theorising and ultimately to introduce them to the killer. Only one slight criticism is levelled at Holmes himself, and even this is invalid and rather unfair. However, the adventure has many interesting features and is not lacking in contradictions and other problems. For the historian delving into the American background of the case there are 'the Molly McQuire outrages in the coalfields of Pennsylvania',[1] and the highly-organised activities of Pinkerton's Detective Agency. Once again the reader is faced with discrepancies that pose chronological problems. And finally we have to contend with Professor Moriarty, who either has appeared before his proper time or else has resurrected himself nearly a decade after his death.

The Valley of Fear was first published by instalments in *The Strand* between September 1914 and May 1915 and is by far the latest of the *Long Stories* to be given to the world. The effect of the narrative is heightened in *The Scowrers* by use of the 'flashback' technique which had already been successfully employed in *A Study in Scarlet*. It is a kind of treatment which might have worked wonders if Conan Doyle had thought of using it to lengthen some of the *Short Stories*. *The Five Orange Pips* and *The Red Circle*, another case in which a Pinkerton figures, immediately spring to mind in this connection.

THE TRAPPING OF BIRDY EDWARDS

The story of *The Scowrers* allows us to dwell for a few moments on what is probably the most tense and exciting piece of writing in all the Holmes literature, 'The Trapping of Birdy Edwards'. The composition of the narrative shows the true master's touch. This is no product of Jack Douglas scribbling his memoirs in the confined quarters and dim light of his 'rat-trap'. This is vintage Conan Doyle. Having built up the tale to its climax, he employs all his artistic skill to create an unforgettable scene with superb effect. Even when read over and over again the episode never loses its thrill. The cautious hush, the strained ears listening for the noises outside, the waiting which seemed interminable, then the silence and utter terror at McMurdo's revelation; a word-picture so brilliantly conceived that it must remain for all time one of the great English literary experiences. Nothing elsewhere in the saga produces quite such a vivid sensation.

But there does exist a repeat performance, this time with Holmes playing the Birdy Edwards part, and one can only ponder on some possible connection. The other case might well be called 'The Trapping of Colonel Walter', from *The Bruce-Partington Plans.* The facts are a little different, but the trap itself is almost the counterpart of the one sprung at Vermissa upon McGinty and his murderous gang. Of course, in *The Bruce-Partington Plans*, the forces of law and order were those who lay in wait, but the false message, the taps on the door, the furtive entrance, all are there. Holmes is not quite the double agent that Edwards was, though he did ultimately act as such when posing as Altamont in *His Last Bow*, but the artistic denouements have some remarkable similarities.

In the actual writing Conan Doyle has allowed himself to employ the same kind of technique, and some of the language is nearly exact repetition. At Oberstein's house the trapping party are 'all seated in the study, waiting patiently' for the traitor. Hours pass, which seem to sound 'the dirge of our hopes' that the final Pierrot advertisement will entice the prey. Holmes remains 'silent and composed, his eyelids half shut'. Then they hear 'a furtive step' and the doubters are hushed: 'He is coming.' There is 'a shuffling noise outside and then two sharp taps with the knocker'. Holmes rises, motioning to his companions to remain seated. He opens 'the outer door, and then . . .'

At Shafter's, 'the men came in good time as arranged'. McMurdo 'had nerves of steel, his manner was as cool and unconcerned as ever'. Then, after a period of waiting, Harraway expresses doubt whether Edwards will come. 'Maybe he won't come. Maybe he'll get a sniff of danger.' 'He'll come, never fear,' McMurdo answers. 'Three loud knocks' are heard at the door. McMurdo raises his hand in caution, leaves the room, opens the outer door, and then . . .

Could one of these well-staged captures have influenced the other? The Vermissa incident happened first, but it is most unlikely that Holmes ever heard of it until some years after *The Bruce-Partington Plans*, which is clearly dated November 1895. Unless it can be established that *The Valley of Fear* investigation was earlier, and as we shall show later there is no reliable foundation for such an assertion, Holmes cannot have copied Edwards, much as he might have wished to emulate the Pinkerton man's brave and efficient methods. The only possible relationship is that perhaps Conan Doyle, when re-writing Douglas' account for publication in 1914, drew upon *The Bruce-Partington Plans* as a basis for the presentation of 'The Trapping of Birdy Edwards', and that he was able thereby so to improve his earlier work that he has left us now with one of the most stirring episodes in our literature.

However, there is a clue that Birdy Edwards influenced Holmes in something else. When the time comes for Holmes to interrupt his retirement and start his campaign against Von Bork in 1912 he goes to Chicago to establish his new identity. Then, continuing to build up his cover, he joins an Irish secret society, this time in Buffalo, and acquires a reputation for giving trouble to the police. Altamont may well have borrowed a few good ideas from McMurdo.

HOLMES AND THE POLICE

To revert now to *The Tragedy of Birlstone*, it is worth examining the conduct of the police and Holmes' relationship with them. For the one and only time in the Holmesian writings we are introduced to Inspector Alec MacDonald, who seems to be one of a new brand of detective officer, ready to take over the reins at Scotland Yard as Gregson and Lestrade prepare for retirement. He was 'a young but trusted member of the detective force', having 'distinguished himself in several cases', though as yet he 'was far from having attained the national fame which he has now achieved'. We are not surprised that, by the time *The Valley of Fear* came to be written, MacDonald had advanced his career so successfully. Holmes obviously approved of him, having assisted him quite gratuitously and anonymously in two of his early cases, and called him by the friendly nickname of 'Mr. Mac'. Lestrade, be it noted, for all his long association with Holmes, was never addressed except with due formality.

Even when MacDonald becomes rather critical of Holmes—the comparison between the theorist and the practical man he had doubtless picked up from Lestrade—they remain on good terms and MacDonald never attempts to stand in Holmes' way. He might, after all, have refused to allow Holmes an evening alone in the Birlstone study, to write the letter about draining the moat, even to join him on the cold January night waiting for some unspecified event to happen in the house. But he didn't; for 'talent instantly recognises genius', as Watson shrewdly observed, 'and MacDonald had talent enough'. Perhaps it was this which most recommended him to Holmes, for the latter possessed a very human streak of vanity. On hearing he had been mentioned by White Mason in his letter to MacDonald, Holmes cannot conceal his pleasure. 'Your friend seems to be no fool,' he remarks. The Sussex officer, too, has recognised the amateur's genius!

It is when the local police officers are considered that certain problems arise. It appears from the outset that White Mason knows all about Holmes and is anxious to have him join the inquiry if MacDonald can get him to come. In his personal letter 'for your private eye' he notes that the 'case is a snorter. Don't waste a moment in getting started. If you can bring Mr. Holmes, please do so, for he will find something after his own heart'. White Mason is obviously familiar with Holmes' tastes as well as having some knowledge of his skill as a detective. He confirms this later when speaking to Watson, remarking that 'when the time comes we'll all hope for a place in your book'.

But how much did he really know? It is most doubtful whether he had ever met Holmes previously and he seems to have had little idea of his methods, or of his attitude toward the police. White Mason looks 'doubtfully at the amateur' and has to be reassured by MacDonald that 'he plays the game'. Holmes then proceeds to explain how he proposes to operate, to which White Mason cordially replies that he is 'honoured by your presence'. Later, when Holmes advises that the police may safely take the day off and 'abandon the case' (an unconscious allusion here, perhaps, to Lestrade's telegram in *The Norwood Builder*), White Mason just looks to the others helplessly, for 'Holmes and his methods were new to him'.

Apparently we are meant to resolve the contradiction by concluding that White Mason's knowledge of Holmes was limited to some past recommendation given to him by his friend MacDonald, and to his own somewhat cursory reading of Watson's published accounts. But if this is so it seems most strange, to say the least, that he should have been so doubtful about working with Holmes. After all, Holmes had been brought in at his suggestion and if he had read only a few of Watson's narratives he would have obtained some notion of how Holmes liked to work. White Mason's curious attitude was not due to any lack of intelligence. He was no worthless or biased local official,[2] but 'a very favourable specimen of the provincial criminal officer', with 'a solid grip of fact and a cold, clear, common-sense brain'. The inconsistency must probably remain a mystery.

The Sussex constabulary seemed luckier than some in the ability of their men. Sergeant Wilson, the local guardian of the law, got quickly to the scene, took 'prompt steps to warn the county authorities that something serious was afoot', and, though he was not unnaturally puzzled and rather nervous, began to investigate along most sensible lines. However, he displayed an amazing lack of local knowledge in being so unsure about the times of the trains. He dismissed any suggestion that the criminal could escape by rail because 'there are no trains before six in the morning', but the inspector was able to send his message to Scotland Yard 'by the five-forty train'. It was, to be precise, 'the milk train', but presumably it carried passengers as well. We cannot but feel a measure of sympathy for the early riser strolling into the station on the sergeant's advice at a quarter to six only to hear that the train has pulled out five minutes earlier.

THE LOCATION OF BIRLSTONE

But where was the station? A minor mystery surrounds the identity of Birlstone, the scene of the shooting. For some reason best known to himself, Watson, with Conan Doyle's connivance, has sought to conceal the actual location. Possibly this was done out of consideration for the feelings of subsequent tenants of the manor-house, a 'venerable building', guarded by a moat which completely encircled it, and 'standing in an old park famous for its huge beech trees'.

There is also a detailed description of the place.

> The village of Birlstone [wrote Watson] is a small and very ancient cluster of half-timbered cottages on the northern border of the county of Sussex. For centuries it had remained unchanged, but within the last few years its picturesque appearance and situation have attracted a number of well-to-do residents, whose villas peep out from the woods around. These woods are locally supposed to be the extreme fringe of the great Weald forest, which thins away until it reaches the northern chalk downs. A number of small shops have come into being to meet the wants of the increased population, so that there seems some prospect that Birlstone may soon grow from an ancient village into a modern town. It is the centre for a considerable area of country, since Tunbridge Wells, the nearest place of importance, is ten or twelve miles to the eastward, over the borders of Kent.

One has to look, therefore, for a picturesque village with a railway station, a moated manor built of brick with modern residential developments nearby, and all situated about ten or twelve miles westward of Tunbridge Wells.

It is not an easy matter to resolve. Watson seems to have been deliberately cryptic about it. A glance at a map reveals the most obvious choice, because almost exactly twelve miles due west of Tunbridge Wells lies the ancient and expanding town of East Grinstead, the older part of which was certainly not lacking in half-timbered cottages. Lest it be objected that East Grinstead could by no stretch of the imagination be termed a village, Watson goes on to confuse his readers still more by later referring to Birlstone as a town. But this contradiction becomes rather unhelpful when we search in vain for the moated manor-house and read of White Mason informing Holmes that he has no choice of lodgings: 'Your room is at the Westville Arms. There's no other place, but I hear that it is clean and good.' This hardly sounds like East Grinstead, which was well provided with hotel accommodation. However, it may be premature to dismiss the claims of East Grinstead to be the original of Birlstone, if only because of the news, reported by *The Sunday Times* in 1971, that a Californian restaurateur was hoping to buy the old railway station there and re-erect it in Massachusetts as a genuine monument to Sherlock Holmes and Dr Watson. A man who backs his theories with hard cash must be worthy of at least a little attention. American businessmen do not commonly light their cigars with five-pound notes.

What are the other possible candidates? Lingfield, just a few miles to the north of East Grinstead, is still only twelve miles west of Tunbridge Wells, and is well endowed with old, timbered houses of many types. It even had a moat for its manor-house, though, alas, the building had been demolished long before John Douglas could have tenanted it. However, Lingfield's claim is open to the apparently insuperable objection that the place lies in the county of Surrey, and not in Sussex.

Forest Row, south of East Grinstead, was another picturesque village; and it lay in Sussex, near the edge of the famous Ashdown Forest, the true name, presumably, of 'the great Weald forest' mentioned by Watson. It satisfies the requirements of having a railway station and being just over ten miles from Tunbridge Wells, but the other features Watson describes seem to be absent.

Edenbridge is just worth considering, though situated a little farther north than the narrative leads one to expect. But Edenbridge can scarcely hope to qualify because, like Tunbridge Wells, it is 'over the borders of Kent'. The same objection may be levelled against the charming village of Groombridge, which has the additional disadvantage of being only four miles away from Tunbridge Wells. But Groombridge re-establishes its claim to be Birlstone by possessing a park with a red-brick country house. And this is just as Watson describes, completely surrounded by the water of an ancient moat. Nevertheless, it seems inconceivable that Watson should have been so sadly mistaken in his distances, quite apart from putting the crime into the wrong county and probably causing no end of confusion for the respective constabularies of Sussex and Kent.

The mystery deepens when we consider the fact that the late James Montgomery, a Baker Street Irregular of Philadelphia, acquired a signed copy of *The Valley of Fear* in which Conan Doyle had written that he had had Groombridge Place in mind for Birlstone Manor. Further discussion of the problem in favour of Groombridge has also been contributed to *The Sherlock Holmes Journal* by Charles Merriman.

Suffice it to say in conclusion of this somewhat unrewarding inquiry that Watson seems to have covered his tracks cleverly enough to compel us to attempt to choose between a town without a moated house—which makes the adventure impossible—and a village in the wrong county—which makes nonsense of almost every other given fact. It is a problem which obstinately defies solution; and the blame may be laid fairly and squarely on Watson's shoulders.

A CRITICISM OF HOLMES

The Valley of Fear contains only one criticism of Holmes, and it scarcely seems a fair one. It comes from Douglas, after he has been unearthed as the killer, and may amount to a bit of professional jealousy on his part. Indicating the piece of plaster on his chin where he has cut himself while shaving, he says, 'You slipped up there, Mr. Holmes, clever as you are, for if you had chanced to take off that plaster you would have found no cut underneath it.' Can this really be taken as a significant omission on Holmes' part?

Despite Baldwin's having 'received the whole charge in the face, blowing his head almost to pieces', Holmes had still been able to observe the small piece of plaster at the angle of the jaw, as a result of which he questioned the butler about it. How can he have been expected to do more? The corpse had already been examined by Wood, the 'brisk and capable general practitioner from the village', who had been seen 'narrowly scrutinizing the body'. The doctor seems to have thought it unnecessary in the circumstances to investigate any further, though the possibility of finding even a small indication of something which could have contributed to the death would have been very much in his mind. The allegation of negligence against Holmes for failing to pursue the point is not, in our view, well founded.

There might have been a more productive line of inquiry had anyone thought it worthwhile to examine the condition of the plaster sticking to the victim's jaw, but the narrative says nothing about it.

One would expect that with both barrels of a shot-gun having been fired simultaneously at such close quarters there would be powder blackening and sprayed wadding from the discharge clearly visible on the part of the face which was not blown away. Also, the bleeding would have been considerable. If the new piece of plaster which Douglas stuck on the corpse was completely clean it is surprising that everyone, including two doctors and two detective inspectors, failed to notice it and to draw the obvious inference. Presumably Douglas camouflaged it suitably after putting it on.

The preparation of the corpse must have been a horrible undertaking. One wonders how Douglas and Barker managed to do it without leaving traces which an experienced detective would have observed. It must have been a gory spectacle. Baldwin had sustained 'appalling injuries', and Douglas himself 'fairly turned sick at the sight'. Yet they contrived not only to remove all the deceased's clothes but also to dress the body so that it could be passed off as that of Douglas. This involved putting on the killer's night clothes and then his pink dressing-gown. The mind boggles in trying to imagine how they did it. Blood was certainly plentiful—'natural enough, considering the condition of the room'—and they must have made a terrible mess. The body might not have become noticeably different from what the investigators would expect to find, but what about themselves? Douglas disappeared into the hiding-place, but Barker went straight off to raise the alarm. Unless he just stood by while Barker did the dirty work his clothes must have been almost ruined, but he left himself no time to change before going out. It is doubtful whether Douglas had an opportunity to wash after going into concealment, where he was 'cooped up two days'. But, oddly enough, Watson makes no comment on his appearance as he emerged except to remark that he 'stood blinking at us with the dazed look of one who comes from the dark into the light'. No mention at all of dirt or blood-stains, either on himself or upon his clothing.

SELF-DEFENCE OR MURDER

All of this may have a perfectly innocent explanation; maybe not. Douglas had been living a lie and Barker telling an untrue story for two days. Was their word to be believed even now, when their subterfuge had been uncovered? Suppose the fight with Baldwin had not ended just as Douglas described. Suppose that when Douglas had got hold of the gun Baldwin dropped it and surrendered. Baldwin is now at the mercy of his deadly enemy. Douglas was a man capable of quick thinking; after all, he took little time, on his own account of it, to realise how much better it would be for him if his pursuers could be persuaded to think him dead. Could he not have thought of substituting one identity for another while holding the cringing Baldwin at gun-point?

Barker, who comes in by chance or is called for, fetches his friend's clothes and then holds the weapon while Baldwin is made to undress and put on Douglas' night attire. If Baldwin was exhausted and terrified, as he probably was while staring down both barrels of the shot-gun, he would have co-operated in anything in the hope of saving his skin. Any prevarication could have been effectively prevented by a timely reminder about the gun being in the hands of a person who was quite prepared to use it. Then, as soon as Baldwin is dressed up to resemble his old enemy his clothes are thrown into the moat, weighted by the dumb-bell, and Douglas takes the gun and fires at point-blank range. Barker and Douglas then have to fiddle with the rings and plaster the victim's face at leisure, whereupon they settle their story before Douglas hides and Barker rushes off to sound the alarm.

Not self-defence perhaps, but premeditated murder. One hesitates to cavil at the jury's verdict, but the acquittal may have been better than Douglas deserved. Our tentative reconstruction of the scene does at least account for the lack of blood-stains upon both Barker and Douglas, and for the fact that neither Holmes nor any of the others who examined the body noticed anything about it to suggest that the corpse had been clothed after death had occurred. To put it no higher, the version postulated here is surely not less consistent with the other data than the accepted version which was given by two admitted liars who, on any showing, possessed first-hand knowledge and every reason to conceal it.

The most important thing concealed was, of course, the bundle containing Baldwin's knife and clothing which was dropped into the turbid water of the moat to sink under the weight of the dumb-bell attached to it. Holmes had no need to stretch his imagination to deduce that 'when water is near and a weight is missing it is not a very far-fetched supposition that something has been sunk in the water'. But the method Holmes used to test the inference, fishing around with the crook of Watson's big umbrella, does seem rather odd. The fabric of the umbrella must have been ruined, yet the good-natured doctor never complained about it.

The bundle was lying in two feet of water, so the top of it must have been at least twelve inches beneath the surface. If we accept the statement that 'the ground-floor windows were within a foot of the surface of the water' the bundle could have been reached with the umbrella, but unless it had been dropped just outside the window Holmes would have had to lean out quite a long way. The moat itself was 'forty feet in breadth', and surely the inclination of anyone attempting to hide a weighted object would be to throw it as far from the edge as possible. Even taking into account the weight of the dumb-bell, the bulk of the package and the general terror of the situation, one would expect Barker and Douglas to have propelled the bundle at least three or four feet from the wall.

In this event, Holmes would have been forced to perform quite a prodigious balancing act, reaching out with his probe and then summoning sufficient energy to land the heavy bundle. We have our doubts about it, but presumably the conspirators were not very clever and, in their panic, succeeded only in dropping the evidence straight down from the window-ledge so that it was easily fished out afterwards. We cannot but feel the greatest sympathy for poor Watson while we try to imagine how he felt as he surveyed the clay stains on what had once been a respectable umbrella.

AN ERROR BY HOLMES?

Another very curious aspect of the investigation is a remark made by Holmes as he returned to his lodgings at the village inn after replacing the saturated bundle he had pulled out of the moat. Watson has gone to bed and is only partially awakened as Holmes enters the bedroom, but he is sufficiently conscious to be astonished at his friend's question, 'would you be afraid to sleep in the same room as a lunatic, a man with softening of the brain, an idiot whose mind has lost its grip?' Holmes is undoubtedly referring to himself, but in terms he usually reserved for dim-witted policemen who failed to draw the right deductions from facts staring them in the face. The suggestion appears to be that Holmes had made some error during the early stages of the inquiry and had only just realised it.

But what error? Look where one will in *The Valley of Fear*, it is impossible to find any mistake or blunder, certainly none sufficiently serious to warrant such bitter words of self-reproach. Was there, perhaps, something which Watson tactfully expunged from the text which had made Holmes so cross with himself? Had he missed some manifest clue, for instance some item which would have exposed the body as someone other than Douglas, something which had been plain as a pikestaff from the outset? Maybe so, but surely nothing truly deserving the opprobrium of idiocy. Whatever high standards Holmes maintained for himself he seems not to have fallen short of them in the Birlstone investigation, which from his point of view was a signal success.

The answer could be that Holmes was not criticising himself, but was throwing sarcasm at the police. That very evening, Holmes has been giving them '*my* reading of the first half' of the story, that is to say that Mrs Douglas and Barker had aided the murderer's escape, but the two detectives can only shake their heads in disbelief. All Holmes wants, for the continuation of his quest, are darkness, Watson's umbrella, and the faithful Ames.

What MacDonald and White Mason said about that is not recorded, but it would be wholly in character with their mood of the moment if one of them had gone so far as to call Holmes a soft-brained lunatic. Or perhaps they teased him with having so lost his grip that he was reduced to behaving like an idiot. Support for the plausibility of this view can be derived from the conversation of the following morning, for when Holmes arranges to meet the police at dusk MacDonald replies that 'that sounds more like sanity'. Had he been party to questioning Holmes' mental capacity the previous evening he might well have made such a remark the next morning as partial atonement

'THEN SUDDENLY HE HAULED SOMETHING IN AS A FISHERMAN LANDS A FISH.'

By Frank Wiles, from *The Valley of Fear*. Holmes, Watson and the police detectives, crouching down behind the screen of laurels, as the sodden bundle is rescued from the moat. 'Watson insists that I am the dramatist in real life,' said Sherlock Holmes.

'THE TALL AND PORTLY FORM OF MYCROFT WAS USHERED INTO THE ROOM.'

By Arthur Twidle, from *The Bruce-Partington Plans*, December 1908. Mycroft Holmes, 'the most indispensable man in the country', closely followed by Inspector Lestrade, who is still wearing his hat. The late James Montgomery thought this illustration by Twidle so good that it 'could easily be mistaken for Paget at his best'.

for an earlier outburst. It is only fair to mention, however, that in the way the narrative unfolds at this juncture the reference to Holmes sounding more like sanity appears to relate to his presumed madness of a moment or two beforehand when he suggested that the police should take the day off.

There seems to be an echo here of an earlier case, *The Reigate Squires*, in which Inspector Forrester remarks to Watson and Colonel Hayter that he thinks 'Holmes has not quite got over his illness yet'. He has been 'behaving very queerly'. Watson replies soothingly that he has 'usually found that there was method in his madness', whereupon the inspector mutters that 'some folk might say there was madness in his method'.

His secretive attitude during an investigation and his love of unveiling a sparkling finale to an admiring audience, like a conjuror pulling the proverbial rabbit out of a hat, caused Holmes to be widely misunderstood, though this kind of behaviour was a natural enough product of his genius. As Watson commented in *The Hound of the Baskervilles*,

> one of Sherlock Holmes's defects—if, indeed, one may call it a defect—was that he was exceedingly loth to communicate his full plans to any other person until the instant of their fulfilment. Partly it came no doubt from his own masterful nature, which loved to dominate and surprise those who were around him. Partly also from his professional caution, which urged him never to take chances. The result, however, was very trying for those who were acting as his agents and assistants.

The period of waiting towards the end of the Birlstone adventure must have been trying indeed to the patience of White Mason and the others.

The exposure of the killer in *The Valley of Fear* shows Holmes once again at his theatrical exploits. Not for him to flourish 'the sopping bundle' and demand that the house be torn to pieces so that Douglas may be dragged from his hiding-place. Tackling the problem with finesse rather than force of arms was his way: letting the conspirators disclose themselves. Not with smoke, as in *A Scandal in Bohemia* and *The Norwood Builder*, but by waiting for the opposition to crack under the mental strain of imminent discovery. Rather similar techniques were employed in *The Second Stain* and *The Reigate Squires*. Despite committing himself to a long wait outside in the cold of a January evening, Holmes assuredly thought it was worth it, even though the police, who had not been apprised of the situation as Holmes knew it, displayed some annoyance. When Holmes arranged a capture along similar lines in *The Six Napoleons* the police were more patient, but of course that case was at a warmer time of year and Lestrade was fairly well aware of what Holmes was trying to achieve.

The philosophy of detection as one of the arts is beautifully expounded by the 'mere connoisseur of crime', as Holmes calls himself in *The Valley of Fear*, when he is urging his companions to possess their souls in patience:

> I am the dramatist in real life. Some touch of the artist wells up within me and calls insistently for a well-staged performance. Surely our profession, Mr. Mac, would be a drab and sordid one if we did not sometimes set the scene so as to glorify our results. The blunt accusation, the brutal tap upon the shoulder—what can one make of such a *dénouement*? But the quick inference, the subtle trap, the clever forecast of coming events, the triumphant vindication of bold theories—are these not the pride and the justification of our life's work?

Strangely enough, it might as well have been the doctrine that inspired Birdy Edwards, himself in his assumed identity of Douglas now about to be trapped by Sherlock Holmes.

THE DATES IN THE CASE

Towards the end of the paragraph from which the philosophy of detection has just been quoted Holmes asks MacDonald the rhetorical question, 'Where would be that thrill if I had been as definite as the time-table?' The same idea could well have been in the minds of Watson and Conan Doyle when they prepared the script of *The Valley of Fear* to send to the publishers. Probably through oversight, perhaps a careless vetting of the text, they have posed for their readers another series of chronological puzzles.[3] This time it is more convenient firstly to examine the case in years and then to consider the separate problems affecting the individual days of the Birlstone adventure.

The part of the book dealing with *The Scowrers* starts with a clear statement that 'it was the fourth of February in the year 1875' when Edwards journeyed by train into the Vermissa Valley. The year is a plausible one, suiting the period of the Molly Maguire outrages, so the inquiry had better begin there.

For three months Edwards carried on his double game until the evening arrived upon which McGinty and his confederates were trapped. The trial of the Scowrers must have taken some time. It 'was held far from the place where their adherents might have terrified the guardians of the law'. Objections to any change of venue and other procedural appeals could have taken a year or more, certainly many months. The main part of the case, when eventually it got started, probably took at least as long again, for the defendants contested every allegation with the aid of wily lawyers, spending money like water in the vain struggle to save themselves. It says a good deal for the skill of their advocates that Ted Baldwin and the Willabys were not found guilty of a capital charge. It is barely credible that all this could have happened within the space of less than eighteen months, so perhaps it is reasonable to infer that the beginning of 1877 at the earliest marked the end of the litigation and the hanging of McGinty and his chief followers.

Baldwin, who escaped the scaffold, was not free for ten years, but Douglas fails to make it clear whether that period was the sentence he served, calculated from the date of conviction, or the total length of his incarceration following his arrest. It is inconceivable that he was ever allowed bail. His release from gaol may therefore have been during the summer of 1885 or about the early part of 1887. Edwards was back to Chicago by then, possibly still in the employment of Pinkerton's, but his foes were out for vengeance, so he migrated to California under the alias of Douglas. There his first wife died of typhoid and the surviving Scowrers made another attempt on his life. The following year he met Barker and for the next five years they remained together as 'partners in a successful mining claim at a place called Benito Canyon'. Within a week of Douglas fleeing from California his enemies were seeking him through Barker. This was 'nearer seven' than six years before *The Tragedy of Birlstone*. These approximate times may be expressed in tabular form as follows:

Chicago—two attempts	¼ year
California—wife's death and another attempt	1 year
California—with Barker	5 years
England	6¾ years
	13 years

These would be the shortest possible times for each period. Edwards might well have remained comparatively unmolested in Chicago for longer than three months and, as Douglas, may have passed a peaceful year or more in the security of his alias before Ettie caught typhoid. But assuming no unnecessary time was lost, a total of thirteen years from the release of the convicts seems about right. If this time span is calculated from the arrests, the killing of Baldwin could have taken place at any time after the middle of 1898; if from the ten-year sentence being imposed, then at about the beginning of 1900. Whichever interpretation is correct, it is beyond dispute that the earliest January for the Birlstone investigation is 1899. This assertion naturally depends for its validity upon the 1875 starting date, but there is nothing inherently wrong in it. Presumably Conan Doyle copied it accurately from the 'bundle of paper' containing 'the story of the Valley of Fear' which Douglas handed to Watson as he advanced from his hiding-place. The fourth of February 1875 was a date Douglas would have been most unlikely to forget.

January 1902 is suggested as the outside limit of time in the other direction. This presupposes an extension to fifteen years of the estimated times tabulated above and the prison sentence of ten years dating from the trial rather than the arrest. It might be argued in favour of an even later date that the trial could have lasted well into 1877 or even 1878, but any contention along that line of reasoning is open to the objection that in January 1903 Watson had contracted a second marriage and moved away from Baker Street, and that by January 1904 Holmes had retired and was living in Sussex.

The evidence against the 1898–1902 dating is contained in the opening chapter of the book. MacDonald is 'ushered into the room' and the narrative states that 'those were the early days at the end of the 'eighties'. What this curiously worded phrase is meant to signify is itself somewhat mysterious. Its construction is highly ambiguous. Apparently some essential words have been omitted. Does it mean that these were the early days of the year, ie, the first week of January, in a year towards the end of the eighteen-eighties? Maybe so. If 'the early days' does not refer to the beginning of January it can only denote either the early days of Holmes' practice as a consulting detective, which is nonsense, or the early days of MacDonald's career at Scotland Yard. The latter theory does at least make some sense, especially when taken in context with the remainder of the paragraph, which goes on to mention the fame which the inspector later achieved. However, any such interpretation leaves unresolved the contradiction between 'the 'eighties' and the additional decade at least that is needed to give Edwards time to cover so much ground after Baldwin's discharge from the penitentiary.

Let us say at once that we believe the reference to the eighties is a misprint which, for some reason, crept into the original text and has been perpetuated in all editions since. Possibly an over-enthusiastic sub-editor without authority altered 'nineties' as originally written by Watson, because *The Final Problem* was in the forefront of his mind and he wanted to inhibit criticism of his periodical for mentioning Moriarty as still being alive several years after his fatal plunge into the Reichenbach abyss. Perhaps the reason is something even simpler—a slip of the pen or a printer's error which nobody troubled to correct.

Of course, the objection may be advanced in reply that if we can arbitrarily decide that 'the 'eighties' really means the eighteen-nineties we might just as plausibly propose that the date when Edwards went to Vermissa should be altered from 1875 to 1865, so as to make up for the same amount of lost time. However, this would not be a very fruitful exercise. It would put the Molly Maguires into the wrong decade and would also involve some confusion with the American Civil War. The economic unrest of the iron and mining areas was essentially an industrial trouble which gathered its impetus during the period following the end of the Civil War. To suggest that the stage was set for Pinkerton to send Edwards to Vermissa in or about 1865 would be an obvious anachronism. The massive growth of Pennsylvania as an industrial centre took place after the war, assisted by increased numbers of European immigrants. Indeed it was within the Keystone state that the labour movements started which gave birth to the great American trade unions. Furthermore, there is the negative evidence that the great conflict between North and South is nowhere alluded to in *The Valley of Fear*, despite the fact that Pennsylvania contained within its boundaries Gettysburg as well as Vermissa.

At all events, it is most unrealistic, when the totality of the evidence is reviewed, even to consider 1889 as a plausible date. This opinion is fortified by the fact that in that year Watson was living at Paddington with his first wife Mary and would not usually have been found at Baker Street at breakfast time.

The virtual impossibility of 1889 as a date for *The Valley of Fear* is made manifest by the appearance at 221B Baker Street of Billy the page, who 'swung open the door' and ushered Inspector MacDonald into the room. Billy's employment dates from the period following the *Return*, probably from around the turn of the century, because, in *The Mazarin Stone*, during which Holmes uses Tavernier's effigy and the Hoffman Barcarolle in a subterfuge to recover the diamond for Lord Cantlemere, Watson alludes to the dummy in the window and remarks that they had 'used something of the sort once before', to which Billy rejoins that this was 'before my time'. This can only be a reference to *The Empty House*, so it would surely be carrying absurdity beyond limits to suggest that Billy can have been on the premises several years earlier than 1894.

The unnamed 'boy in buttons' who figures in *A Case of Identity* (September 1888, or perhaps 1889) can scarcely have been Billy, and was presumably the first of several pages engaged by Holmes during the busier periods of his practice. The mention of Billy in *Thor Bridge* (a case generally agreed as having occurred in 1900 or 1901) does, on the other hand, argue even more forcibly for a late date for *The Valley of Fear*.

The time factor may also be tested by reference to the ages of

Douglas and Barker. At the time of *The Scowrers* Edwards, as Douglas was then known, was 'not far, one would guess, from his thirtieth year'. The logical interpretation of that surmise is that he was thought to be slightly under thirty rather than slightly older. A phrase such as 'not much over thirty' would be the more normal English usage for describing someone slightly older. By the time of *The Tragedy of Birlstone* 'he may have been about fifty', while his friend Barker 'was rather younger than Douglas, forty-five at the most'. If Edwards was twenty-seven when he went to that 'gloomy land of black crag and tangled forest' in February 1875 he would have been fifty-one when, as Douglas, he found that Baldwin had pursued him to his country retreat in Sussex. This calculation involves assuming 1899 as the year of the shooting, but even if 1901 was the correct year Douglas would have been only fifty-three, which is still fairly consistent with both statements.

The only possible disparity is contained in the paragraph which introduces Douglas' narrative of *The Scowrers*: 'I wish you to journey back some twenty years in time . . .' This sentence comes in the middle of a paragraph apparently written by Watson, as indeed the beginning and end of it must have been, but the sentence in the middle makes sense only upon the assumption that it was taken from Douglas' own account and that the editor placed it where it is for the value of the undoubted improvement in literary effect. This can be proved by the way the same sentence continues. Douglas wants his readers to journey backward in time and westward in space, 'that I may lay before you a singular and a terrible narrative—so singular and so terrible that you may find it hard to believe that, even as I tell it, even so did it occur'. Then after that it is Watson, or his editor, who carries on, still within the same paragraph, 'Do not think that I intrude one story before another is finished. . . .'

The 'some twenty years' phrase cannot possibly refer to something that happened two decades before the date of publication of *The Valley of Fear*, but if it has been extracted from the bundle of paper handed by Douglas to 'the historian of this bunch' then it reads naturally enough as belonging to the account of his own adventure which took place just over twenty years before he wrote it. Had the shooting occurred in 1889, less than fourteen years after Edwards ventured into the valley to build up a case against the Scowrers, the expression 'some twenty years' is plainly inaccurate, and for Douglas to have qualified it immediately afterwards by giving the year as 1875 would have highlighted the solecism at once. However, if 1899 was the year of the tragedy, it was indeed 'some twenty years' since the dreadful events at Vermissa.

If the oddly turned phrase about the early days at the end of the eighties which we have previously examined means that MacDonald called at Baker Street in the early days of a year (or of his career) at the end of the nineties, the year can only be 1899, which seems likely enough. *The Valley of Fear* was not published until 1914–15, so there is plenty of time left for Mr Mac so to advance his career as to attain national renown. If a later year had been intended, the idea of a misprint or casual alteration becomes less credible. For instance had Watson written of 'days at the end of Queen Victoria's reign' or of 'days at the start of the century', the alteration becomes far more difficult to explain, unless it was done by the bright, young sub-editor who was frightened about the mention of Moriarty.

Before finally deciding whether 1899 is the right date there are a few other matters to explore concerning the days of the week in that particular January.

It was on 7 January that Holmes received the cipher message from Porlock and later accompanied MacDonald to Birlstone. There was more than one postal delivery to Baker Street that day. The coded warning arrived by the first post and Porlock's letter of withdrawal by the second. Two deliveries of mail by about 10 am means that the day could not have been a Sunday and accordingly 1900 must be discounted. In 1899 7 January was a Saturday. The mystery was solved on the second day, which would be 8 January, but there is no reason why that should not have been a Sunday. The police had received some letters and telegrams, but there is nothing incongruous in that. One Sunday delivery of letters could be expected in any case, and for this kind of urgent investigation the police probably had their own means of collecting mail as soon as it arrived; possibly it was brought by the messenger who delivered the telegrams. During the day the detectives took, or at least were encouraged to take, 'a nice, cheery, country walk' and luncheon 'at some suitable hostelry'—not a bad occupation for a pleasant, winter Sunday.

The day of the killing was 6 January. On that day Douglas had been on guard and never went into the park. This was because 'the day before' the crime he had been shopping at Tunbridge Wells and had caught a glimpse of the vengeful Baldwin. This previous day would have been 5 January. It must have been a weekday, on account of the shopping. This effectively removes 1902 from the reckoning as a possible year, for 5 January then fell on a Sunday.

Thus it seems we are left with only 1899 and 1901 as possible years for *The Valley of Fear*. Despite involving a very tight time schedule for Edwards' movements after the arrest of the Scowrers, we incline towards 1899 as being the more likely, for no other year fits the inference that 'eighties' is a straightforward error for 'nineties', and it also gives the young MacDonald more time in which to achieve national fame before the publication of the story in 1914. Furthermore, 1899 more closely fits the ages of Douglas and Barker than 1901 and coincides more nearly to Douglas writing of the events at Vermissa as having happened 'some twenty years' before the shooting at Birlstone.

THE MORIARTYS

Having now established 1899 as the date of *The Valley of Fear*, an even more intriguing problem must be tackled. How was it that nearly eight years after his death at the Reichenbach Professor Moriarty was still alive and able to pursue his nefarious activities? This conundrum also involves a number of secondary riddles. Is the 1899 date right, after all? Who was Moriarty anyway? Why were the Moriarty brothers, professor and colonel, both called James? And how did Colonel Sebastian Moran avoid arrest in 1891 and escape execution in 1894? All these matters will have to be explored. But, to return to the primary argument, how did Professor Moriarty manage to survive his own death?

The most obvious rejoinder is to beg the question and say that this makes the 1899 date unacceptable. It is true, of course, that if *The*

Valley of Fear did occur 'at the end of the 'eighties', a couple of years or so before the death struggle in *The Final Problem*, Moriarty would indeed have been alive and no query would arise. At first sight this might seem an attractive proposition, though its support for an earlier date would make the chronological analysis even more difficult. But closer scrutiny only goes to refute the suggestion. Any idea that *The Valley of Fear* took place before *The Final Problem* is effectively negatived when Watson's knowledge of Moriarty and his attitude to the super-criminal are considered.

There can be no dispute that *The Final Problem* was an 1891 case, but when Holmes calls on his friend to see whether he can accompany him 'for a week on to the Continent' Watson has never heard of Moriarty. This is not a case of Watson suffering a lapse of memory, since Holmes himself was not expecting the doctor to have any prior knowledge of the master-crook. The conversation behind the closed shutters of Watson's consulting-room makes this abundantly clear:

> 'You have probably never heard of Professor Moriarty?'
> 'Never.'
> 'Aye, there's the genius and the wonder of the thing! The man pervades London, and no one has heard of him.'

Holmes then launches into a long discourse about Moriarty's academic background and criminal tendencies, followed by an account of the professor's visit to Baker Street. If Watson had by any chance been mistaken in having said he had never previously heard of Moriarty he had ample time to recollect and every opportunity of mentioning it. Instead, when the discussion continues the next morning, Watson cannot conceal his astonishment that such cleverly organised vice could possibly exist. Setting fire to Holmes' rooms is really the last straw: 'Good heavens, Holmes! This is intolerable.'

In *The Valley of Fear* there is no such ignorance or amazement on Watson's part. Mention of the name is quite enough to remind him of Moriarty at once. A very different sort of conversation this time:

> 'You have heard me speak of Professor Moriarty?'
> 'The famous scientific criminal, as famous among crooks . . . as he is unknown to the public.'

It is utterly inconceivable that Watson could have known all about Moriarty at the end of the eighties, have had that knowledge increased during *The Valley of Fear*, and yet have been able to say with every ring of truth a mere two years later that he had never heard of him. The dialogues just quoted serve only to offer further proof, if such is needed, that *The Final Problem* was the earlier case and that *The Valley of Fear* took place towards the end of Holmes' active career.[4]

Having disposed of any preliminary objection to the thesis on which the main question is based, we must now consider how it was that Moriarty seems to have become raised from the dead, to live on as the immortal genius of organised crime.

In *The Final Problem* we hear of Professor Moriarty's extraordinary career.

> He is a man of good birth and excellent education, endowed by Nature with a phenomenal mathematical faculty. At the age of twenty-one he wrote a treatise upon the Binomial Theorem, which has had a European vogue. On the strength of it, he won the Mathematical Chair at one of our smaller Universities, and had, to all appearance, a most brilliant career before him. But the man had hereditary tendencies of the most diabolical kind. A criminal strain ran in his blood, which, instead of being modified, was increased and rendered infinitely more dangerous by his extraordinary mental powers. Dark rumours gathered round him in the University town, and eventually he was compelled to resign his Chair and to come down to London, where he set up as an Army coach.

It is with this background that Moriarty achieves his position as the 'deep organizing power' of 'the higher criminal world of London'.

According to *The Valley of Fear*, Professor Moriarty is still 'the famous scientific criminal'. Holmes calls him 'the greatest schemer of all time, the organizer of every devilry, the controlling brain of the underworld'. But here there is no mention of his famous treatise upon the binomial theorem; the professor of *The Valley of Fear* has become 'the celebrated author of *The Dynamics of an Asteroid*'. Inspector MacDonald has 'had a chat with him on eclipses' and borrowed a book which 'was a bit above my head'. We also learn some further details from Holmes about the professor's position in life. 'He is unmarried. His younger brother is a station-master in the West of England. His chair is worth seven hundred a year. And he owns a Greuze.' He is a 'very wealthy man' and pays his chief of staff 'more than the Prime Minister gets'.

MacDonald tells us little about the professor's appearance except that 'he seems to be a very respectable, learned, and talented sort of man', with a 'thin face and grey hair and a solemn-like way of talking'. Holmes, in *The Final Problem*, has described Professor Moriarty more fully.

> He is extremely tall and thin, his forehead domes out in a white curve, and his two eyes are deeply sunken in his head. He is clean-shaven, pale, and ascetic-looking, retaining something of the professor in his features. His shoulders are rounded from much study, and his face protrudes forward, and is for ever slowly oscillating from side to side in a curiously reptilian fashion. He peered at me with great curiosity in his puckered eyes.

Watson's glimpse of Moriarty at Victoria station enabled him only to observe that their pursuer was 'a tall man'. The descriptions in *The Final Problem* and in *The Valley of Fear* could well have been of two different people.

It is obvious that if Professor Moriarty was killed at the Reichenbach Fall in 1891 his namesake who operated on behalf of the Scowrers some eight years later must have been someone different. Before exploring that proposition there is a third Moriarty to mention. This is Colonel James Moriarty, a brother of the Professor Moriarty who lost his life in the adventure of *The Final Problem.* By 1893 Watson's hand was forced, by recent letters in which the colonel was defending his late brother's memory, 'to tell for the first time what really took place between Professor Moriarty and Mr. Sherlock Holmes'. A subsidiary puzzle then appears in *The Empty House* when Watson, quoting Holmes as he is supposed to have spoken in 1894, refers to the victim of Reichenbach as Professor James Moriarty. Can it be at all likely that two brothers should bear the same Christian name?[5]

The basic question to which an answer is required if clarity is to be obtained is: how can we distinguish between three separate Moriartys, two of whom are professors and two of whom, supposedly brothers, are called James? And somewhere into the picture has to be fitted a fourth Moriarty, the West of England station-master.

Before attempting to find an answer to this problem there is other evidence concerning the 'great consultant in crime' and his evil gang which may have a helpful bearing upon the matter. In *The Final Problem* Holmes has arranged with the London police for the arrest of all the organisation's members. 'On Monday we should have them all,' he says. This is something the police can handle without any help from Holmes, 'though my presence is necessary for a conviction'. At Strasburg (in 1891 part of Germany), Holmes receives a telegram reporting that the police 'have secured the whole gang with the exception of' Moriarty. They were not all convicted, which may have been due to Holmes' remaining abroad and not returning to London to give evidence. In *The Empty House*, Holmes admits that 'the course of events in London did not run as well as I had hoped, for the trial of the Moriarty gang left two of its most dangerous members, my own most vindictive enemies, at liberty'. Were these perhaps Brooks and Woodhouse, the two men named by Holmes in 1895 in the preamble to *The Bruce-Partington Plans* among 'the fifty men who have good reason for taking my life'?

Colonel Sebastian Moran, it is interesting to note, was not arrested while Holmes was in Strasburg, because only a few days later he was free to witness Moriarty's death and afterwards to harass Holmes from the cliff above the Reichenbach. The colonel's grim face must have been known to Holmes, who recognised it straight away as belonging to the professor's most dangerous confederate; but did Holmes know beforehand that Moran was involved with Moriarty? Possibly not, because if he did know about Moran his name must have been among those given to the police who would then have arrested him. As against this, Watson says that Holmes endorsed the margin of Moran's biography in his index as 'the second most dangerous man in London', Moriarty himself having presumably been regarded as the most dangerous. A plausible explanation of this apparent inconsistency is that, while Holmes knew well enough that Moran was a tough customer, he had failed to associate Moran with Moriarty until the incident in Switzerland. As Holmes admits in *The Empty House*, 'so cleverly was the colonel concealed that even when the Moriarty gang was broken up we could not incriminate him'.

The connection between Moran and Moriarty, of which Holmes speaks in *The Empty House*, seems to have come to his notice only after *The Final Problem*. If so, this explains why Moran's name was not on the list of wanted men whom the police were to arrest. Holmes was certainly suspicious of air-guns before his departure for Europe in 1891, but he may have possessed insufficient evidence of Moran's involvement with Moriarty to justify having the 'honourable soldier' arrested. Even as far back as 1887 Holmes had only had suspicions that Moran was concerned in the death of Mrs Stewart of Lauder. So cunningly did Moran cover his tracks that it was only much later that Holmes found out about his having been Moriarty's chief of staff. No one need be surprised that the cool, crafty colonel was more than a match for a wounded man-eating tiger.

Moran's position is of some importance because he also figures in *The Valley of Fear*, where Holmes describes him again as Professor Moriarty's chief of staff, employed now at the princely salary of £6,000 a year. How Moran contrived to cheat the gallows for the Adair murder will be explained later, but for our present purposes the evidence of *The Valley of Fear* indicates that the Moriarty gang was reconstituted after *The Final Problem* and was still in active existence around the turn of the century. Moran himself was still alive as late as September 1902, for Holmes refers to him in *The Illustrious Client*, which took place at that time.

How did the Moriarty organisation survive after *The Final Problem*? Moran, together with at least two others of its most dangerous members, remained at liberty after the 1891 trial. Quite possibly there were other leaders and various small fry unknown to Holmes or the police who were never arrested at all.

After Holmes eventually eluded the cascade of rocks sent showering at him down the Reichenbach cliff, Moran must have returned to London to see about re-forming the gang. As chief of staff it would have been his task to take command of the villains as the new Moriarty. To assist in ensuring his authority as leader he assumed the name of his late brother-outlaw as a sort of professional pseudonym. Hence

Watson's reference to *Colonel* James Moriarty and the letters which led to the publication of *The Final Problem.* Watson may have misunderstood the position, but 'brother', in the context of the letters, denotes not necessarily a blood relationship but only the bond of close association; 'the bosom friend of Moriarty', is how Holmes describes it. Looking at it in this light, we can see that Colonel James Moriarty and Colonel Sebastian Moran were actually one and the same person.

Moran's role as the second Moriarty was to gather together the remnants of 'the charming society whose leader lies in the Reichenbach Fall' and to create a new organisation to engage in crime and await the eventual return of Sherlock Holmes. The success of this 'most cunning and dangerous criminal in London' is shown by the fact that Holmes' old enemies were ready to murder him almost as soon as he set foot in Baker Street early in 1894. It is not clear whether Colonel Moran was still leader at this stage or whether he had reverted to his old job as chief of staff. He bore 'the brow of a philosopher' and was paid 'for brains', but the analytical genius of a 'controlling brain of the underworld' may have been lacking in his make-up.

At all events, either before *The Empty House* or as its direct result, a third Moriarty took over the leadership. He was another professor, probably a former university colleague of the gang's founder. As in the case of his academic predecessor, he presumably found that outwitting the forces of the state was a far more satisfying intellectual exercise than teaching undergraduates. The two Professors Moriarty had different learned specialities. The victim of Reichenbach had won a mathematical chair on the strength of his treatise upon the binomial theorem, while the professor who employed Porlock in *The Valley of Fear* and owned the Portalis Greuze was not only a pure mathematician but also an expert on eclipses and the celebrated author of *The Dynamics of an Asteroid.* This second Professor Moriarty probably achieved his academic distinction through scholarships from humble beginnings, so there is nothing inherently improbable in his having a brother who worked for the railway.

The Moriarty of *The Valley of Fear* was the most successful of all. Holmes never caught him, and it may be assumed in his favour that the great detective retired while the professor was still enjoying his ill-gotten gains. It seems that at first he may have taken a little time to make his presence felt on the criminal scene because, in *The Norwood Builder*, a few months after the *Return*, Holmes is heard complaining about lack of work. 'London has become a singularly uninteresting city since the death of the late lamented Professor Moriarty'. But this situation was soon rectified. In *The Solitary Cyclist*, Watson starts the story with the recollection that 'from the years 1894 to 1901 inclusive, Mr. Sherlock Holmes was a very busy man'. And, in *The Golden Pince-Nez*, he refers to 'the three massive manuscript volumes which contain our work for the year 1894'. Doubtless Moriarty was instrumental in furnishing a good deal of the material upon which Holmes had to theorise. Even the slack period immediately after *The Empty House* may not have been due to any lack of effort on Moriarty's part; it may have been merely that Holmes took a little time to re-establish his old connections. Barker, his 'hated rival upon the Surrey shore', who participated a few years later in *The Retired Colourman*, may have picked up some of Holmes' clients during his long absence abroad.

By the time of *The Valley of Fear* the Moriarty gang was as active and evil as ever. Colonel Moran was once more restored to his old rank as 'chief of the staff' and the so-called accident to Douglas when he was swept overboard from the *Palmyra* on the way to Cape Town is cited as a fine example of the Moriarty touch. As Holmes remarked when he heard the sad news, 'you can tell an old master by the sweep of his brush'.

So, the sweep of the brush was made at different times by three successive Moriartys, two professors and one colonel. But what of the colonel? How did he manage to emulate Baldwin the Scowrer and escape the scaffold? The answer to this question is one of the most startling in all the Holmes literature.

A BREAK FOR COLONEL MORAN

At the end of *The Empty House* Moran was arrested by a rather astonished Lestrade for the murder of the Honourable Ronald Adair. The case for the prosecution was 'so overwhelmingly strong', writes Watson, 'that it was not necessary to bring forward all the facts'. All the public knew were those particulars which 'came out' in the

investigation, because 'a good deal was suppressed'. What a very strange state of affairs it was! A murder case, in which 'all London was interested', and the police apparently so cocky about the outcome that they never bothered to bring out all the evidence? It sounds fantastic. And yet we have Watson's word for it that facts were suppressed. Why?

There is no ground whatever for doubting that a considerable body of evidence must have been withheld at Moran's trial, for if the overwhelmingly strong case had been presented to the jury he would have been convicted of the murder and probably hanged. At the very least, he would not have been a free man again within eight or ten years. It must be obvious that the prosecution bungled the trial to such an extent that Moran was acquitted of murder and may have got off altogether. More probably he received a few years' penal servitude for some lesser offence. Perhaps the prosecution made such a mess of its case that Moran was actually allowed to plead guilty to some minor charge so that the capital one was dropped. But, if the colonel was a murderer, why?

When one considers the care and thoroughness with which public prosecutions, especially in serious cases like murder, are prepared, and how many people, not only the police but also their legal advisers and the courts, are involved, the conclusion is inevitable that the suppression of the evidence in Moran's case was no accident. The case was *deliberately* botched, with the specific intention that Moran should get away with it and evade his just deserts. Again, we must ask ourselves the question: why?

There is one clue in *The Empty House* itself. The Adair murder trial was a *cause célèbre* and would have caused public speculation as to why the prosecution fared so badly. Not surprisingly, Watson felt rather uncomfortable about it. He displays a bit of a guilty conscience at having to be less than frank, explaining that the public 'are not to blame me if I have not shared my knowledge with them'. At first, Watson was 'barred by a positive prohibition' from writing the story at all. Only when Holmes lifted the ban, 'upon the third of last month', was Watson free to publicise his friend's escape from Moriarty and the capture of Colonel Moran.

It was once thought that the only reason for the delayed publication of *The Empty House* was reticence on the part of Holmes, coupled with Conan Doyle's reluctance to let it be admitted in *The Strand* that Holmes had survived the Reichenbach encounter. But, as we shall see, there seems to have been an even more compelling reason. *The Empty House*, which provided the background for the *Return*, had to remain a closely guarded secret because to publish that adventure would have involved disclosure of information which might have led to the discovery of the inside story of how Moran avoided paying the full penalty for his crimes. Even in 1903, when *The Empty House* appeared, Watson had to be careful. The story is told purely as a vehicle for introducing Holmes on his return from abroad. Watson makes not the slightest attempt to bring the narrative up to date.

A second clue can be found in *The Illustrious Client.* It may be no accident that this was the case in which Holmes chose to mention 'the living Colonel Sebastian Moran' when speaking to Colonel Damery about the dangerous opponents he had met in the past. Could this have been said because Damery was in the know about Moran's peculiar trial? It is surely significant that Watson chose to include in his account of *The Illustrious Client* an explanation of how Holmes managed to avoid being prosecuted for burgling Baron Gruner's 'architectural nightmare' of a house, that 'when an object is good and a client is sufficiently illustrious, even the rigid British law becomes human and elastic'. Was it, perhaps, Watson's rather cryptic way of letting his readers know how it came about that 'a good deal was suppressed' concerning the death of Ronald Adair? Does it, in essence, imply that it was possible for some pre-eminent personage, even in a murder case, so to mould the workings of the law that only selected facts would be published?

Consider the date of *The Illustrious Client.* It was September 1902. Just a few short months afterwards the ban on Watson from publishing *The Empty House* was withdrawn. And permission to publish was given, we believe, as a reward for services rendered. Having helped to ensure that Baron Gruner never married Violet de Merville, Holmes was told by the illustrious client himself that Watson might now write about the Adair case.

Adair and Moran played cards with Godfrey Milner and Lord Balmoral.[6] All four were presumably well known to one another at their card clubs and in society. Any scandal at that social level would be serious enough; a murder charge absolutely dreadful. But it went further than that, for royalty were involved. Who was the Lord Balmoral who played whist for high stakes at the Bagatelle? None other, of course, than the son of the *châtelaine* of Balmoral, then the Prince of Wales. For one of the prince's associates to face a capital charge was unthinkable. Something had to be done behind the scenes to reduce the prosecution to a smaller compass so that less dire consequences would follow. Steps were therefore taken to ensure that the most damning parts of the evidence were hushed up or, to use Watson's word, suppressed. The prosecution's failure to bring out all the facts can now be understood. Nothing short of pressure from the highest quarters would have sufficed.

The relationship between this and *The Illustrious Client* may now be postulated, though the royal connection can be inferred only through negative indications rather than positive ones; but they present a formidable thesis nevertheless. The Holmesian writings are not reticent about calling noblemen and foreign kings by their correct titles, but an exception is made for the English royal family. For instance, as a reward for his recovery of 'the invaluable Bruce-Partington plans' Holmes 'spent a day at Windsor' collecting 'a remarkably fine emerald tie-pin' as 'a present from a certain gracious lady'. Watson fancied he 'could guess at that lady's august name'—and he was probably right too, though he omits to tell us what his guess was! Nor do we think Watson was so dim as to have been unable to identify the Lord Balmoral whom Moran had defrauded at the card-table.

In *The Illustrious Client* Watson knows the identity of 'the chivalrous gentleman' who had Violet de Merville's interests so much at heart, for he had seen 'the armorial bearings upon the panel' of the brougham which awaited Sir James Damery. As far as can be judged, Watson was no great expert on heraldry. And yet he not only identifies the bearings in the instant before Sir James 'flung his overcoat half out of the window' to conceal them, but he does so in the dark, while the side of the moving carriage is illuminated only by 'the glare of our fanlight'. Instantly recognisable, causing the good doctor to gasp with surprise and to rush upstairs to Holmes, bursting with his great news—could the arms have been other than those of His Majesty the King? We may now conclude with near-certainty that the royal reward this time was not another tie-pin from Windsor but gracious permission to publish the story of *The Empty House*, in which the Prince of Wales, as he then was, had played whist with a murderer.

Which explains why, in *The Valley of Fear*, we can read of Colonel Sebastian Moran being very much alive in 1899, just a few short years after he ought to have been hanged!

NOTES

CHAPTER ONE *A Study in Scarlet*

1 The late Sir Sydney Roberts, first president of the Sherlock Holmes Society of London, said that the date could be assigned to 1852 'with a fair measure of confidence'.

2 This was September 1887, as demonstrated in Chapter 2. Of the major chronologists, Bell and Brend support this year, but Blakeney, Christ, Zeisler, Baring-Gould, Folsom and Dakin all opt for 1888.

3 However, some old Wykehamists loftily assert that Watson's curious description of 'chevying' Tadpole Phelps around the 'playground' with a 'wicket' excludes Winchester. Wellington, with its military tradition, has also been suggested as a possibility, but unfortunately, being in Berkshire, would not fit in with Watson's lyrical nostalgia for the Hampshire countryside.

4 It may even have been as late as the early winter of 1881. As explained later, the commonly held view that Holmes and Watson met in about January and that *A Study in Scarlet* took place in March 1881 is based on faulty reasoning and must be rejected.

5 The canonical chronologists are divided. Bell, Blakeney, Brend, Baring-Gould, Zeisler, Folsom and Dakin favour 1881; Christ favours 1882. My own preference is for 1882, as shown.

6 Reginald Musgrave, who was an undergraduate of the same college as Holmes, was also educated by a tutor, who taught trigonometry of a practical value which even he would have scarcely believed possible.

7 See *The Sign of Four* chapter for argument that *The Five Orange Pips* was prior to Watson's marriage to Mary Morstan.

FIRST INTERVAL *Financial Problems*

1 *The Noble Bachelor.*

2 *A Study in Scarlet.*

3 *Thor Bridge.*

4 *The Bruce-Partington Plans.*

5 *The Sign of Four.*

6 *The Sign of Four.*

7 *The Norwood Builder.*

8 *The Red Circle.*

9 *The Beryl Coronet.*

10 *The Priory School.*

11 *The Priory School.*

12 Later on, as recorded in *The Three Gables*, Holmes had a similar sort of informal arrangement with one Langdale Pike, who became 'his human book of reference upon all matters of social scandal'. Pike made, it was said, 'a four-figure income by the paragraphs which he contributed every week to the garbage papers which cater for an inquisitive public'.

13 The gratitude of royalty was often expressed in kind, rather than in cash. Earlier, Holmes had accepted a remarkable diamond ring 'from the reigning family of Holland' after serving them in a highly confidential matter of great delicacy. Watson noticed, in *A Case of Identity*, that it 'sparkled upon his finger'.

14 Having read the principal works of detective fiction current in his day, which doubtless included the writings of Wilkie Collins, Holmes may possibly have been reminded of Sergeant Cuff who, in his quest for *The Moonstone*, penetrated the seaman's disguise of the murdered villain, Godfrey Ablewhite, by 'washing off his complexion'. Holmes and Watson may also have noticed some similarities between *The Moonstone* and *The Sign of Four*.

15 For a full discussion of this aspect of *The Five Orange Pips*, see the chapter concerning *The Hound of the Baskervilles*.

16 Did Holmes actually say 'compounding'? Later, in *The Three Gables*, he was to remark, with greater precision, that he supposed he would 'have to compound a felony as usual'. The criminal offence would have been *misprision* of felony.

17 Like other heads of state, the Pope may have expressed his appreciation in a non-pecuniary form, perhaps in this instance by presenting to Holmes one of the Vatican cameos!

18 In *Baker Street By-ways*, James Edward Holroyd offers the suggestion that the names in both adventures were echoes of Dr Leander Starr Jameson, leader of the famous raid. Jameson, like Conan Doyle, was born in Edinburgh and, like Watson, took his medical degree at the University of London.

19 See the opening paragraph of *Thor Bridge*.

CHAPTER TWO *The Sign of Four*

1 The chronologists who have opted for 1888 as the date of *The Sign of Four* are obliged to set the date of this and similarly corroborative

stories back a year, even where internal evidence points to a particular year or where a date is clearly given in the text.

SECOND INTERVAL *Some Chronological Problems of the Marriage Period*

1 Within three years, as we learn from *The Final Problem*, the royal family of Scandinavia had also become Holmes' clients, and had rewarded him so generously that he could speak of retirement. Possibly it was the grateful King of Bohemia whom Holmes had to thank for these introductions to European royalty.

2 The quotation here is from the original text in *The Strand Magazine* for December 1893. The collected *Short Stories* omits both the hyphens and the *t* in *coup-de-maître*.

CHAPTER THREE *The Hound of the Baskervilles*

1 It has to be admitted that if our theory about the date of *The Six Napoleons* is correct, the readers of the 'Kensington Outrage' newspaper report would have known that 'Sherlock Holmes, the well-known consulting expert', was very much alive in the summer of 1900. Many other members of the public, including Holmes' clients, must have known too. One wonders who was fooling whom!

2 In writing about Montpelier, Watson presumably relied upon his faulty memory, rather than the gazetteer. His editor, publisher and printer seem to have suffered a similar lapse, for in each succeeding reprint the original spelling mistake has been perpetuated, both in *The Disappearance of Lady Frances Carfax* and *The Empty House*. Perhaps the publishers continue to repeat the error out of devilment, or as proof that Watson sometimes got things wrong. We wonder whether the Mayor of Montpellier, 'in the south of France', has ever protested and whether Great Britain's joining the Common Market will lead to any amendments being made in future editions. The reason for these successive misprints seems even more obscure than the purpose of the detective's 'research into the coal-tar derivatives'. Curiously, though, Watson spells the name of the French town correctly when quoting Holmes, in *A Study in Scarlet*, speaking of 'the notorious Muller, and Lefevre of Montpellier . . .'

3 The actual miscreant may have been Holmes himself, for sending Watson off alone and expecting too much of him. Holmes was well enough acquainted with Watson's limitations and, in *The Blanched Soldier*, was to speak of them as advantages. 'A confederate who guesses your conclusions and course of action is always dangerous, but one to whom each development comes as a perpetual surprise, and to whom the future is always a closed book, is, indeed, the ideal helpmate.' Holmes

was less than fair in these other cases in criticising his 'old friend and biographer' so acidly for the shortcomings which had been so obvious to him all along.

4 This may be an insoluble contradiction in itself. See the discussion about Watson's marriage in the previous chapter, *The Sign of Four*, and the note about the dating of *The Five Orange Pips* which follows the present chapter.

5 Lestrade has told Holmes that 'you are too many for me when you begin to get on your theories . . . I am a practical man'. Watson might also have been thinking of *The Boscombe Valley Mystery*, in which Lestrade remarked very similarly that 'theories are all very well . . . I am a practical man'.

6 For convenience I repeat the years assigned by the major chronologists: 1886 Bell; 1888 Baring-Gould; 1889 Blakeney; 1897 Christ; 1899 Brend; 1900 Dakin, Folsom, Zeisler. Many of the points tabulated in this chapter and elsewhere have already been discovered, discussed and published by these respected experts in arriving at conclusions as to whether the adventure was to be assigned an early or a late date. As a relative late-comer to the study of the Baker Street canon, I salute the patience, the critical analysis and the ingenuity which have been devoted to their researches. It is gratifying to be able to join them as 'a picker-up of shells on the shores of the great unknown ocean', even though one discovers that many of their conclusions are in parallel with one's own research. For example, after I had concluded that the dates in *The Hound of the Baskervilles* had been deliberately, if clumsily, manipulated by Watson and Conan Doyle to conceal the fact that the adventure occurred late in the saga, I found from Martin Dakin's book that a writer in *The Sherlock Holmes Journal* had independently arrived at a similar solution.

CHAPTER FOUR *The Valley of Fear*

1 See Conan Doyle's *Preface* to the collected *Long Stories* (1929). It is strange that he should use abnormal spelling for the Molly Maguires, as they are generally known.

2 'Local aid is always either worthless or else biassed', Holmes told Watson as they set forth on *The Boscombe Valley Mystery*.

3 Once again the difficulties are shown by the wide variations in the chronologies. Although the authors broadly agree on 7 January as the date of the opening of the adventure at 221B, the actual year is divided as follows: 1887 Bell; 1888 Baring-Gould, Dakin, Zeisler, Folsom; 1889 Christ; 1890 Blakeney; 1900 Brend.

4 In case it may be argued to the contrary—ie, that Holmes has not seen

Moriarty in *The Valley of Fear* but has already encountered him in *The Final Problem*—let me say at once that this does not involve any contradiction. As will be made clear later in this chapter, the Moriarty of *The Valley of Fear* was a totally different person from the Moriarty of *The Final Problem*, and there is no evidence to suggest that Holmes was telling anything but the strict truth when he denied having seen him before. There is no basic inconsistency here which need worry us into supposing that *The Valley of Fear* must, or even might, have been the earlier case.

5 Dr W. S. Bristowe, in his essay 'The Truth about Moriarty' in *Seventeen Steps to 221B*, has collected a number of examples of brothers bearing the same Christian name, but this does not seem to be a matter of sufficiently common occurrence to make it at all likely that the two brothers Moriarty with whom Holmes was concerned came within that very limited group.

6 Lord Balmoral was, of course, well known in racing circles. One of the runners in the Wessex Plate, the Duke of Balmoral's Iris, ran a bad third to Silver Blaze and Desborough. The reference to Lord Balmoral as the duke may have been one of Watson's errors of transcription.

SELECT BIBLIOGRAPHY

Baring-Gould, William. *The Chronological Holmes* (published privately in the USA, 1955)

—— (ed). *The Annotated Sherlock Holmes*, 2 vols (1968)

Bell, H. W. *Sherlock Holmes and Dr Watson* (1932)

—— (ed). *Baker Street Studies* (1934)

Blakeney, T. S. *Sherlock Holmes: Fact or Fiction?* (1932)

Brend, Gavin. *My Dear Holmes* (1951)

Christ, Jay Finley. *An Irregular Chronology* (Michigan, 1947)

Dakin, D. Martin. *A Sherlock Holmes Commentary* (1972)

Folsom, Rev Henry T. *Through the Years at Baker Street: A Chronology of Sherlock Holmes* (rev ed privately printed Washington 1964)

Hall, Trevor H. *Sherlock Holmes, Ten Literary Studies* (1969)

——. *The Late Mr Sherlock Holmes* (1971)

Holroyd, James Edward. *Baker Street By-ways* (1959)

—— (ed). *Seventeen Steps to 221B* (1967)

Peck, Andrew Jay. *The Date Being?, a comparative compendium of chronological data* (privately printed New York 1971, Supplement 1973)

Roberts, S. C. *Holmes and Watson, a Miscellany* (1953)

Sayers, Dorothy M. *Unpopular Opinions* (1946)

Smith, Edgar W. *Baker Street and Beyond* (New Jersey, 1957)

—— (ed). *Profile by Gaslight* (New York, 1944)

——. *Introducing Mr Sherlock Holmes* (New Jersey, 1959)

Starrett, Vincent. *The Private Life of Sherlock Holmes* (1934)

—— (ed). *221B Studies in Sherlock Holmes* (New Jersey, 1956)

Warrack, Guy. *Sherlock Holmes and Music* (1947)

Zeisler, E. B. *Baker Street Chronology* (Chicago, 1953)

There are several chapters devoted to Sherlock Holmes in Pierre Nordon's *Conan Doyle* (1966)

ACKNOWLEDGEMENTS

For permission to quote from the Sherlock Holmes stories and novels I am much obliged to Baskervilles Investments Limited and to the Conan Doyle publishers, Messrs John Murray and Jonathan Cape.

It is also a pleasure to acknowledge with grateful thanks the assistance so readily placed at my disposal by that eminent Sherlockian James Edward Holroyd, who read the manuscript with a constructively critical eye, kindly suggested a number of improvements, and drew my attention to several points which I had missed. My enthusiastic acceptance of nearly all his proposals is a clear indication of how very much I have valued his help. This is not to say that he is responsible for any opinions or conclusions of mine with which the reader may disagree. For instance, such a kind man as James Holroyd would probably not have been so hard on Dr Watson as I, in one passage particularly, have thought justified.

Finally, my thanks to my publishers, Messrs David & Charles, for their unfailing courtesy and encouragement from the moment I first approached them, not least in saving me immense trouble by answering my many and various queries by return of post.

Ian McQueen

Bournemouth
1974

INDEXES

INDEX TO THE SHERLOCK HOLMES STORIES

The Abbey Grange, 29, 42, 62

The Beryl Coronet, 51, 52
Black Peter, 29, 30, 40, 42, 58, 59, 148
The Blanched Soldier, 60, 61, 215
The Blue Carbuncle, 55, 56, 93, 95, 97
The Boscombe Valley Mystery, 35, 41, 54, 93, 96, 165, 216
The Bruce-Partington Plans, 44, 47, 68, 180, 181, 205

The Cardboard Box, 42, 69, 87–91, 98, 165
A Case of Identity, 39, 53, 105, 111, 150, 198, 214
Charles Augustus Milverton, 49, 164
The Copper Beeches, 14, 40, 45, 46, 52, 81, 97, 99
The Creeping Man, 151
The Crooked Man, 54, 76, 77, 93, 96, 138, 142

The Dancing Men, 43, 154, 157
The Devil's Foot, 23, 31, 32, 37, 44, 71, 148
The Dying Detective, 39–42, 94

The Empty House, 33, 45, 70, 100, 103, 124, 198, 204–12, 215
The Engineer's Thumb, 29, 44, 64, 93–5, 168

The Final Problem, 45, 56, 81, 90, 94, 97–100, 117–26, 153, 197, 202–7, 215, 217
The Five Orange Pips, 19, 30, 43, 54, 58, 86–9, 104, 132, 150, 154–8, 171–6, 179

The Gloria Scott, 26–8, 44
The Golden Pince-Nez, 42, 57, 59, 67, 208
The Greek Interpreter, 25, 44, 142

His Last Bow, 25, 71, 180
The Hound of the Baskervilles, 29–31, 101, 120, 129–70, 215, 216

The Illustrious Client, 151, 206 210–12

Lady Frances Carfax, 60, 152, 163, 215
The Lion's Mane, 44, 60

The Man with the Twisted Lip, 52, 95, 96, 103, 104, 111
The Mazarin Stone, 62, 69, 70, 198
The Missing Three-Quarter, 31, 42–4, 66, 83
The Musgrave Ritual, 17, 26–8, 35, 37, 47, 103

The Naval Treaty, 13, 30, 38, 55, 93, 95, 135
The Noble Bachelor, 40, 53, 68, 75, 76, 85–7, 150, 162
The Norwood Builder, 30, 37, 57, 59, 84, 151, 165–7, 183, 193, 208

The Priory School, 61, 102

The Red Circle, 44, 179
The Red-Headed League, 52, 94, 99, 113–16, 118
The Reigate Squires, 17, 42, 193, 194
The Resident Patient, 53, 86
The Retired Colourman, 30, 43, 152, 163, 208

A Scandal in Bohemia, 55, 80, 92, 95, 108–11, 150, 160, 173, 193
The Second Stain, 51, 98, 194
Shoscombe Old Place, 40, 59, 99, 109
The Sign of Four, 13–15, 40, 43, 45, 50, 52, 65, 66, 75–107, 148, 149, 214
Silver Blaze, 42, 55, 69, 86, 91, 217
The Six Napoleons, 42, 166, 167, 170, 215
The Solitary Cyclist, 59, 60, 151, 152, 208
The Speckled Band, 20, 29, 47, 48, 164
The Stockbroker's Clerk, 52, 53, 92–5
A Study in Scarlet, 13–37, 39, 41–3, 48, 80, 99–103, 164, 179, 213, 215
The Sussex Vampire, 14, 60

Thor Bridge, 30, 62, 63, 156, 174, 198
The Three Gables, 60, 214
The Three Garridebs, 63–7, 148
The Three Students, 99

The Valley of Fear, 30, 42, 179–212, 216, 217
The Veiled Lodger, 44

Wisteria Lodge, 59

The Yellow Face, 49, 156, 173

GENERAL INDEX

Ablewhite, Godfrey, 214
Adair, Ronald, 208–11
Adler, Irene, 55, 109, 110, 160
Afghanistan, 15–18, 92
Aldershot, 93, 96
Allahabad, 77
Alpha Inn, 55
Altamont, 25, 181
Amberley, Josiah, 43, 152
Ames, 190
Angel, Hosmer, 111
Anstruther, Dr, 93
Armstrong, Dr, 44
Ashdown Forest, 185
Audley Court, 35
Australia, 15

Backwater, Lord, 50
Baker, Henry, 55, 56
Baldwin, Ted, 186–8, 195, 196, 197, 199, 201, 208
Ballarat, 15
Balmoral, Lord, 211, 217
Barclay, Col, 76, 77
Bardle, Inspector, 61
Baring-Gould, William, 10, 28, 114, 147, 213, 216, 218
Barker, Cecil, 187–90, 195, 196
Barker (detective), 208
Barrymore, Mr and Mrs, 120, 137, 139–41, 144, 145
Barts Hospital, 16, 17, 33, 69
Baskerville Hall, 134, 140, 142, 143, 145, 168
Baskerville, Sir Charles, 120, 130, 139, 160, 161, 163, 168
Baskerville, Sir Henry, 60, 130–5, 137, 140–6, 147, 151–4, 159–64, 168
Baskerville, Sir Hugo, 136, 139, 142
Beckenham, 142
Bell, H. W., 10, 28, 82, 114, 142, 213, 216, 218
Bellinger, Lord, 51
Benito Canyon, 195
Bennett, Trevor, 151
Beppo, 167
Bhurtee, 77
Billy the page, 69, 198
Birlstone, 182–6, 200
Birmingham, 92, 93, 95
Blackheath, 14, 148
Blakeney, T. S., 28, 147, 213, 216, 218
Blessington, 53, 54
Bohemia, King of, 36, 55, 109–11, 151, 215
Brackwell, Lady Eva, 49
Bradley's, 136, 139, 143
Brend, Gavin, 10, 28, 147, 213, 216, 218
Briony Lodge, 95
Bristowe, W. S., 217
Brixton Road, 18

Brussels, 125

Calhoun, Capt, 175, 176
Cambridge, 14, 31, 83
Candahar, 16
Canterbury, 119, 122–6
Cantlemere, Lord, 62, 198
Cape Town, 208
Carfax, Lady Frances, 60
Cawnpore, 77
Chicago, 181, 195, 196
Christ, J. F., 10, 28, 114, 147, 213, 216, 218
Clay, John, 113–17
Clayton, 153
Clotilde, Princess, 109
Collins, Wilkie, 214
Coombe Tracey, 101, 134, 141, 145, 164, 165
Criterion Bar, 16, 21
Croker, Capt, 62
Cubitt, Hilton, 154–8
Cuff, Sgt, 214
Cummings, Joyce, 63
Cushing, Miss, 90

Dakin, Martin, 28, 31, 112, 142, 147, 213, 216, 218
Damery, Sir James, 151, 210, 211
Dartmoor, 86, 132–4, 142, 143
De Merville, Violet, 210, 211
De Reszke brothers, 159
Devoy, Nancy, 77
Dodd, James, 60, 61
Donnithorpe, 28
Douglas, John, 180, 186–96, 199–201, 208
Dover, 119, 122–6
Doyle, Sir A. C., 9, 67, 88, 103, 104, 108, 109, 129–34, 170, 171, 172, 179–81, 183–6, 194, 196, 210, 214, 216

Dunbar, Miss, 62, 63

East Grinstead, 184, 185
Eccles, J. S., 59
Edenbridge, 185
Edwards, Birdy, 179–81, 194–201
Emsworth, Col, 60
Emsworth, Godfrey, 60
Evans, Killer, 63

Farintosh, Mrs, 47
Farquhar, Dr, 94
Ferguson, Robert, 14, 60
Fleet Street, 113, 115
Folsom, Rev H. T., 28, 147, 213, 216, 218
Fordham, 172
Forest Row, 185
Forrester, Inspector, 193
Forrester, Mrs Cecil, 50, 87, 89, 91, 98
Frankland, 145, 163

Garrideb, John, 64
Garrideb, Nathan, 64
Gelder & Co, 167
Gibson, J. Neil, 46, 62, 63, 174
Gilbert, A., 174
Gregory, Inspector, 42
Gregson, Tobias, 20, 23, 24, 33, 181
Greuze, 70, 204, 207
Grimpen, 135, 153
Groombridge, 185, 186
Gruner, Baron, 210

Hall, Trevor, 218
Hanover Square, 76
Harden, J. V., 59
Hargreave, Wilson, 154, 157
Harraway, 180
Hatherley, Victor, 29, 44, 64, 93
Hayter, Col, 17, 193

Holborn Restaurant, 16, 21
Holder, Alexander, 51, 52, 150
Holdernesse, Duke of, 57, 58, 60–2, 102
Holdhurst, Lord, 14, 38
Holmes, Mycroft, 25, 26, 44, 47, 57, 68, 142, 192
Holroyd, James E., 214, 218, 220
Hope, Jefferson, 18, 20–3, 80
Hope, Trelawney, 51
Hopkins, Stanley, 29, 42, 62
Horsham, 175
Hudson, Mrs, 30, 39, 40, 57, 58, 69, 111, 149
Huff, Darrell, 123
Hunter, Violet, 40, 45, 52, 97
Hutchinson, George, 22, 24, 34
Huxtable, Dr T., 61

Jackson, Dr, 93
Jameson Raid, 214
Jones, Athelney, 65, 82, 92
Jones, Peter, 116, 117

Kensington, 57, 93–5, 98, 99, 151
King's Pyland, 87
Knox, E. V., 23
Knox, Ronald, 31

Lauriston Gardens, 19
Lestrade, Inspector, 20, 23, 24, 33–5, 41, 42, 54, 59, 64, 84, 90, 101, 131–6, 141, 165–7, 181–3, 192, 194, 208, 216
Le Villard, François, 43
Lewisham, 152
Lingfield, 185
Lucknow, 77
Lyons, Laura, 130, 141, 145, 146, 156, 163, 164

Maberley, Mary, 60
MacCarthy, Sir Desmond, 79
McCarthy, James, 54
MacDonald, Alec, 181–3, 190, 194, 197–201, 203, 204
McFarlane, J. H., 33, 59
McGinty, John, 180, 195
McGowran, Bill, 136
McMurdo, John, 180, 181
McQuire, Molly, 179
Maguire, Molly, 195, 197, 216
Maiwand, 16–19
Marcini's, 159
Martin, Inspector, 157
Mason, John, 59
Mason, White, 182–4, 190–3
Maupertuis, Baron, 51
Melas, 44, 142
Merriman, Charles, 186
Merripit House, 131, 144, 145
Merryweather, 116, 117
Merton, Sam, 70
Metcalfe, Percy, 18
Meunier, Oscar, 70
Milner, Godfrey, 211
Milverton, C. A., 49
Montague Street, 27, 35
Montgomery, James, 185, 192
Montpellier, 152, 215
Moran, Col, 70, 201–12
Moriarty, Col, 201–8, 217
Moriarty, Professor, 33, 70, 90, 116–26, 129, 153, 179, 197, 200, 201–9, 217
Morley, Christopher, 100
Morstan, Capt Arthur, 78, 79, 106
Morstan, Mary, 15, 33, 45, 52, 75–105, 149, 168, 171, 198
Mortimer, Dr, 132, 136, 137, 143–7, 149, 151, 160–3, 168–70
Moulton, F. H., 76
Mount-James, Lord, 44
Munro, Grant, 49, 156

Murphy, Major, 54, 142
Musgrave, Reginald, 26, 27, 47, 213

Narbonne, 56, 118
Neill, Col, 77
Netley, 16
New Forest, 14, 90
Nîmes, 56, 118
Norberton, Sir Robert, 59
Nordon, Pierre, 219
Northumberland Avenue, 76
North Walsham, 154
Norton, Godfrey, 55
Norwood, 79

Oberstein, 180
Old Deer Park, 14
Openshaw, Elias, 172, 176
Openshaw, John, 54, 55, 88, 89, 157, 158, 171–6
Openshaw, Joseph, 176
Overton, Cyril, 42, 43
Oxford, 26, 117
Oxford Street, 58, 94, 136

Paddington, 93, 94, 96, 98, 168, 198
Paget, Sidney, 83, 84, 101, 102, 119, 120, 137, 138, 139–42, 155, 156, 173
Peck, A. J., 218
Pennsylvania, 179, 198
Peshawur, 15
Peterson, 55, 56
Phelps, Percy, 13, 30, 55, 92, 93, 135, 213
Pierrot, 180
Pike, Langdale, 214
Pinkerton, 179, 195, 198
Pondicherry Lodge, 15, 66, 79, 81
Porlock, Fred, 200, 207
Prendergast, Major, 54, 55, 176
Prescott, Rodger, 64
Princetown, 135
Pycroft, Hall, 52, 92

Regent Street, 139, 143
Reichenbach Fall, 33, 88, 122, 124, 129, 197, 204–7
Ricoletti, 48
Ridling Thorpe, 157
Roberts, Sir Sydney, 10, 213, 218
Robinson, Fletcher, 130, 133
Ronder, Mrs, 44
Ross (Herefordshire), 42
Ross, Col, 42, 55
Ross, Duncan, 115

St Clair, Neville, 52, 112
St Simon, Lord Robert, 50, 53, 75, 86, 162
Savannah, 175
Sayers, Dorothy, 10, 103, 114, 218
Scandinavia, King of, 50, 57, 109
Selden, 130, 135, 143–6, 153, 154
Sholto, Major, 79, 80, 105
Sholto, Thaddeus, 106
Slaney, Abe, 154, 157
Small, Jonathan, 80–2, 105–7
Smith, Edgar, 10, 218
Smith, Violet, 59, 60
Smith's Wharf, 81
Southsea, 14, 90
Spalding, Vincent, 114
Stamford, 16, 17, 21–3, 39
Stanford's, 143
Stapleton, Mr and Mrs, 130–5, 145, 153, 163, 169
Stark, Col Lysander, 64
Starr, Dr Lysander, 64
Starrett, Vincent, 218
Staunton, Godfrey, 43, 44
Stoner, Helen, 29, 47
Stradivarius, 69
Strasburg, 125, 205